Where Is Here?

Where Is Here?

Canada's Maps and the Stories They Tell

Alan Morantz

PENGUIN
CANADA

PENGUIN CANADA
Published by the Penguin Group
Penguin Books, a division of Pearson Canada, 10 Alcorn Avenue, Toronto, Ontario,
Canada M4V 3B2
Penguin Books Ltd, 80 Strand, London WC2R 0RL, England
Penguin Putnam Inc., 375 Hudson Street, New York, New York 10014, U.S.A.
Penguin Books Australia Ltd, 250 Camberwell Road, Camberwell, Victoria 3124, Australia
Penguin Books India (P) Ltd, 11, Community Centre, Panchsheel Park,
New Delhi – 110 017, India
Penguin Books (NZ) Ltd, cnr Rosedale and Airborne Roads, Albany, Auckland 1310,
New Zealand
Penguin Books (South Africa) (Pty) Ltd, 24 Sturdee Avenue, Rosebank 2196, South Africa

Penguin Books Ltd, Registered Offices: 80 Strand, London WC2R 0RL, England

10 9 8 7 6 5 4 3 2 1

Illustration for endpapers, *The coast of southwestern Baffin Island* by Simeonie Qapappik,
Cape Dorset, 1990. Courtesy Norman Hallendy.

Printed and bound in Canada on acid free paper. ∞

NATIONAL LIBRARY OF CANADA CATALOGUING IN PUBLICATION

Morantz, Alan, 1958-
    Where is here? : Canada's maps and the stories they tell / Alan Morantz.

Includes index.
ISBN 0-14-301351-3

1. Maps—Canada—History. 2. Cartography—Canada—History. I. Title.

GA471.M67 2002   912'.0971   C2002-903268-7

Visit Penguin Books' website at **www.penguin.ca**

To Mollie and Joe, for latitude,
and Suzanna and Katie, for longitude

CONTENTS

Acknowledgements

"EVERY BOOK HAS AN INTRINSIC impossibility, which its writer discovers as soon as his first excitement dwindles."

That bit of wisdom comes from the pen of American author Annie Dillard, and it is an observation that I hereby confirm. As far as I can tell, the ways to deal with such literary impossibilities are to maintain the initial excitement for as long as you can — thereby denying the awful truth — and to surround yourself with smart folk who help make the impossible possible.

Fortunately, the Canadian world of maps is populated with knowledgeable and generous people who were important sources of information. A great many contributed beyond the call of professional duty or friendship, but the following deserve special recognition. They acted as my go-to panel of experts and last line of defence: Norman Hallendy in Carp, Ontario, who inspired me to take a wide-angle view of map-making and acted as an all-round finishing school; Conrad Heidenreich in Toronto, who offered a primer on the history of cartography and read draft chapters in the comfort of his cottage; Jeffrey Murray in Ottawa, who led a tour of the National Archives backrooms, arranged for photographs and shared his hard-won research into Western Canada's maps; and Lou Sebert in Ottawa, who plotted out a map for my book, corrected innumerable mistakes (including the spelling of his name) and taught me how to calculate latitude by observing the sun at noon. Lou, I am sad to say, will not have the chance to read this heartfelt acknowledgement; he passed away on August 1, 2002, just as the book was in a late stage of production. Lou had a mountain-sized love of Canadian maps, and a particular fondness for the Three-Mile Sectional Maps of the Canadian West. His loss is keenly felt by Canada's entire cartographic community.

The following people, map lovers from coast to coast to coast, enthusiastically agreed to share their thoughts and resources on the subject: Mark Adams; Rod Bantjes; Bill Barry; Bart Campbell; Izzy Cohen; Terry Cook; Marlene Creates; Edward Dahl; Nelson Martin-Dawson; Glen Gilbert; David Gray; Philip Hiscock; Stan Knowlton; Tony Lea; Samuel Ludwin; Landon Mackenzie; Hooley McLaughlin; Paul Manley; Lisa Morriss-Andrews; Briony Penn; Brian Shipley; Matthew Sparke; Boon Tan; Fraser Taylor; Iain Taylor; Ron Whistance-Smith; and Hap Wilson.

Thanks go to Marlene Creates, who gave permission to use text panels from *Places of Presence: Newfoundland kin and ancestral land, Newfoundland 1989–1991* (Kilick Press, 1997), and to Landon Mackenzie, who allowed me to use performance script from *Accounting for an imaginary prairie life* (1997). John MacDonald kindly granted permission to quote from *The Arctic Sky: Inuit Astronomy, Star Lore, and Legend* (Royal Ontario Museum and Nunavut Research Institute, 1998).

One person who was not interviewed for this book, but who deserves acknowledgement nonetheless, is Don Thomson. Don wrote *Men and Meridians*, the epic three-volume history of the mapping and surveying of Canada to 1947; *Men and Meridians* is still the point of departure for anyone needing to learn the lay of the land. As president of the Canadian Authors Association, he also worked diligently for the right of authors to receive royalties for public use of their books. Don passed away in January 2001.

My thanks go to Francis Backhouse, in Victoria, and Brent Harris, in Kingston, for their research assistance and ability to uncover gems. Thanks too to all those eBay nuts who bid against me for city and highway maps and who almost always won. I could not have afforded writing this book without them.

Where Is Here? is an outgrowth of work I did as project editor of *Canadian Geographic*'s seventieth anniversary issue. I am grateful to Rick Boychuk, editor of *Canadian Geographic*, and his fine crew for asking me to come aboard for the special issue on mapping. Cynthia Good, Penguin's publisher, and Jacqueline Kaiser, formerly its senior editor, were enthusiastic early supporters of the book, while Diane Turbide, Penguin's editorial director, and copy editor Sharon Kirsch offered many astute observations that strengthened the manuscript.

Finally, my wife, Suzanna, and daughter, Katie, were wellsprings of editorial and emotional support. They have learned a few things about the maps of Canada, while I have learned, yet again, how lucky I am to experience joy and serenity on the home front, all the more treasured when the "intrinsic impossibility" of writing inevitably sets in.

Introduction

C. J. MORGAN VOLUNTEERED AS A "laundry lady" at a group home in Edmonton. Twice a week, she would arrive at the front door and be greeted warmly, offered a cup of tea and invited into the residents' lives. Some lives remained off limits.

One evening, while Morgan worked in the laundry room, Stevie showed up carrying an atlas from an encyclopedia set. Stevie was twenty-five years old and had the face of an angel. He was also autistic, and had a limited ability to interact with the laundry lady. The two had made eye contact only about ten times, Morgan wrote in an essay published in *The Globe and Mail*, and six of those times were accidental. In her essay, Morgan recounted what happened that evening: "I don't remember what I said to him as I eased over to stand beside him, but I know I was talking. He traced a road with his finger, then a river. Then he allowed me to turn the pages so I could show him where he lives, where he was born, where I was born. But mostly he was just tracing paths. His eyes followed his finger. That's the first time I have seen him focus on anything."

Who knows where Stevie travelled when he traced the lines on the map. Maps have a strange way of blending into the deepest wells of imagination. They are created to serve the most utilitarian of purposes, but once born, they take on lives of their own in the most surprising of ways. Just ask C. J. Morgan.

Where Is Here? tries to pick up on the wonder that Morgan and Stevie experienced that Edmonton evening by looking at how the maps we make in turn make us. The intent is to present a soulful picture of how maps and the act of map-making have shaped us as Canadians and what they reveal of who we are.

A definition is in order. By "maps" I mean the familiar historical and modern documents that show political divisions, resource locations and travel routes but also the songs, stones, scrawls and art that we create and employ to find our way, and some sort of meaning, in the world. The definition is loose enough to include hobo drawings, Blackfoot cosmological body-part place names and modern art, along with Jesuit maps and road guides published before the building of the Trans-Canada Highway.

Maps are socially significant in many ways. They were a primary means of transferring the knowledge of Aboriginal civilizations to the Western world. They are essential for survival and part of an oral storytelling tradition. They are used to seduce motorists and exploit consumers, are a form of identity for small-town burghers, and a means of creative expression and recreation.

Maps, too, are sources of comfort. No one is more keenly aware of that than Canadians. We have geography imposed on us by breadth of land mass, rushing waterways and bracingly cold winds. We turn to maps seeking comfort and reassurance in familiar lines and place names. To this day our resonant memories are not of revolutionaries but of settlers and explorers — those who brandished not muskets but maps. Among Canada's truest national heroes are the La Vérendryes, among the first North American–born explorers to venture deep into their continent; and David Thompson, called "the greatest land geographer who ever lived," his magnificent accomplishment of mapping nearly four million square kilometres of the Northwest appreciated only after his death. Our cartographic obsession has made us prolific developers of mapping technology, from the mapping camera calibrator to geographic information systems. It has even affected Canadian novelists and artists — Aritha Van Herk and Marlene Creates prominent among them — who time and again probe themes of exploration and mapping as routes to self-identity.

In many countries, early maps were fine works of art, drawn to grace the library walls of royalty and the powerful. In Canada, maps were almost always hard-won working documents, whether to lead explorers ever farther inland or to help surveyors blaze a path for railroads. As such, Canada's maps are highly revealing. They are windows on worldviews, assumptions and dreams. They are mirrors of the best and worst in human nature.

Turning the focus around, *Where Is Here?* is a window on the maps themselves, or at least on an eclectic selection of Canadian maps that are stories in their own right. How was a given map produced? What and whose reality did it reflect? What reality did it call into being?

Studying a map, we can always find another subtlety that can be read between the contours. Each line, each dot, each colour that is on a map represents a conscious act and decision by the map-maker. Ed Dahl, the former map curator with the National Archives of Canada, once said: "The richest appreciation one can have of a map is to know what prompted that conscious decision to put it there. It's not easy to do that. They say a picture is worth a thousand words. I would say a map is worth a thousand pictures."

And a thousand stories.

1

SURVIVAL

*It seems to me that Canadian sensibility has been profoundly
disturbed, not so much by our famous problem of identity...as
by a series of paradoxes in what confronts that identity. It is
less perplexed by the question Who am I? than by some riddle
as Where is here?*
— Northrop Frye in *The Literary History of Canada*

To TELL THE TRUTH, Northrop, I would be just as happy to find a
certain gazebo, the one that sits by the stream that meanders
through the lush park in the middle of Perth, on the eastern flank of
Ontario. In place of a road map and precise directions, I had these
rather informal coordinates that, my friend Norman Hallendy
assured me, would guarantee that that day's meeting would not end
as yesterday's had, which is to say with both of us driving up and
down highways muttering to ourselves.

You would think we could get our act together, given the motive
for our meeting. I had been mining for insights on the social

1

significance of maps. Who better to interview than Norm Hallendy, who has forty-five years' experience travelling with traditional Inuit in the eastern Arctic and observing their ingenious strategies for navigating their world? We were supposed to meet in Westport, the midpoint between my home in Kingston and his in Carp, west of Ottawa. To spare both of us embarrassment, I will say only that the meeting did not happen, owing to a misunderstanding of the rendezvous time and a misinterpretation of the word "emporium." Undaunted, we made new plans to meet in Perth the following day, guided by directions even more vague than the day before's. But as I drove through Perth looking for a gazebo by a running body of water, it occurred to me that Norm was trying to teach a lesson. Navigation does not have to involve a printed map with a familiar grid. Sometimes, you need only feel the way to your destination.

It is a worthwhile, if not roundabout, exercise. When we finally did meet by the sparkling stream, Norm delivered his point in a more explicit way by telling me about the demanding nature of travel on a beguiling Arctic landscape. Instead of formal maps or compasses, he said, the traditional Inuit read variations in light or patterns made in the snow. They sang *aya-yait* songs that acted as Triptiks, and built *inuksuit* stone figures to relay information to other wayfarers. They devised visual place names to evoke a picture in the mind: An island could be called "where seals lie upon the ice" or "that which resembles a woman removing her parka hood." Norm offered an Aristotelian maxim: "There can be no thought without an image."

He recalled a day trip made in early spring between Cape Dorset and Inuksugalait. "I was travelling on a snowmobile with carver Ohito Ashuna and his sixteen-year-old son," Norm said. "I could never have made that trip alone, even with the finest maps and GPS [Global Positioning System], because the route wasn't a straight line and we had to take into account prevailing conditions each hour. If the sun came out, you would get snow melt and you'd have to go on another route."

Ashuna was continually reading cues and clues, Norm said. Occasionally, Ashuna would stop and point something out to his son. At this time of the day, the shadow falls this way in the valley. These hills look like two breasts; do not go through that inviting pass because it will lead you to the wrong place. Farther on is an upwelling of spring water and it could be very dangerous. "We were zigzagging all the way along, and each time we changed routes the pictures in his mind would be shuffled around," said Norm. "I was desperately trying to record in my memory the essential information that would guide me, but I was totally lost. I did not have the mental ability to observe subtle elements in context of one another. I was reading positions and Ohito was reading the landscape."

Norm said he once asked an elder how a mutual acquaintance became so adept at reading the weather. The reply was deceptively simple. "He said, 'Because he was afraid. He was afraid of drowning.'"

TENSION IS INDEED A GOOD motivator. It is the frisson that comes from disorientation, from being aware of shifts in the shadows that may point the way to safer ground. French philosopher Albert Camus said, "What gives value to travel is fear," and there is little doubt that fear — of the unknown, of imminent disaster — was in the hearts of North America's early explorers, be they the Vikings of a millennium ago or the later European seafarers. It is out of such primal fear that the first maps of what we now know as Canada were imagined.

But that sort of fear would not match the day-to-day efforts to survive in such an austere environment as the Arctic. The Inumariit, the Inuit who once lived in the traditional manner before communities were fixed in one location, were used to travelling huge distances, four to five thousand square kilometres in a lifetime. They travelled on foot, with sleds, or *komiteks*, and in flat-bottomed boats, or *umiaks*. In the strict sense of the word, they were not nomads; they followed known routes defined by the forces of nature: the weather or the migration of caribou or other animals. There were movements within a familiar area, from base camp to lakes in order to fish or hunt seals. There were travels that took several days, still within familiar areas. Then there were movements between distant but known areas, say from Cape Dorset to Pangnirtung.

To describe such a life as hard would be trite yet accurate. The fear of starvation — of caribou herds collapsing, of disaster in the face of extreme cold — was a guiding force, as was the fear of the unexpected: an unknown sound, an unexperienced atmospheric condition. In Norman Hallendy's travels with the Inumariit, such fears surfaced time and again. One elder, a respected hunter, spoke of desperate times when, long after the dogs were eaten, the only food left was so rotten it would disintegrate when pinched between fingers. "The one thing I do not have to be reminded of is starvation," he told Norm in a conversation in the late 1970s. "You will never know what it's like to be starving." He continued,

> *Starving is something I have known more than once. I can still remember the burning pain in my stomach. You become so weak that there is no outward sign of suffering. You know that you are dying and you are helpless to even try to find food. Finally, you say to yourself, It's too bad but nothing can be done; it's too late. And you accept the coming of death. All you can do is wait, and you know that death is about to swallow you.*

Having to be constantly alert to danger forced the Inuit travellers to respect everything around them, and to be acutely sensitive and knowledgeable about the shapes of rocks and clouds, the sounds of wind, the properties of snow crystals. In the Arctic, there are three prevailing "seasons." There is winter, the best and safest time to travel, when bodies of water are frozen and the greatest distances are covered. There is summer, when travel on often-soggy land is more difficult and risky; you zigzag and turn like a mouse testing the corridors of a maze. Travel is often by sea, which is a much riskier venture that requires knowledge of where the shallows are at various times of the season. And there are transition seasons, the most perilous times, when the land is thawed, when the sea is rubbery and the rivers partially frozen. The greatest risk of hypothermia is during this time. It should be no surprise that the Inuktitut word for weather and knowledge is the same: *sila*.

No topographic map or satellite image, no sophisticated handheld GPS, is of much use in navigating in such variable environments. In middle latitudes, the sun's orderly movements during the year help define the cardinal points of "north," "south," "east" and "west." In northerly latitudes, where the sun does not even rise above the horizon for a number of months, the cardinal references must be based on other environmental factors, primarily the wind. "By and large you can read maps in the Arctic but they're of limited use to me," said Norm. "The map is from a bird's-eye view and I'm not a bird. I'm walking on the land and I can't see the base, the points. If I'm flying over it, no problem." A map made in the mind, however, was another matter. It was the ultimate in portability, created and carried in the heads of the wayfarers. "It was not really a material culture. Cartographers in our world transfer images onto paper. For the Inuit, the landscape was rendered in words. They created images that could be transferred from one mind to another."

Such maps served generation upon generation of Inuit exceedingly well, in ways that are almost impossible to comprehend for the modern city dweller. It is no understatement to say that urbanites have short memories: Who among us knows that in the recent past, passenger pigeons made up the great majority of birds, congregating in such quantity that they would darken the daytime sky? For us, oral history has a limited horizon.

In place of longitude or latitude, the coordinates on the mental maps of the Inuit were snowdrifts, wind direction, stars and the general lay of the land. There was a map for calm days, another for windy. The direction of ripples on fresh water, patterns made in the snow, tides, phases of moon, time of day or night, movements and shapes of clouds, colour of the landscape — all were parts of the Inumariit's cognitive cartography.

It is said that some old hunters could even read the clouds, although Norm never observed this himself. In the simplest form, the hunters would know that certain cloud formations appeared over certain landforms or bodies of water. According to Robin McGrath, a Newfoundland researcher who did twenty-two years of research in the Arctic on language and culture, sky maps at times actually guided Inuit hunters. In the polar springtime, when the earth begins to melt and the sea is still frozen, the dark land mass reflects up into low-hanging clouds; with such transient charts, the Inumariit could observe in the clouds a mirror view of the landscape ahead. The same phenomenon held true during wintertime, according to McGrath. When travelling over a white landscape after a snowfall, caribou hunters could spot herds by looking into the clouds and seeing them in the moisture in the air.

Ever since Inuit mapping was first studied in detail some thirty years ago, researchers have noted how map-making was an elemental part of Inuit life, for young and old, men and women. Shamans had their own maps of areas perceived to be inhabited by malevolent spirits, locales that must be avoided. But the forms of cognitive maps were quite different, particularly between men and women. Being hunters, men carried with them information on moving over the land or the sea. Women knew the elements that made for the safest camps, in particular natural resources such as berries and seaweed. "The moment we reached camp the women took over," said Norm. "She's now giving the orders; where and how the tent is set up, where the grub boxes are put. They know where the berries are, where to find the plants used to make fires. It's a different cognitive mapping." On longer trips, though, women would join the men breaking trail and leading the dogs forward, and they often needed to be mindful of the details of the territory.

Academics who have studied map-making by traditional societies in African, Australian, Pacific or American cultures offer useful distinctions among the various forms of cartography. Cognitive cartography relates to thoughts and images. Performance cartography comes in the form of rituals, speech and dance, while material cartography reveals itself in rock art and sketches on crude media. It is a maddeningly difficult area to study, since most of such traditional societies are held together by a rather tenuous testimony of oral knowledge. In Canada's eastern Arctic, it is even more difficult, since there is little material cartography to study, and there are few, if any, Inumariit still living who can talk about the rhythms and rhymes of living traditionally on the land.

To some extent, they still speak through Norman Hallendy. Since making his first trip to the Arctic in 1958, working for the Department of Northern Affairs and National Resources, Norm has returned year after year to the eastern Arctic, particularly the Cape Dorset area, befriending elders, who took him on many arduous trips and shared their oral history. In his workaday world down south, Norm amassed a sort of master-of-the-universe curriculum vitae: accomplished industrial designer, one-time ministerial delegate to NATO war games, senior federal civil servant who helped shape Canadian housing policy. In the north, he was known as "Apirsuqti," the Inquisitive One. And inquisitive he was, asking questions that grew ever more nuanced over the years. What prompted reticent

Inuit elders to trust a southerner enough to confide in him and show him places of power? "I don't know how one is certain confidence is truly gained without first giving it," he once told me. "You know, the sharing of information is much like the sharing of food. The best feast is when everybody brings something to the occasion. My grandmother's tales of life's perils and pleasures were listened to with as much attention by my Inuit friends as I listened to the same kind of life's adventures in the Arctic."

With the wonder of a child and the precision of a scientist, Norm recorded his field observations and audio and video interviews with the elders with whom he grew old. After more than five decades of observations and interviews, he now has a body of primary research that is unique in Arctic studies. That research has not been hermetically sealed in academic journals but instead packaged into popular articles and presentations to diplomats, the public and scientists. He is particularly engaging with youth, both from the north and south. To some extent, his stories represent sheets in an atlas embodying the cognitive cartography of the elders he knew and respected.

Many of the stories relate to *inuksuit*, the modern icons of northern identity. Although they are generally thought of as flat stones and igneous boulders stacked and arranged into human-like figures, traditional *inuksuit* come in all sorts of shapes and sizes. Some are as tall as an adult and in the shape of a window, used for sighting and aligning; others can be unmistakable phallic symbols, indicating a rich spawning area. There are *inuksuit* made up of two stones standing side by side and holding up a third stone, creating a doorway or window. An *inuksummarik* was made of rounded boulders and acted as an important directional indicator at headlands, entrances to bays, transitional points between water and land, and high hills. Many of the *inuksuit* acted as maps, but others were elegant expressions of joy or gratitude and even objects of veneration, as Norm

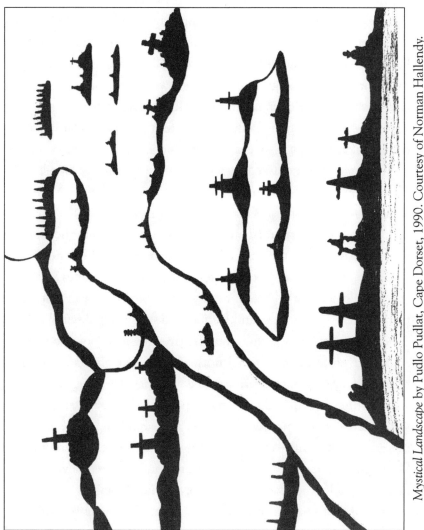

Mystical Landscape by Pudlo Pudlat, Cape Dorset, 1990. Courtesy of Norman Hallendy.

artfully shows in his comprehensive book, *Inuksuit: Silent Messengers of the Arctic*, published in 2000.

Norm was an astute observer while travelling with his mentors, and he devised some shrewd exercises to win a deeper understanding of their perceptions. In 1990, for example, he asked Pudlo Pudlat of Cape Dorset to draw a map of a place that was important to him. Pudlat produced what Norm calls a "mystical landscape." He placed the horizon in the foreground, evoking a world beyond, and encircled an island with six *inuksuit*. Pinnacles are shown marking dangerous passages along the Baffin coast. Norm can spot Itiliardjuk at the top left, the West Foxe islands in the upper right corner.

The same year, he asked his old friend Simeonie Qapappik to indicate on a map places he knew. Qapappik pushed aside Norm's maps, took out a blank sheet of paper, and began drawing the south coast of southwest Baffin Island from Inuksugalait, where there are some two hundred stone figures, to Ammaarjuak, where he was born, some three hundred kilometres to the east. To the lines on the page he added favoured locations of seals and walrus, the migration path of geese and caribou, and, curiously, a string of *inuksuit* placed "where one must be respectful," though Qapappik would not elaborate. As Norm wrote in *Inuksuit,* "I noticed that, though his drawing resembled my map, there were seeming discrepancies in his vision of the coastline. Compared with my map, Simeonie's chart depicted some places quite large while others were rendered more insignificant." Later, while travelling in the area, Norm realized that on Qapappik's map, places of particular importance were drawn large and places of less significance were proportionately small.

The kind of mind map that Norm most often describes seems more like a running film than a static chart imprinted with lines and words and on which images are arranged sequentially. This point was brought home in vivid fashion during his 1995 field season. That year, he tried to locate a site inland on southwest Baffin Island's Foxe

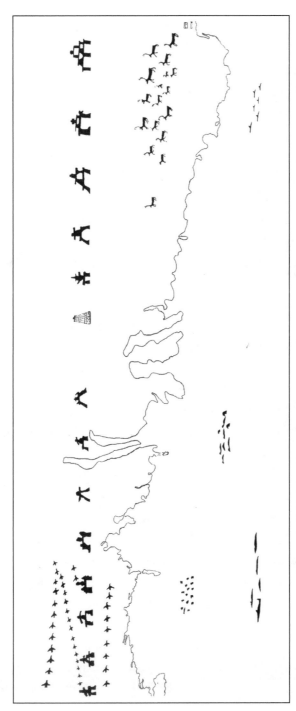

The coast of southwestern Baffin Island by Simeonie Qapappik, Cape Dorset, 1990. Courtesy of Norman Hallendy.

Peninsula, where he heard there were hundreds of *inuksuit*, said to be where people waited for caribou and hunted with bows and arrows. He enlisted one of the elders, Paulassie, who was one of the few who had a vague recollection of where the site might be located. The problem was that Paulassie travelled to the site only in winter, by dogsled. But on this trip, Norm and Paulassie were exploring the area in the summer from a helicopter, the only real option for that time of year.

Much to their frustration, they could not locate the site; Paulassie seemed perplexed by the landscape far below. He asked the pilot to land the helicopter on an outcrop. They got out and Norm stood there as the Inuk just looked around, scanning the horizon and trying to find a profile he could recognize. "He knew generally where he was," said Norm, "and if we crashed he could walk out of there. There would be enough cues to get him to the coast. Nature makes its own maps. Tides. Big islands become small islands. But on that first trip we never found what we were looking for."

Only after the fact did Norm realize what the problem was. Sitting in the chopper, Paulassie was facing the back and looking out a small window. He was referencing the landforms in reverse sequence; it made it very difficult to relate one hill to the next. When you look at a map, you study a page. When you map in the mind, the landscape is what is important.

The following year, Norm and Paulassie got another chance. This time, the elder sat in front with the pilot but still had problems orienting. Now the problem was that they were flying too high, and Paulassie had never seen the land at such a scale. Norm recalled, "We saw some boulders on the outcrops far below, and it was a huge plain, so I said, 'Maybe there's something there.' I told the pilot to come down very low, fifty feet above the ground, and then we could see the *inuksuit*. The moment he saw the place all the pictures came back and the reels were running." (Interestingly, Norm took a precise GPS reading of the location but has never published it, knowing full well the implications of placing a location's coordinates on a map. "Someone will go there, scratch, sniff, and dig," he said. "Some of these sites are better revered by thinking of them rather than trampling on them." He said he would only reveal the location of the site if there were a compelling reason to do so.)

In cognitive cartography based on not only physical maps but also oral history, place names are crucial yet elegantly subtle in their use. More often than not, the place names on Western maps are inspired by luminaries of our Eurocentric past. Rarely is an Inuit place name given to commemorate a person. In *The Arctic Sky*, a comprehensive book of Inuit astronomy and star lore, John MacDonald, who manages the Igloolik Research Centre for the Nunavut Research Institute, refers to the important role of language in place naming. "In striking contrast to the European approach — particularly that of explorers who tended to fill out their maps in memory of monarchs, mentors and friends — Inuit place naming sought to portray the physical, biological, or ecological significance of the land. Inuit rarely named places in honour of persons, and only occasionally to commemorate events. Many of these place names are disappearing, signifying the destruction of libraries of maps."

Inuktitut place names conjure images. If you were to ask Norm if he had ever been to the place where the rocks are warm from the bodies of walrus, he would know precisely what you were referring to, exactly how far it was from the shore, and that it was a dangerous place where the tide was going out. It certainly beats a name like Norman Hallendy Bay. Place names could also have layered meanings. *Nurrata*, for example, means flat land in the most literal sense, which is hardly evocative. But for those with a deeper understanding of the term, *nurrata* also means the place where the land and sea look continuous in the middle of winter.

Experiential maps and place names were shared during the course of trips when an elder needed to convey the nature and behaviour of phenomena along the way. Strung together, traditional Inuktitut place names perform in similar ways as stories told by one generation to the next. I asked Norm for an example and he began to relate a tale of the time a number of years ago when he was planning a trip to a place known as Igalaalik, a location that at one point was home to a powerful shaman. It was not that far from Norm's base at Cape Dorset, perhaps a one-day journey. After much effort, he arranged for a guide who was born in Igalaalik and was therefore not afraid to make the journey to what many considered a haunted place. "So we made arrangements but he said, 'We've got to go very early in the morning at sunrise because we're going all down the coast and there's a narrow passage and we have to get through it exactly at the right time to get to the big bay and then we'll go across the bay and finally get there.'" Norm then told two versions of the same journey:

The next day we got down to the beach, the tide was just coming in. We started out, the sun was just coming up. We came to the first island on the coast and then we came to the first unnamed mountain to the left and there was another little island and the place where Peter Pitsolak had a camp further along. We travelled further and further and then finally off to the right were the West Foxe islands. About that time the day got kind of lousy but then the sun came out. We began to feel kind of good about this. Then we came to the narrows, the tide was exactly right, and we wiggled through, which saved us a heck of a long time. As soon as we got through the narrows, off to the left-hand side was an enormous vein of white marble as far as you can see down the coastline. So we crossed Andrew Gordon Bay, we got to this point of land and arrived at the camp of Qiatsuq. I made several photographs and we were tired so we went to bed quite early. The next day we turned around and went back to Cape Dorset.

Next Norm described the same trip as if the guide's father were speaking:

We left at the feet of the high mountains when the lamp was lit. First we came upon the island where the dogs are left in summer. After that was the beautiful mountain that pushes against mist. Then the island where the old ladies were left when the men went hunting. Past there we saw to the left Kiattuq, which means where this place is warmed by the embrace of rocks. Travelling still further down the coast we came to the islands that look like a seal basking on the ice and then there was the island that looks like a woman removing her parka hood. After that there were the little fart islands. And at that time sunbeams penetrated dark places and we rejoiced. We came to the place where the tip of the finger almost touches the armpit. We made our way across and immediately to our left saw the place that looks like a great river frozen in summer. We crossed the great bay and in time arrived at the imagined window, but by then we were tired and devoured by sleep. The next day we did what we had to do and returned to the place of high mountains.

While he spent parts of forty-five years travelling on the land in the company of elders and speaks admiringly of the Inuit's traditional mind maps, Norm has a deep affection for the conventional maps of Western society. Out of comfort or habit, he always carries maps when travelling on the land in the eastern Arctic, even though they are of limited practical use. "I always carried maps," he said. "I felt comforted by maps. It's nuts because when we're travelling I never look at maps. It's only at the end of the journey that I take them out."

Those conventional maps have come in handy in other ways. Norm took out a photocopied map from a thick plastic pouch. Prepared by him for the Kinngait Cultural Society, it was a simply adorned contour map of about seventy kilometres of fractured coast-line of Andrew Gordon Bay, on the south-central limit of Baffin Island. The few place names on the map itself provide a revealing window into European exploration in the Arctic: Cape Willingdon, Hume Island, Coatesworth Island. But Norm has added another layer by placing the numbers 1 through 101 on the map. Each number represents an Inuktitut place name collected from elder Pudlo Pootoogook. Some define small islands, others areas just inland. When you examine the place names in their context, the map becomes rich and subtle. Some names are functionally expressive: a cove island is called Sapujjuat, place of the stone weirs; Taliruat, the place shaped like a seal flipper; Innaarulik, where there is a steep cliff; Qainnguarialik, where you must travel along the shoreline in spring-time. Other place names hint at stories: the islet Arqvavik, the place where the sperm whale was taken; a spot on a well-protected bay called Aqiatulaulakvik, a place where one got full from eating; Qajugiaq, where big waves could sweep over the island.

With Western eyes, you can easily look at this map of the Andrew Gordon Bay coastline and be oblivious to the other layers of map staring back at you. You see a still image; Norman Hallendy sees a motion picture.

THE INUMARIIT HAD OTHER MAPPING tools besides *inuksuit* and place names. Songs and tongue twisters, for example, were fun ways to deliver spatial information in context and proper sequence, easily remembered and passed on. Norm has heard of the story of an old hunter who travelled from Taloyoak to Ikpiar-juk (Arctic Bay) by himself, on a trip he had never made to a place he had never been, armed only with a song, a travelling *aya-yait*. An *aya-yait* could go something like this: Now we go to the place that looks like a seal lying on the ice, and then we see the walrus coming out of the water.

Songs figured significantly in other cultures based on oral traditions. Newfoundland seafarers, for example, had their own versions of *aya-yait*. Philip Hiscock, folklore archivist at Memorial University in Newfoundland, says mariners used navigational songs with mnemonic rhymes as part of mapping by oral tradition to help them navigate the foggy and serrated coastline of the island. As he points out, mariners in the nineteenth century might have had access to published charts, but they were considerably expensive, likely out of reach for most. As an alternative, ocean-going captains "tapped on oral heritage few of us can comprehend today." No one knows how many such songs existed; few survived on the vector of oral tradition and fewer still were put to paper.

Hiscock offered an example of a navigational rhyme that appeared in Annie Proulx's novel *The Shipping News*:

When the Knitting Pins you is abreast
Desperate Cove bears due west
Behind the Pins you must steer
'Til the Old Man's Shoe does appear.
The tickle lies just past the toe,
It's narrow, you must slowly go.

The most famous navigational rhyme is "Wadham's Song," likely written by a mariner named Wadham in 1756. In eleven verses, it sings the way from Bonavista one hundred kilometres north to Fogo, pointing out the "sunken rocks," the "damned rugged isles" and the "house on Syme's Isle."

It begins:

From Bonavista Cape to the Stinking Isles
The course is north full forty miles,
When you must swing away northeast

Till Cape Freel's Gull Island bears nor'-nor'west.
Then nor'-nor'west thirty-three miles,
Three leagues offshore lies Wadham's Isles,
Where of a rock you must take care;
Two miles sou'-sou'east from Isles bear.

And eight verses later, ends:

When Pilley's Point you are abreast,
Starboard haul, and steer sou'-sou'west
Till Pilley's Point covers Syme's Stage;
Then you are clear, I will engage.

Many years later, of course, widely reproduced mariners' charts were in every ship rounding Bonavista Cape. They might have been improvements on navigational rhymes, but no one would say they were as memorable. The fact that so few rhymes or *aya-yait* still exist points to one simple truth: They may be portable over land and sea and between generations, but if you don't sing your maps, your maps will no longer sing for you.

"BECAUSE HE WAS AFRAID." Norman Hallendy's simple explanation for his mentor's finely honed navigational skills came to mind when I talked with Bart Campbell. By day, Campbell is a medical technologist, living with his wife and three children in Vancouver. But like Norm, Campbell has a hobby that he pursues with a rare passion — the collection of oral history from elders with experiences from a different time. In Campbell's case, the focus of his fascination is the hobo, that restless soul who tramped the Pacific Coast during the heyday from 1890 to 1920. Like the Inumariit, hoboes lived an itinerant, rather than nomadic, life, their movements guided by the seasons and hardscrabble opportunities. Hoboes, too, were motivated

A brief dictionary of hobo "mapping" signs.

by fear: fear of being beaten, fear of being trapped in a reefer (refrigerated boxcar) and freezing to death, fear of being turned over to the authorities. Their fears were expressed in utopian dreams of living atop Big Rock Candy Mountain, where handouts grow on bushes, the bulldogs have rubber teeth and little streams of alcohol come a-trickling down the rocks. One way of coping with those fears was to devise a system of mapping the zones of danger and refuge for the benefit of other hoboes to follow, a system based on chalk drawings and oral accounts to pass on their meaning.

Campbell's fascination with the hobo way of life may have something to do with his own itinerant childhood. Born in Edmonton, Campbell figures he had moved seventeen times before he reached his fourteenth birthday, giving him an appreciation not only of the geography of Canada, but also of how it felt to bounce around the country like tumbleweed. As an adult, he moved to East Vancouver and began frequenting the bacon-and-egg neighbourhood diners that were the favourite hangouts of old-timers who used to work on the docks a couple of blocks away. He talked them up and collected their stories. And he spent time with his grandfather, Fred Dubbin, a former hobo himself who told Bart about the hobo culture that prevailed in turn-of-the-century Vancouver.

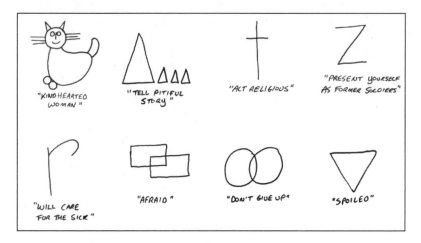

During the summer and fall, hoboes (or boomers, as they were called in the days before demography gave the word new meaning) followed opportunity: Some worked as miners, loggers, bridge snakes or tunnel builders, sleeping outdoors and begging meals. Some hoboes crossed the continent in search of work, taking turns in a number of industries. For most, though, life involved movement through agricultural areas; they followed harvests, picking fruit and harvesting crops. "I take my hat off to the hobo," Rev. Andrew Roddan of Vancouver's First United Church wrote at the time. "He has been an indispensable factor in the building of Canada. Without his strong muscles the railways, canals, bridges, tunnels, and public works of many kinds could never have been carried out." Roddan added,

> As a rule they are a good class of men, rough and uncouth on the outside, but when you come to know them they are very human, generous, and responsive to a touch of kindness, especially when they know there is nothing of cant or insincerity about it. The irregularity of their work has a very serious reaction on their outlook on society and life in general. The lack of permanence tends to demoralize the man, and while in the vigor of his manhood he is

*able to stand the racket, the advance of years begins to tell on him
and he goes down physically.*

(Roddan also offered a handy distinction among the various
homeless people in turn-of-the-century North America: A hobo was
a migratory worker; a tramp was a migratory non-worker; and a bum
was a stationary non-worker. Another version of the pecking order
went like this: The hobo works and wanders, the tramp dreams and
wanders, and the bum drinks and wanders.)

In the winter, hoboes would camp in Vancouver's mild but moist
urban "jungles"; in the case of Campbell's grandfather, in the ravines
along the False Creek Flats. Thousands would live in the melting pot
of transient villages, in crowded lean-tos made of soggy cardboard
and old carpets. In the jungles, they would learn some of the finer
points of the hobo life. They would try to stay one step ahead of
police and their hounds, who would be on the prowl for "volunteers"
for unemployment relief camps. "During the worst years of the Great
Depression," Campbell wrote in an article for *Canadian Geographic*,
"men were drifting, using rumours of jobs someplace else as an
excuse for wandering and seeing new things, living at large like wild
dogs, begging and stealing and getting drunk whenever they got a

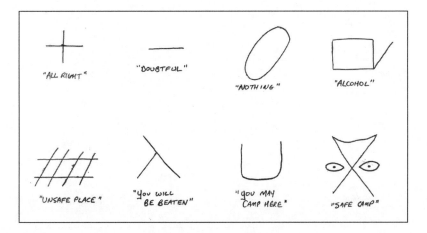

chance." Abused by employers and demonized by the public, hoboes needed a quick and dirty language. "Nouns and written languages just could not accurately communicate the fluid universe in which the unemployed and homeless existed — their harsh worlds of constantly transforming things, places, people and choices for survival," Campbell said.

Hoboes lacked the financial resources to provide themselves shelter, but fear and necessity fed a certain resourcefulness. They developed their own cognitive cartography and backed it up with scrawled "maps." These maps, drawn in chalk, were seemingly crude signs on fence posts, gates, sidewalks, trees and car tires, and for those who understood the signs, they imparted crucial wayfaring information. As Campbell learned from his grandfather and other elders, the chalk figures were most commonly placed on water towers near train stations, the places where hoboes jumped off and needed to know the lay of the land. (In the hobo heyday, movement was largely by railroad and not road.) "Gypsies had many of the same signs," said Campbell. "Signs at the crossroads were very important to them, and obviously some of those signs made their way to North America and Canada."

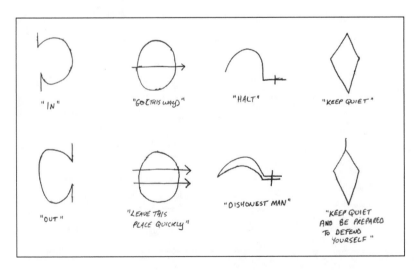

Most of the chalk signs were intuitive, many others less so. A top hat represented a "gentleman," a stick figure "a woman," a smiling cat with six whiskers "a kind-hearted woman." Five circles arranged in a paw print said "hospitable people," while a bird signalled "telephone." A circle with one arrow drawn through said "go this way," while two arrows warned "leave this place quickly." Intersecting circles implored "don't give up," a large triangle next to three small triangles advised "tell a pitiful story." A "Z" meant "present yourselves as former soldiers." Horizontal rectangles with a central dot carried a malevolent warning when combined with other figures, such as a wavy line (poisonous water). The train hoppers learned how to interpret the signs out of desperation, Campbell said. Their meanings were also passed along in the hobo jungles and relief camps and became "living, associate map keys for orienteering in strange places."

But like *inuksuit* and *aya-yait* songs, the hobo signs were more than merely functional navigational cues. They were evocative, their shapes and lines conjuring happy or bittersweet memories, but memories and stories nonetheless. An old-time Inuk hunter explained the phenomenon to Norman Hallendy in a simple yet poetic way: "This [*inuksuk*] attaches me to my ancestors and to this place." Bart Campbell expressed it in a similar manner: "They were a way of using the full range of the imagination to discern the real meanings about the places where people lived."

When Campbell talked of the hoboes' chalk "maps," I realized he could just as well be referring to the Inumariit's *inuksuit*. Hornblende boulders rearranged to tell a story; finger-sized cylinders of white limestone scratched over a wooden piling to point the way to refuge. Survival and stone.

2

EXPLORATION

THE FIRST EUROPEANS IN THE NEW WORLD used entirely different mapping techniques to impose political order on the Aboriginals
they met. In the vanguard were the Jesuit missionaries who came to
the New World primed to save souls, guided by the same strategy
they used in China and South America. It so happened that the missionaries ended up redrawing the lines of Native civilizations.

Not that the Jesuits and other explorers of the time seriously
believed that the Aboriginal nations they encountered in the St
Lawrence River and Great Lakes regions had any cartographic sense
of their own world. The Europeans barely trusted their hosts' wayfaring advice. Steeped in mathematics and astronomy, the explorers
developed maps and charts that helped them travel over vast seas.
The Aboriginals they met had no such material evidence.

Or perhaps the evidence was not noticed. *Inuksuit* and mnemonic
tunes were just a few mapping techniques Aboriginals used to
impose temporal order on yawning spaces, twisting waterways and

Drawing a map on birchbark by W. G. R. Hind. In this 1861 painting, a Montagnais named Domenique prepares a map of portages on the upper Moisie River for the Labrador Peninsula Expedition. Metropolitan Toronto Reference Library, John Ross Robertson Collection (T31956).

imagined shamanic worlds. Long before systematic European exploration of Canada began in the fifteenth century, Native groups used fragments of their world to understand their surroundings. The medium and the message varied widely. But in an exercise of imagination, if you were to bundle those maps together, what would the resulting "atlas" of Native cartography show? You would find maps that were used to prepare for war, to teach young hunters and wayfarers the shape of tribal territory, and to bridge a gap between heaven and earth. They might have been scratched in the sand or snow or sketched on the inner bark of paper birch trees. For the Iroquois and Ojibway, such maps, engraved with a hardwood or bone stylus or smeared with charcoal and bear's grease, formed part of an archived collection kept in central repositories, along with wampum belts and other artifacts. On the prairies, Aboriginals drew maps on the skins of elk, beaver, bison or deer. Records of journeys were etched on moose antler.

The "atlas" would include maps of a more spiritual nature as well. The Ojibway, for example, produced esoteric migration scrolls on birchbark illustrating the geographic spread of their belief system, in which snakes represented rivers. The Montagnais of the lower St Lawrence created maps on the scapula of caribou by holding the bone over hot coals and then interpreting the resulting cracks. According to one researcher, cracks leading to charred patches of bone were interpreted as maps of tracks, which were followed on the ground.

For the most part, the details of such mapping are just hinted at in legends or accounts of early European travellers. Occasionally, the importance of maps to Natives shines through. Hugh Brody, in his masterful *Maps and Dreams*, wrote of an electrifying encounter at the conclusion of formal hearings in 1979 between Beaver Indians and officials of the Northern Pipeline Agency, the body that studied the impact of a pipeline on traditional life in northeast

British Columbia. At the end of the day of hearings, a husband and wife came forward with a moose hide bundle, which they proceeded to untie and empty. Inside was a dream map as large as the tabletop. As Brody recounted it, the fascinated white officials of what was known as the Berger hearings after Justice Thomas Berger, gathered around the table amazed and confused by what they were hearing. "Abe Fellow and Aggan Wolf explained. Up here is heaven, this is the trail that must be followed; here is a wrong direction, this is where it would be worst of all to go; and over there are all the animals." They explained that all of what they had recounted had been discovered in dreams. A corner was missing, however, which prompted one of the officials to ask how the map was damaged. "Aggan answered: someone had died who would not easily find his way to heaven, so the owner of the map had cut a piece of it and buried it with the body. With the aid of even a fragment, said Aggan, the dead man would probably find the correct trail, and when the owner of the map dies, it would all be buried with him."

It is interesting today to speculate how different European exploration and colonization would have been had Native maps been less transitory and instead codified in a series of atlases, a graphic language the peripatetic westerners knew well. But for all the many motivations to map, there seem to be few, if any, records of Native groups using maps to establish title to land or to fix boundaries.

Instead of maps being declarations of land ownership, they were the primary means of transferring the intelligence of one civilization to another. With sticks and stones arranged on sand or charcoal etched on a boat deck, Native people told the story of their lives and lands, and showed explorers what lay ahead beyond the bend in the river or height of land. The maps not only served to help explorers move along rivers and over land, but also revealed cultural knowledge and, as the episode at the end of the Berger Inquiry showed, they provided a window into Native spiritual life. The European explorers of Canada, purposeful and pragmatic all, took whatever navigational intelligence they could glean from Native peoples and layered their own maps on top of that. They then asked their Native guides to fill in the blanks. Exploration and discovery have always worked that way. The Greek geographer Strabo wrote that humans are informed of the nature and content of their world "through perception and experience alike."

The most dramatic cartographic contacts came in the Arctic, between British explorers and the Inuit. They spoke to each other through their maps, but the vocabulary could not have been more different. The British, in their *Oxford Dictionary*, define map as "a representation of earth's surface, showing physical and political features." Western grid maps rely on coordinates of latitude and longitude. The Inuit term for map is *piusituqait nunannguartangit*, meaning that which imitates the land. Their maps eschew fixed positions in space for a pattern of interconnected lines, where the premium is on tracing a continuous path between geographic features.

The world's archives hold almost two hundred maps drawn by Inuit on paper for explorers and ethnographers between 1818 and 1924. A look at the maps through Western eyes reveals the unique cartographic rules of scale, orientation and legend used by the Inuit. In the 1820s, Inuk Iligliuk, who lived on Melville Island, drew charts for Captain Edward Parry, commander of the British exploration ships *Fury* and *Hecla*. With no experience mapping, Iligliuk created a map of the peninsula where she was born. She indicated place names, the location of resources such as a peat bog and a soapstone quarry, caribou crossings, villages and hunting sites, and environmental conditions such as high and low tides. Her maps did omit, however, topographic elements and the scale seemed as if a drunk had handled the sketching pen.

Puzzled, Parry gave Iligliuk lessons in how to use a drawing compass to scale off distance and showed her a small-scale map of Repulse

Bay and Winter Island. Iligliuk then drew a map that Parry could more easily understand and that he could decorate with cardinal points and hachuring (shading with short lines) to show surfaces in relief. Researcher Renée Fossett drew the distinction between the two styles: "While European cartography sought to describe physical reality objectively, Inuit mapping attempted to describe practical reality subjectively."

As in any communication between vastly different peoples, something could be lost in the translation. Native North American maps were unlike the topographic or thematic maps the Europeans were familiar with. Complex and serrated coastlines were represented as straight lines, while areas with special significance, such as hunting or spiritual sites, were exaggerated. Certain sections of a route might have been more hazardous to negotiate and so were magnified in representation. Place names were embedded with geographical information. John Spink and D. W. Moodie prepared a monograph with a number of Inuit-derived maps. In one, the map-maker considerably reduced the width of Baffin Island since it could be crossed in three days, and expanded out of all proportion a portage from Lyon Inlet since fifteen "sleeps" were required to reach the coast. Few mapmakers actually acknowledge the peril in cartographic translation. Perhaps the only example is Philippe Buache's *Carte physique des terreins les plus élevés de la partie occidentale du Canada*, published in 1753, which includes along the top the map drawn by the Cree informant. While Buache's would look familiar to Western eyes, the Cree version looks like a necklace of lakes of varying sizes strung together by a river.

Barbara Belyea, an English professor at the University of Calgary who has written forcefully about the clash of cartographic conventions, has described European explorers as translators, trying to understand Native spatial intelligence and to package that intelligence in European terms. "They could gain information only by

finding European equivalents for the map structure and topographical details which the Natives provided," she has written.

> As translators, the explorers occupied a middle position between
> the two cultures, slipping from one convention to the other as they
> guessed what the Native maps "meant." The information was
> lopsided: explorers were ignorant of the territory long familiar to
> its Native inhabitants. As well, the explorers wanted this knowledge
> not as it came structured in Amerindian ways of seeing and experi-
> encing, but broken down into data which they could fit into their
> own geographical scheme.

EXPERIENCE AND IMAGINATION fuel the explorer, and that was
certainly the case in the unfolding story of Canada. The very rare
European ventured inland without a map or Native guide. "I
don't think there's any explorer, French or English, who ever
went into new country without knowing where they were going
or what they were going to find," said Conrad Heidenreich, an
emeritus professor at York University, Toronto, and the leading
expert on the cartography of New France. In Heidenreich's mind,
it was Samuel de Champlain who laid down the template for all
to follow.

There are many reasons why Champlain has a rather high perch
on the list of Canadian explorers. Proficient at estimating latitude,
distance and compass direction, Champlain was the first person
hired specifically to explore and map Canada, and he produced the
country's first scientific documents. Conrad Heidenreich considers
Champlain's 1612, 1613, 1616 and 1632 maps the "mother maps" of
Canadian cartography. But no less significant is the fact that Champlain was the first to systematically question Natives and use the
maps they made for him to learn about the geography of the areas
beyond the St Lawrence River.

Within a couple of days of landing at Tadoussac on his first expedition in 1603, for example, Champlain learned of the existence of Hudson Bay. Through an interpreter (Champlain never learned to speak any Native languages), he found that if he followed the Saguenay River and connecting river systems, he would come upon a major lake and eventually end up at a salt sea. Champlain reasoned that there must be a huge bay from the Atlantic Ocean that led inland and maybe to a Northwest Passage. This was many years before Henry Hudson sailed into the bay that would bear his name. One month later, at the Lachine Rapids, Champlain questioned a Native informant about the upper St Lawrence, and he was rewarded with a tidy map of Lake Ontario and told of Niagara Falls, information that he would later test and confirm. "It set up the process of exploring Canada," said Heidenreich. "Champlain knew that without the Natives, he couldn't have done it."

In July 1615, on his way to meet the Huron, Champlain came upon a chief of the Ottawa at the mouth of the French River. The chief sketched out the western lands, information that made its way the next year onto Champlain's 1616 map of New France, which gave Lake Ontario (Lac St Louis) its first realistic shape. "I gave a hatchet to their chief," Champlain wrote, "who was as happy and pleased with it as if I had made him some rich gift and, entering into conversation with him, I asked him about his country, which he drew for me with charcoal on a piece of tree-bark. He gave me to understand that they had come to this place to dry the fruit called blueberries..."

Champlain's maps were not merely illustrations but working tools. Yet as navigational aids, they had to be accurate only until the mariner reached the mouth of the St Lawrence, at the Gaspé Peninsula, when he began to sail by landmark and soundings. Once inland, the challenge really began, and this is where Champlain relied on Native informants. It was a sort of exploration on the run: Interior surveys were made in the company of Natives on the warpath, usually against the Iroquois. Champlain had to leave instruments behind and rely more on intuition and practical experience.

Thanks to the rapport built up with Native groups, which began with Champlain, the French were all over the interior before the English ever saw Lake Ontario. The English seemed content to hunker down in their Hudson's Bay Company forts and wait for the Natives to come calling with goods. "The English first saw Lake Ontario in 1686," said Heidenreich. "Sixteen eighty-six! By that time the French had been down to the Gulf of Mexico and mapped the entire Great Lakes system." Some English maps issued as late as 1701 showed only a single large lake at the end of the St Lawrence River. Even after a century of trade on the coast of Hudson Bay, the English still knew little of the inland drainage area.

If it was Samuel de Champlain who showed how the New World could be possessed with the help of its own Native peoples, it was left to a determined army of Catholic missionaries to put the plan into action. Anxious to impose a Christian face on the "savage" north country, Champlain in 1615 eagerly arranged for the first missionaries, the Récollet, to come to New France. Thirteen years later the first Jesuits arrived, and for the next century, they managed to map, with impressive acuity, much of the northeastern part of the continent. In particular, the remarkably detailed map of Lake Superior (*Lac Supérieur et autres lieux où sont les Missions des Pères de la Compagnie de Jésus. . .*), created by Jesuit Fathers Claude Dablon and Claude Allouez and published in 1672, is considered one of the most impressive maps of New France in the seventeenth century. Its delineation of Lake Superior and the northern parts of lakes Michigan and Huron was not surpassed until the detailed British hydrographic surveys of the nineteenth century.

The Jesuits based their missions in Canada on their successful experience in Brazil and Paraguay. The primary motive was to convert Natives to Christianity, but the missionaries did have to get around and identify the locations of tribes and their seasonal movements. Maps were essential to accomplish that. Jesuit-inspired maps of the New World, published in Paris, were also useful for attracting resources to the cause. In 1632, the Paris Academy of Sciences asked the Jesuits, most of whom were university professors trained in mathematics and astronomy, to make systematic geographical observations more precise than Champlain could offer. Father Le Jeune, for example, made one of the earliest distance calculations between New France and Dieppe, the centre of French cartography, using the recently invented spherical trigonometry. Le Jeune, who, as the Superior of the Mission at Quebec, delivered the eulogy at Champlain's funeral, was one of the few people in the world using such advanced calculations.

More important than their mathematical or observational skills was the Jesuits' ability to extract geographical intelligence from the Huron, Algonquin and Montagnais. Unlike Champlain, who was always at the mercy of translators, the Jesuits realized that they would have to learn Native languages in order to convert the Natives to Christianity. Father Le Jeune wrote in the 1638 Jesuit *Relations*: "First we make expeditions to go and attack the enemy on their own ground, with their own weapons — that is to say, by knowledge of the Montagnais, Algonkian, and Huron languages." Le Jeune himself resolved to accompany the Montagnais as they set out for the winter hunt in the autumn, after the close of the eel fishery, and to winter with them, to offer comfort at a vulnerable moment, to distribute a drop of baptismal water, but mostly to master the language.

Having learned the Native languages, the Jesuits then imitated Native ways. It was a matter of survival: They had little but their wits and the generosity of their hosts when travelling overland and preaching the gospel. In determining time, distance and direction of travel, they, like other explorers, had nothing but a magnetic compass and their own eyes to observe natural phenomena. As historian D. B. Quinn wrote,

> In the exploring process, the Indian was normally essential to the European trapper, explorer, and missionary; he supplied the canoes and the skill to repair them; he propelled their canoes, if the European had insufficient skill or strength, or else the paddling and steering was shared. He knew the portages far beyond the limits of the explorer's knowledge. When he was in strange territory he was often still the guide, picking up animal trails, indications of changes of soil, rock, and vegetation, co-operating in determining direction, giving advice about weather prospects and the means of mitigating the effects of bad weather.

In their quest to expand their flock, the Jesuits journeyed westward in the seventeenth and eighteenth centuries to the Great Lakes. They did the best they could to make sense of the many lakes and lowlands, sketching prominent features or broad outlines of areas and writing up descriptions in the *Relations*, which were sent to Quebec for editing by the Superior and then on to France for publishing and distribution to an eager audience there and in the rest of Europe. The widely read periodical, containing the finest travel writing of the time, directly influenced prominent seventeenth- and eighteenth-century cartographers. Read today, the *Relations* show how the Jesuits were eager to map, with the help of Native geographical intelligence, not only the physical features of their new territories but also the political distribution of the Native groups they encountered.

The map *Nouvelle France* is a good example of how maps seamlessly incorporated these varied streams of information. *Nouvelle France* is the earliest surviving map that shows the distribution of

Native groups of the eastern Great Lakes prior to the disruption caused by the Iroquois wars. Although its author and date are mysteries, Conrad Heidenreich, in a scholarly whodunit, determined that Quebec surveyor Jean Bourdon, the only trained map-maker in New France at the time, created the map in 1641. Bourdon took the map, sketched on skin, to France early in the 1640s to show the court the geopolitical situation in the colony. The map covers the area between the Saguenay River in the east and the eastern reaches of a large lake west of Lake Huron, and shows the area north from the headwaters of the Ottawa River south to the mouth of the Hudson River.

Bourdon undoubtedly started with Champlain's benchmark map of New France of 1632 and his published writings. A second piece of information, Heidenreich says, was a rough map of the Lake Champlain route, likely obtained from two Frenchmen captured by the Mohawk in the autumn of 1640 and released at Trois-Rivières in June 1641. A third and crucial body of information was the Jesuit *Relations* of 1640, an energetically written travelogue by Father Le Jeune. A keen geographer, Le Jeune recounted his and his colleagues' travels with the Montagnais in the hill country south of the St Lawrence River between Quebec and the Gaspé Peninsula, a time when he encountered many different Native groups. He wrote of a Montagnais chief from Tadoussac who, in April 1637, drew a map of Iroquois country for Governor Montmagny. He said the chief took a pencil and sketched the country where he was going, stating, "Here is the river which is to take us into a great lake; from this lake, we pass into the land of our enemies; in this place are their villages." Most significantly, Le Jeune wrote in his *Relations* of information he received from "Une carte Huronne," a Huron-made map brought to him by Father Ragueneau. Heidenreich surmises that *Nouvelle France* is a partial copy of that Huron map.

Novae Franciae accurata delineatio, produced in 1657 and attributed to Italian Jesuit priest Francesco Bressani. This left sheet of the map, reflecting Bressani's own travels among the Huron, is the most accurate delineation of the Great Lakes prior to 1670. National Archives of Canada (NMC-6339).

Whenever they could, the Jesuits tested the information they received from their Native guides, though on occasion they did not necessarily practise due diligence. Father Pierre Laure, who worked in the Chicoutimi district, clearly never ventured into the interior, judging from his *Relations*. But his maps show details such as portages, a cave and Indian rock paintings. "He had an old Montagnais woman who kept house for him who helped him make maps," said Heidenreich. "He always hoped that one day they would travel into the interior for missionizing. Those maps, like others, were sent to Europe and incorporated into maps of New France ten years later." The maps were accurate enough to help modern archaeologists locate the cave and rock paintings.

Most missionaries, however, based their sketches and manuscript maps on direct experience. Father Francesco Bressani is a classic example. His 1657 manuscript map of New France is often thought to be the most decorative seventeenth-century map of the area, which is made even more incredible considering the travails he experienced. Bressani arrived in New France in 1641 to make astronomical observations of eclipses from which longitude could be calculated, as well as to missionize. In April 1644, at the age of thirty-two, Bressani was on the way from Quebec to the Huron Mission when a party of twenty-seven Iroquois just outside Trois-Rivières captured him. For the next two months, he was tortured, burned and beaten with unremitting fury, mutilated, and left naked and bound to a stake. On the day when he thought he was to be taken out of his misery and mercifully killed, he was given over as a slave to "an Old woman" of the tribe who had lost a grandfather at the hands of the Huron.

On the fifteenth of July, Bressani wrote the following letter to his Father Superior: "I know not whether Your Paternity will recognize the letter of a poor cripple, who formerly, when in perfect health, was well known to you. The letter is badly written, and quite soiled, because, in addition to other inconveniences, he who writes it has only one whole finger on his right hand; and it is difficult to avoid staining the paper with the blood that flows from his wounds, not yet healed: he uses arquebus powder for ink, and the earth for a table. He writes it from the country of the Hiroquois, where at present he happens to be a captive." For good measure, his letter included a sketch of his mutilated hands. Somehow, Bressani survived and was ransomed to the Dutch for several hundred francs and sent back to France.

The next year, Bressani was back in New France, and spent four years in the Huron Mission before returning, for good, to Italy. He wrote an account of his experiences and, in 1657, published his remarkable map, *Novae Franciae Accurata Delineatro*, covering New France west to the eastern reach of Lake Superior. As a base, Bressani modified the map of the Great Lakes published a year earlier by Nicolas Sanson, who, in turn, had based his on Jesuit information and unpublished Jesuit manuscript maps. Bressani's richly decorated map, considered the rarest map of Canada, is most interesting for its insets rather than what it showed of the territory. In one inset, Bressani described the Huron country northwest of Lake Ontario in good detail. Almost one-quarter of the map is taken over by a vivid illustration of the martyrdom of fellow missionaries Jean de Brébeuf and Gabriel Lalemant by the Iroquois; the missionaries were fitted with red-hot hatchets, slashed with glowing bark, "baptized" in boiling water and cut up alive. In the opposite corner is another inset, this time with a Huron family worshipping in front of a cross. It includes remarkably accurate pictures of Native life, such as canoeing, hunting with bow and arrow, and meeting in council.

More than one person has wondered who actually drew the famed illustrations on *Novae Franciae*. Most assume that Bressani was responsible, considering the well-informed detail. They are the most accurate and unique pictures of Native life in the seventeenth century to have emerged. But there is the small matter of Bressani's hands, burned and mutilated as a result of the torture inflicted by the Iroquois. Was he physically able to draw? As well, Bressani's name does not actually appear on the map. The name that does appear is that of Giovanni Frederico Pesca, an Italian portrait engraver famous at the time.

Looking at the story from all the angles, Heidenreich believes Bressani did indeed inspire the illustrations. For one thing, Pesca never left Italy and therefore was in no position to picture life in New France. Someone — Bressani — must have supplied him with superb sketches. Heidenreich then turns his attention to Bressani's sketch of his hands, which the emeritus professor says, the priest included out of religious pride.

Bressani's letter to his Superior is a curious thing. "It is in the form of a confession," says Heidenreich:

> I was told that his hands were so badly mutilated that he couldn't do Mass properly, like pour the wine. So when he returned from captivity, he made his way to Rome to see the Pope, and the Pope gave him a dispensation to say Mass without the use of his fingers. That's why his sketch of his hands was included. He sent it along not only as an excuse for his bad handwriting but he knew that as a priest he is mutilated. I think if he could draw his hand and write a letter he probably supplied the sketches that Pesca used to render it onto the map.

Bressani's map, like most Jesuit charts, is replete with Native place names and tribal locations. In the context of the times, such a strategy was highly unusual and was not followed by the French or English. Jean-Louis Baptiste Franquelin, a respected cartographer in New France in the 1670s, was an early agitator for precise surveying and French place names. In a memoir to the French court in March

1689, he wrote, "It appears necessary to divide this huge country into provinces which would be delimited and designated by permanent French names, as well as special rivers and spots; for this we would suppress all Indian names which bring confusion only because they are changed very often and because each tribe gives its own designations, so that one place has always many names." After the conquest of New France, the English started systematically to change some of the French place names to English. "Look at Northern Ontario, which is still full of Native place names," said Heidenreich. "You won't find that in the United States, where they were taken out."

Studying Bressani's map today, with continued tension over Native land claims in mind, it is tempting to see in it a rare and accurate picture of Canada as a confederation of tribes living in tightly defined and unchanging territories. That might not be too far off: Bressani, in creating such a detailed map of Native territory in his campaign to save more souls, allows us, three hundred and forty-five years later, to appreciate the territorial dominion of the Huron, Iroquois and Montagnais, in relation to one another and to the dominant waterways. Tempting, but Conrad Heidenreich offers few words of caution. For one thing, some Native groups were known by more than one name. For another, Native names in early seventeenth century sources are given in French, Iroquoian or Algonquian. Since Native languages were strictly oral and featured many regional dialects, "the name of any particular Native group had to be recorded phonetically and could therefore be spelled in a variety of ways." Compounding matters was the fact that the Europeans who recorded the names were often less than competent in other languages. The location of Native groups was also problematic. Some groups were seasonally mobile, and most underwent population dislocation at some period in their history. "Since most maps are compilations, it makes them untrustworthy as evidence for Native locations unless the information on the map can be dated," Heidenreich has written.

WHILE THE GEOGRAPHIC intelligence and unpublished manuscript maps amassed by the Jesuits made a great impact on administrators, traders and other explorers in Canada, their greatest influence was on a new generation of cartographers back in France. Cartographers such as the Delisle family were applying new and more rigorous standards to the act of producing a map, and the maps they created gave those in the Old World a picture of the mysterious and wild lands across the ocean. At the time, a newly published map was the equivalent of a video report from a CNN news crew on location. And one of the greatest sources of material for that crew were the maps and *Relations* of the Jesuits.

It helped that French authorities recognized the value of maps produced on the fly in New France, and took steps to harness the power of information. After Governor Frontenac appointed Jean-Louis Baptiste Franquelin the first royal cartographer in New France in 1686, a law was enacted that everyone travelling in the interior had to deposit diaries and sketch maps, which were then sent to France to the Ministry of the Marine.

The act of making a map back in France was very much like the act of exploring, a combination of experience and imagination. Just as the Jesuit had to interpret and divine from the Native testimony, the cartographer in Paris had to sift through Jesuit testimony and all the other information coming out of the young colony and consolidate it. Some of the cartographic information flowing into Europe was decades old, since there was no system in place to get information onto printed maps regularly. The printed maps were often an outgrowth of a chaotic ad hoc process, for reasons that had nothing to do with North America and everything to do with engravers and print shops in Europe having to make money to survive.

The famous *La Carte du Canada ou Novvelle France* of 1703 reveals the dynamics often at play. The work of Guillaume Delisle, it is lauded as the first map to accurately depict the latitude and longitude of Canada. Based on seven years of thorough research (although not including a personal visit to the New World), *La Carte du Canada* had a huge impact when it was published, highlighting the height of French power in Canada at one moment in time. Overnight, the map became the standard that formed the basis of maps to come. It was remarkable not only for the research that went into its creation but also for its sound mathematical basis; Delisle used precise calculations of the eclipse to fix the precise longitude of Quebec, where previously it had been only guessed at. *La Carte du Canada* is hailed as an early example of a cool, dispassionate, almost scientific map, very different from the impressionistic and cruder maps that came out of Canada in the sixteenth and seventeenth centuries. But even though it does not overtly show it, Delisle's 1703 map still containes a substantial amount of Native information and reflections of an imperial power.

Known as the first modern cartographer, Guillaume Delisle learned the trade from his father, Claude, a celebrated history and geography teacher who founded the family cartographic business. Guillaume learned his lessons well, applying scientific methods and scrupulous examination of original sources. Unlike earlier cartographers, Delisle left blanks representing unknown areas rather than fabricating hypothetical features.

In *L'Atelier Delisle* (2001), Nelson Martin-Dawson, associate professor in the department of history and political science at the University of Sherbooke, studied the work behind the scenes of the Delisle map, showing how Delisle made sense of all the information at his disposal: the voluminous travelogues in the Jesuit *Relations* and elsewhere, intelligence about certain waterways, distances between villages, anything that would supplement the hard scientific observations and maps already published. Which information should be trusted? How should contradictions and inconsistencies be handled? As Martin-Dawson pointed out, the Delisles professed to care little about the political dimensions of their work, considering such matters nothing but geographical ornaments ("qu'un accessoire, un ornement & une broderie que les historiens ajout[ai]ent au canevas qui leur [était] donné par les géographes").

On his preparatory sketch maps, Delisle would make marginal notes of certain consistencies and inconsistencies in distances or place names, and try to work out a concordance for the different scales and measurements used in Spanish, English and French maps. He would have to work his way through meanings of words in different languages, though it helped that Delisle was comfortable with many languages, and was aware of North American Native geographical terms.

Delisle produced twenty-six sketches of varying detail based on the Jesuit *Relations*, some highly annotated. Delisle appreciated the Jesuits' ability to make mathematical measurements based on astronomical observations for latitude and longitude. When concerned about dubious or inconsistent information, he compiled a list of questions to pose to explorers on the ground, in particular Pierre Le Moyne d'Iberville, through an exchange of letters and visits to Paris. Delisle knew many of the missionaries and explorers himself, which greatly enhanced his ability to query them on their judgment. What did the "savages" mean in terms of distance when they said there are two nights' journey between locations? D'Iberville tried to help:

When it takes one day to get from one place to the next, the Natives (savages) say one day. But when you have to sleep before arriving,

in other words, it takes two days, they call that one night. When
they sleep six nights it means seven days.

In at least one case, according to Martin-Dawson, Delisle was
willing to include Native information not necessarily confirmed by a
European. On the map, Lake Winnipeg (Lac des Assenipoils) is
shown with its water communication down to Hudson Bay, but this
was from an Indian report rather than from European discovery.

Martin-Dawson says that, to the Delisles, the natural divisions,
such as mountains and waterways, were of more interest than
political features, since borders and people move and disappear,
unlike mountains. Still, the Delisles took great care to identify the
locations of many Native groups, information that had commercial as well as purely scientific dimensions. Martin-Dawson found
that about fifty Amerindian nations were identified in the twenty-
six sketches drawn from information in the *Relations*, plus two
other sketches from other missionaries. But on the final map of
1703, only fifteen of those nations were identified. Why were
so many omitted?

In some cases, such as the Algonquins along both sides of the
Ottawa River, Delisle consolidated a number of related bands into
one heading. In other cases, such as the Mistassini Cree, in the
middle of present-day Quebec, traditional grounds identified in
earlier maps or Jesuit testimony had been abandoned, either due to
famine, disease inadvertently introduced by Europeans, or the collapse of hunting grounds. The one omission that Martin-Dawson has
trouble explaining is that of the Montagnais, one of the best-known
Aboriginal nations. Among the first to meet the French, and likely
the most open to the missionaries' offerings, the Montagnais were
laid low by epidemics and by warfare with the Iroquois. Formerly
strong on both sides of the St Lawrence River, they were shown on
earlier maps and still existed in the Tadoussac region when Delisle

was working on his map. Martin-Dawson is convinced it was not an accidental omission, but he does not offer an alternative hypothesis.

Delisle might have disdained politics and anything unscientific, but his landmark 1703 map showcases a large cartouche in the upper left corner, complete with impressionistic scenes from the New World that may suggest imperial claims — albeit not as transparent as the 1788 wall map of the Western hemisphere by L'Abbé Jean Baptiste Louis Clouet, showing Jacques Cartier setting up a cross to claim Canada for the King of France. The work of artist N. Guérard, the Delisle cartouche carried the symbol of French royalty. Other elements in the cartouche included a Jesuit missionary baptizing an Indian and a Récollet missionary showing Natives the road to heaven, an Iroquois brandishing a scalp from a French head, Iroquois on a bed of thistles, a Huron brandishing a rosary, and beaver. On a map otherwise laden with scientific pretension, this is one of the few spots where Native faces were depicted, albeit as a flamboyant adornment.

THE ERA OF LARGE-SCALE French surveying and mapping ended with the fall of Louisbourg in 1758, but significant mapping by French missionaries carried on to the last days of Canada's exploration. Taking up the challenge of the Jesuits more than two hundred years later, and using many of the strategies employed in the early days of New France, the Oblates made their own mapping mark on the Northwest in the late nineteenth century.

The Religious Institute of the Oblates of Mary Immaculate was founded in Paris in 1816. Twenty-five years later, the Oblates established their first foreign mission in Canada and, guided by their motto, *Usque ad extremum terrae!* (Right to the ends of the Earth!), set their sights on converting the Native peoples of the Mackenzie Valley. The long-bearded Oblates, with their distinctive black robes, earned a reputation among the Metis, Dene and Inuit as independent and passionate religious pioneers. For more than a century they, along with the RCMP and the Hudson's Bay Company, represented the white presence in the Canadian North.

Like the Jesuits, the Oblates missionized Native people while they were on the move between seasonal activities. Many of the itinerant missionaries could not survive the rigours of the tundra and the boreal forest, and either died travelling overland or returned to France. Still others developed a dim view of those they were trying to "save." But like the Jesuits, many of the Oblates were fascinated by the Canadian world and absorbed by their studies of the North. Men such as Father Van de Velde made observations of polar bears, and Father Guy Mary Rousselière worked at archaeological digs at Pelly Bay, Chesterfield Inlet and Baker Lake. They were particularly fascinated by the Amerindian view of the land.

Well into the nineteenth century, the only things known, geographically speaking, of the western Arctic and the Mackenzie watershed were fruits of the efforts of famed explorers such as Sir John Franklin, Alexander Mackenzie and Peter Warren Dease. Theirs were high-profile projects, eagerly followed in Canada and Britain. These maps, hard won to be sure, essentially were road maps in that they sketched the main arterial waterways of the region. Fairly well-known were the large lakes of Manitoba, the west coast of Hudson Bay, and the Assiniboine River valley and the prairies. There was knowledge of a chain of mountains beyond the Saskatchewan River and of extensive prairie grasslands to the south of the Saskatchewan forks. But the interior of the country remained little known to Europeans.

In 1875, seemingly out of nowhere, two maps published by the Société de Géographie de Paris revealed what was between the waterways, from the Rockies east to the Coppermine River and the Arctic coast south to Great Slave Lake. Just as surprising was the source of these maps: not a professional explorer or surveyor but an Oblate missionary by the name of Father Emile Petitot.

Among a colourful crew of missionaries, Petitot was a standout. Respected among the Native people, feted by the geographical societies of England and France yet feared and loathed by his colleagues, Petitot was one of Canada's greatest amateur geographers, ethnographers and map-makers. Until aerial surveying was conducted later in the twentieth century, Petitot's maps of the Northwest Territories were considered the standard for all others. He compiled a French-Eskimo dictionary, based on the dialect spoken by the Tchiglit, who lived at the mouths of the Mackenzie and Anderson rivers, and a dictionary of the major Athapaskan languages — including the Chipewyan, Hareskin and Loucheux dialects — that is still used today. Petitot's mapping and other scientific achievements are all the more remarkable considering the missionary spent much of his time on the thin edge between sanity and madness while trying to stay one step ahead of the Superior who wanted to banish him from Athabasca country.

In 1862, only two weeks after he was ordained as an Oblate priest, Petitot found himself on a ship headed for Quebec and then on to the Mackenzie River, where he lived for the next twelve years at missions in Fort Providence, Fort Resolution and Fort Good Hope. Not that he stayed long at any of these locales. Most of the time he travelled with Native companions in the uncharted areas of the North, places between the well-surveyed rivers and coastal regions. Using Fort Good Hope as his base, Petitot travelled from Great Slave Lake to the Arctic Sea and between the Mackenzie and Laird rivers.

He was a keen observer of both the land and the people who guided him. In books that he would later publish, he described Amerindian weapons, housing construction, sleeping arrangements, detailed physical characteristics, tattooing, cannibalism, incest and the trafficking of women. Of the small tribe known as the Loucheux, "the mountain dwellers" who were nearly all cross-eyed, Petitot observed, "It was among those Indians that I saw the first Redskins who were hump-backed, misshapen or with tooth trouble." Elsewhere he added, "The number of stammerers among the Dindjie: 5 stammerers out of 150 people."

Petitot also set down important observations of Native cosmology and wayfaring. While exploring around Good Hope in 1878, he learned that the Tchiglit named the north *Kanoug-argnerk*, meaning the "desolate, unfortunate baneful" point of space, that the Eskimo call the Orient *Tcanera-nerk*, the foul point, because it is from the east that arrive hail, blizzards and snowstorms, the long summer rains, and sleet, and that they call the south the "previous point," towards which aspirations and desires are directed. To the Tchiglit, the west is *Ouavan-nerk*, the initial point, the point of departure, of origin; to the Eskimo, the west is simply unknown.

He clearly learned much about living off the land in their company. In a letter to J. Fabre in June 1868, Petitot wrote: "At the ends of all islands or deltas of the river, where there is wood, the Eskimos drive wooden shafts into the river bottom, to serve as guiding-marks. These are fir trees from which some of the limbs have been trimmed off. Every channel having only one such guiding-mark is a dead end. The presence of many guiding-marks shows that the channel is a safe route and leads to one of the four outlets of the river."

Like the Jesuits farther east, Petitot put a Native face on the maps of the Northwest. His two maps (one redrawn by a cartographer and a second manuscript map done in Petitot's own hand) completed the cartographic work of Sir John Franklin. They cover the Arctic basin area between the Coppermine River and the Rockies and from Great Slave Lake to the Arctic Sea. They include geographical data of the interior between Great Bear Lake, the Mackenzie River and the Arctic, showing the hunting territory of the Dene-dindjie tribes, permanent trails, boundaries of tribal territories and "Indian names of all localities." They also revealed the Rivière à Roncière-Le

Noury, discovered by Petitot in 1868. For eighty years, geographers denied its existence until aerial photography proved Petitot right.

In *The geography of the Athabaskaw-Mackenzie region and of the Great Lakes of the Arctic Basin*, Petitot revealed how he compiled his maps. Since he had no other instruments than a compass and a watch, and had no means of getting any, he used the Franklin Expedition maps as a foundation on which he added his own geographical data. "I therefore preserved the data that I had checked with the aid of my own instruments (such as they were) and made no change in the general delineation of the Mackenzie River and the Rocky Mountains, nor in the location and general outlines of Great Bear and Great Slave Lakes," he wrote. "Given two points whose positions had already been well established by means of instruments, and whose distance one from the other, in geographic miles, was known to me, I set down within that particular area my own geographic material." Periodically, he would compare his compass north with the North Star to keep track of the local compass variation caused by variation in the magnetic field.

Besides taking Paris by storm, Petitot became the toast of Ottawa and London. He addressed a Canadian Senate committee looking into the geological makeup of the Mackenzie basin, while the Royal Geographical Society awarded him the Back Prize in 1883. Lieutenant-General Sir J. H. Lefroy addressed the Geographical Section of the British Association in Swansea in 1880 and spoke glowingly of the special contributions of Petitot:

> He has on foot or in canoe, often accompanied only by Indians or Esquimaux, again and again traversed that desolate country in every direction. He navigated the Mackenzie ten times between Great Slave Lake and Fort Good Hope and eight times between Fort Good Hope and its mouth. We owe to his visits the disentanglement of a confusion which existed between the mouth of the Peel

*River and those of the Mackenzie, owing to their uniting in one
delta; the explanation of the so-called Esquimaux Lake, which has
no existence, and the delineation of the course of three large rivers
which fall into the Polar Sea in that neighbourhood. Petitot also
traced and sketched several lakes and chains of lakes which support
his opinion that this region is partaking of that operation of elevation
which extends to Hudson's Bay.*

Petitot was clearly an explorer at heart, and travelling on the land
had the added bonus of being far from the watchful eye of his superiors. According to University of Ottawa religion professor Robert
Choquette, after living with Petitot for a year, the coadjutor bishop
of St Boniface said, "He dreams only of long voyages. He often asks
me to send him to the Eskimos . . . He charges carelessly into the
greatest dangers. Last fall, I had to invoke religious obedience to pre-
vent him from going skating on ice that was only one inch thick . . .
He is even more careless on a canoe or barge. He had to freeze his
fingers before agreeing to wear mittens. . . . He has a great facility for
learning, and an even greater one for walking, but . . . he must be
made into a good missionary."

It does not appear that Petitot was made into a great missionary.
Perhaps that is why he seemed to be so popular among the Native
people with whom he travelled. If you believe his own memoirs, his
hosts respected him. The Hareskin called him *Yat-ci-Nezun* (Father
Good), while the Trakwel-Ottiné looked upon him as a great physician, *Intranzétchot*. This was no small feat, and likely was a factor in
his success as a map-maker and observer of the natural world. As
retired Canada Land Surveyor and map historian Lou Sebert
pointed out in the journal *Geomatica*:

*It appears that he had no difficulty in getting Native people to dis-
close the names they had given to geographic features. This is in*

marked contrast to the experience of Dr. Bell and other geologists working in northern Ontario and Quebec at about the same period. They found that the Indians of their area were rather reticent in disclosing place names and in fact were rather casual about consistency in naming features. In some cases, a place had a winter name that was quite different from its summer name. Petitot seems to have experienced no such difficulty but it must be remembered that he could speak the Native dialects while Bell had to work through Native interpreters.

But for his colleagues and superiors, Petitot was a handful. His sexual longing for young Indian men caused consternation, and when he ignored his promise to stay away from one particular boy, Bishop Faraud in 1866 pronounced a sentence of excommunication. It was later lifted when the young man in question married. Petitot also exhibited erratic and violent behaviour; he was convinced the Indians and whites were trying to kill him. He would swerve between normalcy and madness; and when darkness came, as it did in the winter of 1868, he became stark raving mad. He predicted the end of the world, accused his Superior Father Séguin of murdering Jesus Christ and the Virgin Mary, and proclaimed that he was a Mohammedan, Jew, pagan, Antichrist or angel. During these crises, Petitot was frequently tied down and placed under guard after having run around naked outdoors at temperatures of minus forty degrees Celsius. On two occasions, he tried to murder Séguin by strangling him or butchering him with an axe, in order to offer him in sacrifice for the salvation of the world — all the while screaming and howling. In October 1881, he was directed to return to France, an order he ignored. It was not until 1882 that Petitot was surreptitiously registered in a Montreal hospital for the mentally ill, and spent two years there before returning to France and living out his days. The era of missionary mapping of Canada was drawing to a close.

IN THE CULTURAL TRANSACTION between the Amerindian and the map-making missionary/explorer, it is hard to see what enduring benefits accrued to the Native peoples beyond, some would say, an introduction to Christianity. For their part, the Jesuit and Oblate missions failed in their efforts to convert the "savages" in any great numbers, although, in the case of the Oblates, they did benefit from gaining a better appreciation for Native worldviews.

The maps that were born of this exchange have a greater legacy. For one, they were tangible evidence of Native dominions in the inland regions; Jacques Bellin's definitive 1744 map of New France, *Carte de la Partie Orientale de la Nouvelle France ou du Canada*, based largely on Jesuit information, rightly refers to these areas as "pays" — countries, or nations. But the maps were also the prime means by which images of the New World were fixed in the minds of Europeans; with their royal seals, images of barbarians in Elysian Fields and Euro-derived place names, maps served as subtle and overt symbols of possession. Consigned to ghostly memory were the dream maps of another civilization.

3

MISDIRECTION

THE MISSIONARY MAP-MAKERS had one motivation: to convert
Canada's Native people and to save souls. As soldiers in God's army,
they were passionate believers, flag bearers not for reason but for the
Bible and the ancient texts that defined their world. Yet as map-
makers, they were cool, dispassionate and highly effective observers.
Their charts, built from on-the-ground experience or Native intelligence, are paragons of accuracy, despite being created by primitive
navigational tools. By contrast, professional cartographers in London and Paris, worldly and enlightened, all too often turned out
maps of the New World shot through with sloppiness and wishful
thinking. And saying that is being kind.

To be unkind is to say that many of the notable maps of the age
were cynical constructs designed to get financiers to part with
money, to boost sales of atlases and to further imperial designs. Perhaps the best way to look at this chapter of map-making is to view
eighteenth-century maps of Canada as elaborate paintings, with

brush strokes of fantasy and misinterpretation of Native accounts filling in the blank spaces in Europe's cartographic imagination. Rumours were accepted as fact and set down on maps, leading to more wild speculations. Faked maps were copied in whole or in part with even more errors mixed in with reality. Although some impressive coastal charting was produced, often such maps were not published, since the market was much more developed for maps of speculative geography. These cartographers, historian R. A. Skelton once wrote, worked at "the uncertain boundary between knowledge and ignorance."

Nowhere is this more evident than in the mapping of western North America. Instead of the fantasy of sea monsters or mermaids populating the North Atlantic Ocean, the unknown western part of North America was filled with invented rivers and mountains. The power of wilful imagination over experience ruled the maps of this time. Map-makers, who rarely had first-hand information, accepted the exaggerated accounts of travellers, who in turn sometimes based their stories on hearsay. The New World was simply a roadblock to seafaring nations that craved a share of the lucrative Eastern spice trade. Spain and Portugal had claimed the southern sea routes; France, England and the Netherlands desperately sought a western sea route to the Pacific and, from there, to China and the Spice Islands. The St Lawrence and Great Lakes drainage system could get them only halfway there. The anxious Europeans wanted to get to Asia at all costs, hoping that beyond the ken of "unruly savages," beyond the tall grass prairie, beyond the mountains, lay Cathay or El Dorado. Canada was merely the back of beyond.

Perversely, once those fantasies and impulses were brush-stroked on maps, they became a reality that shaped further exploration and nation building, and led to bona fide exploration and mapping.

IF YOU ARE PRODUCING A map of an area for which there is only incomplete information, you have a number of choices. You can draw elaborate cartouches filled with illustrations of the royal seal or of the people, fauna and flora of the area. The Dutch were particularly good at this. Or you can fill the blank spaces with elaborate geographical theories and pass them off as fact, a trick that both the English and French map-makers practised with Canada.

In the case of the English, official policy was to leave the financial initiative for exploration and settlement to private investors. Maps, then, served as glossy come-ons. "Maps that promoters commissioned contained analogous embellishments, depicting enticing water routes for which no evidence actually existed," American map historian Stephanie Abbot Roper has written. "Cartographers drew their maps to emphasize marketable commodities such as furs, timber, grape vines (for producing wine), and sassafras trees (for silk worms). In their maps they also stressed similarities with England and deemphasized any natural hazards that might deter investment."

When making such points, Roper had in mind the quintessential English cartographic huckster, Michael Lok. Lok was a high-class promoter, gambler, entrepreneur, and likely swindler. He and Richard Hakluyt were the leading promoters of English expansion to North America during the Elizabethan era. Lok is perhaps best known as the impresario behind Martin Frobisher and that explorer's efforts during three expeditions to discover the eastern entrance to the Northwest Passage and to mine gold in Arctic Canada. Like Don King pumping interest in his latest heavyweight fighter, Lok paraded Frobisher and his boat, as well as many other artifacts from the "Orient": souvenirs such as flowers, grasses and other foreign plants and small black stones that, Lok whispered, could be gold. He tried to convince the English public that Frobisher was not a pirate but a loyal and brave agent of the Crown. He enlisted troubadours to compose ballads praising Frobisher's valiant exploits.

The centrepiece of Lok's efforts to drum up support for expeditions and colonization of northeastern North America was his 1582 map of the north polar region, published in Hakluyt's *Divers Voyages Touching the Discoverie of America*. Lok's map is a blend of fact and fiction: There are mythical Atlantic islands of Brasil and St Brendan, the fictitious Sea of Verrazanao in the Chesapeake area, names of discoverers such as Cartier and the location of a planned colony. Lok pictured Canada as a motley assortment of huge islands and loosely connected peninsulas; Frobisher's travels in 1576, 1577 and 1578 are more or less correctly laid down, including Frisland (Greenland) and the Baffin Island discoveries. The landforms on either side of the newly discovered Frobisher's Strait are named for Queen Elizabeth and, rather immodestly, Lok himself. The map shows the location of Meta Incognita, the Unknown Shore, although in greatly simplified form, and omits the northwest part of the continent to imply ease of access to the South Seas.

Nothing on Lok's map indicated that he was also a major promoter and principal investor in the Northwest Passage exploration. On the contrary, this was how Hakluyt described his cartographer friend in the accompanying text: "The mappe is Master Michael Lockes, a man, for his knowledge in Divers languages, and especially in Cosmographie, able to doe his countrey good, and worthie, in my judgement, for the manifolde good partes in him, of good reputation and better fortune."

Frobisher's unsuccessful ventures ruined Lok the financier but did nothing to discourage Lok the map-maker. In April 1596, Lok arrived in Venice for business meetings with the Levant Company, where he met Juan de Fuca. De Fuca was a Greek pilot in the service of Spain, and he had a fantastic tale for Lok. De Fuca, who was then about sixty years old, had sailed in the West Indies for forty years, and during his return from the Philippines to Mexico had been robbed by English explorer Thomas Cavendish, losing goods to the value of sixty thousand ducats, a substantial amount of money at the time. He also stated that he had been sent from Mexico with three ships and a hundred men to discover the Strait of Anian, but a mutiny broke out, preventing further progress. In 1592, however, the viceroy sent him back again to follow up the previous voyage, on this occasion with greater success. De Fuca apparently sailed through the alleged strait, between forty-seven and forty-eight degrees North, which led into a broad body of water. He reported that at the entrance to the strait there was a great headland, or island, with a high pinnacle or spired rock, like a pillar. De Fuca returned to Acapulco hoping for a reward for his discovery, but after two years, was sent to Spain, where he was given a royal welcome but no compensation.

He apparently also looked to the English for support: If the Queen would furnish him a vessel of forty tons, he guaranteed to sail through the strait in ninety days. That offer was not taken up. In meeting Lok, he again offered to repeat his voyage in return for a certain payment, but despite Lok's efforts, de Fuca never did return to the Pacific Northwest.

With hindsight, de Fuca's voyage is of doubtful authenticity. De Fuca might have spun the yarn from information he picked up on a voyage to the Pacific Northwest that really did happen. The strait now bearing the name of Juan de Fuca was identified in 1787 by Charles William Barkley, who recognized it as that discovered by the Greek mariner. But the strait that bears his name is a full degree farther north than what de Fuca described, an error that is often regarded as too large. Whether or not de Fuca actually made the discovery that he claimed, his tale would loom large in the carto-graphic imaging of the Pacific Northwest for the better part of the seventeenth and eighteenth centuries, especially so once even more dubious tales were added to the canvas.

WHILE ENGLISH MAP-MAKERS could not decide whether Canada was a get-rich-quick scheme or a geographical barrier to the Orient, the French let their imagination loose. Although the work of France's best map-makers showed marked advancement in accuracy over the English, the French, too, were consumed by finding an easy passage through Canada via a great river to the west, and by increasing their stake in the fur trade by encouraging westward exploration. Perhaps the earliest backer of this vision was Louis-Armand de Lom d'Arce, Baron de la Hontan. La Hontan was a lively rogue and classic pamphleteer, lovable only until he tried his hand at drawing a map. He arrived in Canada in 1684 as a seventeen-year-old lieutenant to serve in an expedition against the Iroquois. He spent a decade fighting the Indians and commanding posts, and had the opportunity to explore the Mississippi. At the age of twenty-seven, he was forced to flee the colony after being charged with insubordination by the governor of Acadia, under whom he served (he replied to the charges with "scurrilous songs"). La Hontan was not reluctant to stir the pot of controversy. In one of his writings, La Hontan delivered a devastating critique of Christianity through the mouth of a Huron Indian named Adario, who considered Jesuit teachings to be full of contradiction and Christianity as nothing more than a social custom.

While religious dogma had little hold over La Hontan, an idea that captured his imagination — and captivated the elite of the Old World — was the possibility of discovering a west-flowing river slicing through the continent and emptying into the ocean. It was one of the most romantic geographical concepts of the day, since it represented the best chance for an efficient route through the northern part of the continent. The earliest written accounts of a passage to the west appeared in the travelogues written by the Jesuits in 1640. The missionaries wrote that they had heard from Natives living in the Lake Superior region of a sea north of present-day New Mexico that allowed access to Japan and China. The information caught the interest of the famed Delisle family of map-makers. In 1697, they placed what they called *Mer de l'Ouest* on a globe, where it took on the shape of the Mediterranean Sea.

A western passage to riches was too irresistible a narrative for La Hontan to pass up. In 1703, he published a widely read and influential volume, *Nouveaux Voyages*. In it, he depicted an imaginary waterway named Rivière Longue flowing into the Mississippi from a ridge of mountains, on the reverse side of which another waterway flowed, with sizable cities running into a salt lake nearly a thousand miles in circumference. And he had the Ottawa River merging with the Abitibi, which in turn flowed into the Albany River and then to Lake Superior and James Bay. The publication sold well in both France and England; it eventually appeared in thirteen editions in French, English, Dutch, German and Italian. *Nouveaux Voyages* has been widely derided; map historian Louis Karpinski wrote in 1931 that La Hontan was a cartographer "for whom the real facts were only incidental or accidental."

Karpinski was perhaps unduly harsh in his assessment. Speculative map-making in La Hontan's day was akin to creative nonfiction in ours — liberties were taken and understood as such. It is true, however, that La Hontan's successful book did much to undo the sound information published in earlier maps by Jesuits Claude Dablon and Louis Hennepin. La Hontan's imaginary geography made its way onto the otherwise celebrated 1703 map by Guillaume Delisle, *La Carte du Canada ou de la Nouvelle France*, and was still showing up on maps until late in the eighteenth century. This was partly because penny-pinching map-makers used existing copperplates of maps for as long as possible, changing the date but leaving in stale information.

French officials desperately wanted to believe La Hontan's claims, particularly after they appeared to be validated by the sober and professional Delisle family. And they set out to prove these claims.

Between 1731 and 1742, the French government sent Canadian-born Pierre Gaultier de Varennes, sieur de La Vérendrye, on several expeditions into Western Canada to establish trading posts and to find a route to the Pacific Ocean.

La Vérendrye eagerly accepted the challenge, particularly the challenge to find the inevitable passage to the Orient. In all his travels in the interior, La Vérendrye could usually be heard prob-ing the Native people he encountered for information on what lay in the unknown West. A Cree chief named Ochagach finally told La Vérendrye what he wanted to hear. Ochagach said that he himself

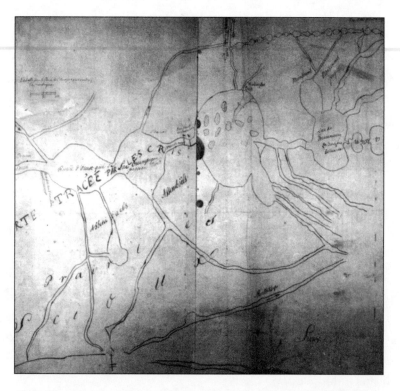

Carte Tracée par les Cris was likely compiled in 1729 by Pierre Gaultier de Varennes, sieur de La Vérendrye from three Cree maps. It depicts the region around present-day Lake Winnipeg and Lake of the Woods. National Archives of Canada (NMC-24556).

had been on a great lake lying west of Lake Superior, that out of it flowed a river westward, and that he had paddled down this river until he came to water that, as La Vérendrye understood, rose and fell like the tide. Ochagach said he had never ventured to the mouth of this river but that he was told it emptied into a great body of salt water upon the shores of which lived many people. To back up his story, he drew maps for La Vérendrye, one of a number that La Vérendrye commissioned from Cree and Assiniboine Indians. La Vérendrye consolidated the information into a large map extending some two thousand kilometres west of Lake of the Woods until just before the Pacific Ocean.

Like so many other explorers, La Vérendrye and his three sons who accompanied him misinterpreted much of what they transcribed from the Indian maps and oral testimony of Ochagach and other Cree chiefs. They came to believe that a "Rivière de l'Ouest," River of the West, connected with an opening on the Pacific coast discovered by Martin d'Aguilar in 1603, and that the river flowed into an inland sea called La Mer de L'Ouest, first mentioned by the Delisles. Unfortunately, neither the River of the West nor La Mer de L'Ouest existed; the Indians were likely referring to the Nelson River and Lake Winnipeg. Likewise, La Vérendrye perpetuated the myth of Montagne de Pierre Brilliante, a "small mountain, the stones of which sparkle night and day," from information received from Indians. On the other hand, La Vérendrye did not appear to put much weight on another Indian story about lofty mountains beyond which was a lake "of which was not good to drink." (The Rocky Mountains would not show up on maps until the second half of the eighteenth century.)

Emboldened by the Native intelligence, La Vérendrye set out in 1731 for the West with three sons, a nephew, a Jesuit priest, and Ochagach as guide. By 1739, La Vérendrye had reached the Mandan villages on the upper Missouri. That year, his son François explored the

Saskatchewan River. François and another son, Louis, explored the area southwest of the Mandan villages to the Rocky Mountains. But there was no great western river or sea, just the inconvenient Lake Winnipeg that empties into the Atlantic, not the Pacific, via Hudson Bay.

Like all the maps and charts produced by explorers and missionaries in New France, the cartographic documentation from the La Vérendrye expeditions was sent to the Dépot des Cartes, Plans et Journeaux de la Marine in Paris, the main depository of documents relating to French exploration in North America. Jacques-Nicolas Bellin was the senior hydrographic engineer at the Dépot. Bellin made several maps of North America, including one for the Jesuit scholar Father Charlevoix, sent by the regent of Louis XV to collect all information on lands to the west of Lake Superior. Bellin incorporated La Vérendrye's misinformation, including the Rivière de l'Ouest, La Mer de l'Ouest and Montagne de Pierre Brilliante, in the maps he made in 1744 for Charlevoix's *Histoire et description générale de la Nouvelle France*. For good measure, he threw in the mysterious Juan de Fuca Strait. His River of the West flowed westward just north of latitude fifty degrees North via present day Rainy Lake and Lake of the Woods into Lake Winnipeg. Speculation was turning into certainty.

IF THERE WAS ONE GROUP of cartographers willing to rise above fantasy map-making, it would have been the Delisle family firm. Yes, the Delisles placed the Mer de l'Ouest on a globe in 1697, over the objections of Claude Delisle, who remained skeptical because the information was not based on first-hand accounts. Significantly, the Mer did not appear on the family's famous 1703 map of Canada.

But apparently there was a black sheep hiding in the Delisle flock. Joseph-Nicolas Delisle did not share his family's reluctance to engage in geographical fantasy. In the days when the French and Russian elites were close, Joseph-Nicolas held the position of

Russian Academician and was deeply involved in Russia's efforts to confirm that Siberia was not connected to America, something that Russian sailors and *zemleprokhodsty* (pathfinders) knew for certain. (In fact, in 1648 a Cossack by the name of Semyon Ivanovich Deshnev set out in an open boat from the river Kolyma on a fur-hunting expedition, rounded Cape Chukchi, the outermost point of Asia, and then was driven out to sea; by the time he had reached land he had discovered that Asia and America were not connected to one another. The report of his travels was filed in an office in Yakutsk in northeast Siberia and forgotten.)

The Russians were anxious to be regarded as equal to Europeans, and figured one way to do this was to produce a reliable map of the north Pacific and announce it in European circles. The Kamchatka expeditions of 1725 to 1742, led by Vitus Bering and Alexei Chirikov, were successes, almost despite Joseph-Nicolas Delisle's contributions. In 1731, Delisle was asked by the St Petersburg Academy of Sciences to produce a manuscript map as a guide for the second Bering expedition. Prudently, he did not show the coastline north of California, since it was terra incognita at the time. But indulging in some wishful thinking, he could not resist inserting a chain of imaginary lands south of Kamchatka, such as Staten Island, Company Land and de Gama Land. When Bering actually used the map ten years later, he looked for these islands, and in the process, his two ships went too far out to sea and got separated. Sven Waxell, a Swede who served as a lieutenant on Bering's voyages for sixteen years, reflected the frustration and fury of the crew when he later wrote in *The American Expedition*:

> *I think it would be only reasonable were such unknown lands first to be explored before they are trumpeted abroad as being the coasts of Yezo or de Gama, for unless such investigations are first undertaken, many a good sailorman will be most unwarrantably*

deceived. Those who produce uncertain things of that kind would do better than hold their peace, or, if they must exercise imagination and speculation, let them keep the results to themselves and not put them into the hands of others. I know that I am writing all too much about this matter, but I can hardly tear myself away from it, for my blood still boils when I think of the scandalous deception of which we were victims.

In April 1750, eight years after the conclusion of the Kamchatka expeditions, Delisle discussed the expedition's findings in a paper to the Royal Academy in Paris. But it was hardly a rigorous report; Delisle spent more time discussing the dubious voyage of Spanish Admiral Bartolomeo de Fonte who, in 1640, was said to have discovered a bay or inlet on the Pacific coast at latitude fifty-three degrees North, an inlet that supposedly originated on the Atlantic coast. In reality, de Fonte's account appears to have been a piece of fiction that first appeared in 1708 in the London periodical *The Monthly Miscellany or Memoirs for the Curious*, and caused little interest at the time. Spanish authorities long insisted that there was no 1640 voyage and no de Fonte, and in fact, the letter likely was a creation of the editor. Delisle probably resuscitated the story to enhance his reputation at the expense of the Russians; in 1754, Delisle produced an entire atlas devoted to de Fonte's experience.

When Delisle retired from the Russian Academy and returned to Paris (with a stash of maps purloined from the Russians), he found a kindred spirit in his brother-in-law, Philippe Buache, who was just as excited about the new geography offered by the Mer de l'Ouest and the accounts of de Fuca and de Fonte. Perhaps they wanted to stimulate new expeditions to confirm that there existed a clear passage through Canada between the Atlantic and Pacific oceans; perhaps they wanted to cash in on the high interest in Europe in Bering's discoveries by adding the speculative but provocative theories.

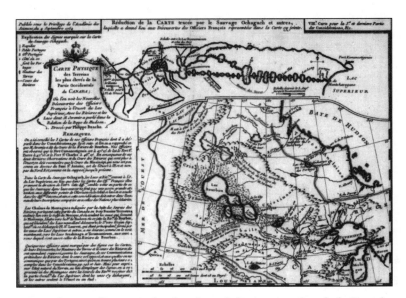

Carte physique des terreins les plus élevés de la partie occidentale du Canada by Philippe Buache and published in 1753. By incorporating the map of a Cree informant, Buache offered rare acknowledgement of Native cartography. National Archives of Canada (NMC-13295).

Whatever the motive, Delisle and Buache's series of thirteen maps, published in 1752, and Buache's follow-up map of 1754, certainly caused considerable interest. One shows the course of the Bering expedition but adds the hypothetical Anian Strait. De Fonte Passage is shown leading inland to a large lake, Lac de Fonte, which is in turn connected by a waterway to Hudson Bay. To the north, Mer de l'Ouest connects with the de Fonte water system.

It was a ghoulish goulash: French, English, Spanish, Russian and Chinese information and place names, stories true and false. The map triggered a storm of controversy — Russian scientists spent considerable effort refuting and correcting Buache's accounts, and French explorers in Western Canada had already realized that they were chasing a myth — but that didn't stop Delisle's fantasies from being reflected in maps into the eighteenth century. (Buache claimed his dead father-in-law, Guillaume Delisle, had drawn the map, but there is suspicion that Buache used Delisle's name to boost the credibility of Buache's own geographical speculations.)

Though ridiculed, Buache's map has a certain latter-day charm. Along the top third of the map is an inset that contains a rendering of the map made by the Cree chief Ochagach for La Vérendrye, which the explorer forwarded to French officials. Taken as a whole, the map is a compilation of many voices screaming to be heard. The result is a lot of noise.

The English, too, got into the spirit of speculative map-making in Canada in the eighteenth century. La Hontan, de Fonte and the other chestnuts of best-selling maps were very useful in the inevitable campaign to challenge the supremacy of the Hudson's Bay Company. The challenger was Arthur Dobbs, a wealthy Irishman who resented the Company's control of the crucial Hudson Bay watershed. In 1744, he plucked out of obscurity de Fonte's account of a powerful snake of a river to the Pacific and used it to support his claim of a Northwest Passage. Conceived with the help of Joseph LaFrance, a coureur de bois who travelled from the Great Lakes to Hudson Bay in 1739, Dobbs's map showed the western side of Hudson Bay draining into a large body of water that gradually became the Pacific.

His map was a polemical challenge meant to undercut the big company's claim that it was still worth royal patronage, and was a crucial part of a campaign to revoke the monopoly granted to the Hudson's Bay Company. In 1748, a petition to the Privy Council asked that Dobbs's North West committee be incorporated into a company trading to the Hudson Bay area; when the petition failed, the matter went to Parliament, which set up a committee to investigate.

The Hudson's Bay Company responded with its own lamentable map, the most hapless of charts. Titled *Map of North America with*

Hudson's Bay and Straits, Anno 1748, engraved by R. W. Seale, it was privately issued by the Company to be used as evidence in the inquiry. Its specific purpose was to take the heat off the Company for not being more active in exploration. The map bears both the Royal Coat of Arms and the Arms of the Hudson's Bay Company, although not even those insignia could prop up the shaky foundation of geographical information. The intent of the map was to prove that the Northwest Passage went through and beyond the Great Lakes to La Hontan's mythical Long River. Heading west, another short portage from that river would allow access to the Western Sea. De Fonte's fanciful travels show up as "de Fonts Track," heading off in the direction of Alaska. Many of the errors were known at the time: The western end of Lake Superior lies at the same longitude as California, Florida is one thousand kilometres east of its true position, Lake Huron looks as if it has eaten several lakes and poor New Brunswick is reduced to an island. To add insult to injury, there are even errors in the placement of Hudson Bay.

Up until this map, Seale did not have a bad reputation, and historians generally assume that he was merely following orders from an officer of the Hudson's Bay Company. We will never know if the 1748 Seale map was born of ignorance or fraudulence. Apparently, almost all the copies were destroyed, with the survivors becoming among the rarest of engraved maps in North America. Which leads us to the final irony: In death, the map achieved the value and appreciation that eluded it in life.

WHILE MANY OF THESE myth-laden maps were hits in the salons of Europe, travellers who actually had to live by the information were not so amused. The man who put an end to the imaginary cartography was Captain James Cook, who saw the craggy and arcing Pacific coast of North America with his own eyes.

When Cook set out in the spring of 1778 to search for the Pacific entrance to the Northwest Passage, he had a stash of maps, charts and intelligence reports to guide him along the coast, together with the well-established apocryphal tales that were passed off as facts in a century's worth of maps. A map of Samuel Hearne's journey to the Arctic via the Coppermine River in 1771 was of some use; but a promising Russian map published in 1744, showing Bering Strait and what appeared to be a route to the Arctic, proved to be of much less value. The map and accompanying commentary, published in *Account of the New Northern Archipelago*, was the handiwork of Jacob von Stahlin, secretary of the St Petersburg Academy of Sciences, and it purportedly was based on the discoveries of Lieutenant Synd and Russian traders. Von Stahlin called it "a very accurate little Map." It showed Alaska as an island, not a peninsula, and between Alaska and the continent, fifteen degrees east of Bering Strait, was a wide and welcoming strait.

Reaching the area, Cook and his fellow mariners searched in vain for the rivers and straits leading inland described by de Fuca and de Fonte. No matter, his instructions were to sail to at least latitude sixty-five degrees. They traveled north, past the peaks of Mount St Elias, which loomed inland, then followed the shore as it veered sharply west and then south. With von Stahlin's map in hand, Cook each day anxiously expected to see the opening that would allow them to "separate the Continent." Cook rounded the Alaska peninsula and found himself in a strait that bore no resemblance to the strait pictured in von Stahlin's map. When ice closed in, Cook was forced to retreat, never having found the island of "Alaschka." A disgusted Cook described von Stahlin's chart as "A Map that the most illiterate of his illiterate Sea faring men would have been ashamed to put his name to."

Cook was infuriated and perhaps a little embarrassed, but his expedition could hardly be considered a failure. He had charted the coastline from Mount St Elias to the Bering Strait and determined the true shape of the Alaska peninsula. Most important of all, Cook was a real person and not a rumour, and he had a true travelogue with a map to back it up. Through his maps and lavishly illustrated accounts, readers in Europe got an accurate view of the Pacific Northwest. As *The Exploration of North America* pointed out,

> *Any publication about Cook was likely to sell well in a half-dozen European languages. The official account, lavishly illustrated, was priced formidably . . . yet one London periodical noted of its sale: "We remember not a circumstance like what has happened on this occasion. On the third day after publication, a copy was not to be met with in the hands of the bookseller; and to our certain knowledge, six, seven, eight, and even ten guineas, have since been offered for a sett."*

Carte de l'Amerique Septentrionale . . . by Jacques-Nicolas Bellin and published in 1743. On this map, Bellin pictures both the fabled — and false — Mer de l'Ouest and two fictitious islands in Lake Superior: Phillippeaux and Pontchartrain. National Archives of Canada (NMC-13814).

Cook's discoveries should have delivered the final nail in the coffin of great west-flowing rivers and salty seas. But these fictitious features still managed to appear on maps well into the nineteenth century, making great fodder for map dealers. "I recently sold an anonymous French world map dated 1826 that clearly showed the River of the West and still suggested a Sea of the West," said one map dealer in the autumn of 2001. "No wonder it was anonymous, I wouldn't want my name on it either. That map had other inaccuracies that had been clearly mapped before the date on the map. Many cartographic myths continued to be depicted long after they had clearly been disproved. In the case of the French world map, I think that it was left over from a much earlier printing, then a date added and it was foisted on some unsuspecting geography student."

THE CARTOGRAPHER WHO GAVE the Mer de l'Ouest fiction credibility, Jacques-Nicolas Bellin, has yet another distinction: He also created islands in Lake Superior that did not exist.

Because of its size and deep waters, and fierce and unpredictable winds, Lake Superior has always been the most fabled of the Great Lakes. It is the one mariners fear most, from even the earliest days of European exploration. The map titled *Lac Supérieur*, produced in 1672 by Fathers Claude Dablon and Claude Allouez, is widely considered the greatest cartographic accomplishment of the Jesuits of the time.

Bellin was a respected map-maker himself, having worked on the Mississippi Delta in 1700 and on Cape Breton Island in 1713. Being respected, however, means having your map copied by fellow map-makers with less-than-rigorous standards of accuracy. When Bellin's map — *Carte des lacs du Canada* — was published in Charlevoix's well-read *Histoire et description générale de la Nouvelle France*, his peers did not have to squint to find two new islands in Superior near the already known Isle Royale: Isle Phillipeaux and Isle Pontchartrain. These two fictitious islands were to appear on maps for the next century.

How did such a mistake happen? A number of years ago, Conrad Heidenreich took the map apart and investigated where Bellin got the information on the two islands. Bellin's sin, Heidenreich discovered, was not in cynically perpetuating a hoax but in blindly mapping features he had not seen. "He should have known better," said Heidenreich.

Heidenreich started by looking at whose names grace the phantom islands. "Phillipeaux" was named for Jean-Frédéric Phélypeaux, Comte de Maurepas, Minister of the French Marine from 1723 to 1749 and Bellin's boss. "Pontchartrain" was named for Phélypeaux's father, the former minister, Jérome Phélypeaux, Comte de Pontchartrain. It was natural to assume that either Charlevoix or Bellin, or both, were responsible for the errors, perhaps to curry favour with the leaders of the day.

But Heidenreich dug deeper and came up with another explanation. By rooting through archives, Heidenreich identified three manuscript maps likely used by Bellin. The three maps were themselves redrawn based on information and intelligence in New France submitted to the cartographers. By deductive reasoning and a close examination of goings-on in the colony, Heidenreich identified the originator of the material as Louis Denys de La Ronde. La Ronde was an officer in the navy and commandant of the fur post at Chagouamigon on Madeline Island near the southwest shore of Lake Superior. La Ronde had prepared a report on the possibilities of copper mining around Lake Superior. In it, Heidenreich said, "La Ronde repeated Indian stories of several islands full of copper and suggested that he build two ships to find and exploit these deposits. In return for his efforts to help finance his mining ventures, La Ronde requested a nine-year monopoly on the fur trade at Chagouamigon free of licencing fees," a request that was granted.

The mining operation never panned out because of the high cost of transporting the ore to Montreal, but throughout his efforts, La Ronde relied on the favours of others, people such as Jean-Frédéric Phély-peaux, which explains how the islands were given the names. As to why the two islands were identified in the first place, Heidenreich figures the error is due to La Ronde's misinterpretation of the Native account. La Ronde never laid eyes on the islands described by the Indians, although he continued to look for them right up until 1738.

Once committed to a map by a cartographer with the stature of Bellin, however, the phantom islands of Lake Superior took on a life of their own. They appeared on the standard map in the second half of the eighteenth century, A *Map of the British and French Dominions in North America*, produced in 1755 by Dr John Mitchell. Mitchell's map was used to settle the boundary between the United States and British North America during negotiations in 1782–1783. The ensuing Treaty of Paris awarded Isle Phillipeaux to the United States, while smaller Isle Pontchartrain was handed to Canada. The phantom islands were finally excised on Aaron Arrowsmith's 1801 A *Map of America*. But they could still be seen on lesser maps published until at least 1852, fifty years after the extra islands were known to be imaginary and more than a century after the mistake was first widely published.

MAPS CAN POWERFULLY misinform or misdirect by what they do not show as much as by what they do. Rumours used or intelligence withheld can both be effective weapons, something politicians know very well. Samuel Bawlf might have seen these dynamics when he was a Cabinet minister in the Social Credit government in British Columbia between 1975 and 1986. As an amateur maritime hist-orian, though, he certainly sees subterfuge in the history of discovery and how travels were laid down on maps.

Even before his graduate-student days in the geography depart-ment at University of British Columbia, Bawlf was fascinated by the history of exploration. During the second half of the 1990s, he was consumed by everything surrounding the movements and history of Sir Francis Drake, the most celebrated British explorer of Elizabethan times, who circumnavigated the globe between 1578 and 1580. Bawlf sensed that there was a story hidden in the maps and maritime records from those remarkable years of exploration. After five years of study, Bawlf developed a rich, if controversial, yarn of cartographic cover-up and imperial conspiracy.

Bawlf first publicized his findings in a series of articles for the *Vancouver Sun* beginning on August 5, 2000, then enlarged upon them in a book published in 2001. He drew a wide and diverse audience. The storyline of cartographic deception is still a seductive yarn for conspiracy theorists and whodunit lovers. But Bawlf also attracted a rabble-rousing crowd of naysayers convinced that he was the second coming of Baron de la Hontan. Where the Baron chose to fantasize about a riparian expressway to the Orient, Bawlf set out to redeem Drake's pirate image. The key, Bawlf was convinced, lay in maps kept secret by the British royalty.

It is a matter of historical record that Drake, sailing in the *Golden Hinde*, probed the west coast of North America, but it is assumed he travelled only as far north as California, claiming "Nova Albion" (near present-day San Francisco) for Queen Elizabeth I before leaving for home. Bawlf's case is that Drake in fact travelled much further north in an effort to find the Northwest Passage from the Pacific. Bawlf paints a surprising itinerary: He says Drake reached the mouth of the Stikine River, sailed up to southeast Alaska, explored the Strait of Georgia, and came down the Inside Passage, where he identified important islands. He argues that the "Nova Albion" that Drake claimed for Queen Elizabeth I was not in the San Francisco Bay area but on the east coast of Vancouver Island.

At the beginning, Bawlf's curiosity was aroused by the fact that the records for Drake's voyage were missing several months of the expedition from the summer of 1579. Bawlf also thought it odd that before Drake arrived on the scene in the Pacific, maps of the

northwest coast had few features. After his voyages, many details —
bays, rivers, headlands, place names and, most significantly, islands
— began showing up on English maps.

Bawlf then set out to study the maps of the period. He examined
handwriting on previously unidentified documents, putting manu-
scripts under spectral photography to detect hidden changes. He
examined Spanish intelligence reports that were intercepted by the
English. And he travelled to sites in Oregon to determine if the land
and landmarks matched up with the maps of the area purportedly
drawn by Drake.

Bawlf learned, for example, that the Spaniards off Argentina later
captured Drake's cousin John, who was on the voyage. John told his
captors that Drake sailed north some five thousand kilometres until
they reached latitude forty-eight degrees, and that between forty-six
degrees and forty-eight degrees Drake discovered a handful of islands
"of good land," which they called San Bartolome, San Jaime and,
the largest, Nova Albion.

Drake also scrutinized an unsigned manuscript, dubbed *The
Anonymous Narrative*, believed to be written by promoter Richard
Hakluyt and based on the journal of sailors with Drake's expedition.
It devotes few words to seven and a half months of Drake's travels,
and mentions travels up to forty-eight degrees but nothing about
islands or Nova Albion. Bawlf noticed something odd in the document: It appeared that the latitude of forty-eight degrees had been
written over. He asked the British Museum to photograph the
numerals using spectral analysis, which can reveal alterations to
documents. Much to Bawlf's surprise, the analysis showed that the
numerals in the manuscript had been altered not once but twice.
The latitude originally read fifty degrees (the latitude of Vancouver
Island), and then was changed to fifty-three degrees (the latitude
of the Queen Charlotte Islands) and was finally altered to read

forty-eight degrees. This seemed to be strong evidence that Drake had travelled farther north than officially acknowledged.

Bawlf then studied maps that he says Drake had privately drawn to show to patrons and important people. One was the so-called Drake-Mellon map, which shows that Drake travelled north at forty degrees on a peninsula, behind which an English flag is planted at the head of an inlet. And Bawlf looked at two other maps drawn from this template and, he presumes, vetted by Drake. One, known as the French Drake map, depicts Drake's stopping place still at forty degrees but at an island, one of a chain of four islands stretching eight hundred kilometres along the coast. A second map, the Dutch Drake map, shows a chain of islands bearing a strong resemblance to the coastline from the Olympic Peninsula to Prince of Wales Island. "When I saw this long chain of islands on these maps, I was thoroughly intrigued," Bawlf wrote. "Although the latitudes for the islands were wrong, the unmistakeable impression was that Drake had formed a comprehension of the great archipelago extending northward from Cape Flattery that explorers two centuries later acquired only after numerous expeditions." Looking closer, Bawlf could see a strait running east to west, corresponding to Johnstone Strait, while a body of land with a concave east coast and distinctive southern tip is, to Bawlf's eyes, clearly Vancouver Island. He is convinced that the flag denoting the future colony site was planted near the northern end of Georgia Strait, not at a bay in California.

How was Drake's itinerary supposedly suppressed? On his return, all of Drake's charts and illustrated journals were placed under guard, and publication of the particulars of his journeys was strictly forbidden, Bawlf says. The English actions are similar to what the Russians did to keep Bering's discoveries of Alaska secret from Spain. The British, too, were in competition with Spain and its leader, King Philip.

That embargo was apparently to be broken by Richard Hakluyt, who teamed up with Lok to promote the Frobisher voyages. In 1589, Hakluyt promised, says Bawlf, to give a full account of "Nova Albion upon the backside of Canada, further than any Christian hitherto hath pierced."

Albion was an ancient name for Britain, Bawlf wrote, so Hakluyt was in effect announcing that "New England" was located on the Pacific coast of what is now Canada. Only when Hakluyt's book was published, the promised account never appeared, and Nova Albion's location was later moved south. Suddenly Drake had only travelled as far north as forty-two degrees before turning back and harbouring near present-day San Francisco, a claim that archaeologists have never been able to authenticate.

In 1603, once both Drake and Queen Elizabeth I had died, a Dutch cartographer who had worked with Drake in producing his commemorative maps collaborated on a globe. According to Bawlf, that globe revealed the true track of Drake's northwest voyage, illustrating a large indentation that matches the shape of the mainland behind Vancouver Island. The distinctive and hidden inner coastline could not have been depicted with such clarity unless Drake had sailed the length of the straits separating the island from the mainland, Bawlf claims. As well, place names started appearing on maps from Dutch cartographers, names such as "coast of objections" at fifty-three degrees and "cape of good fortune" at fifty-five degrees.

Bawlf's claims were sufficiently controversial that historical cartographers and Drakeophiles began taking sides. On one side, Richard Ruggles, a leading expert in the history of map-making, told the *Vancouver Sun*, "I thought, 'My God, this is a completely new approach which nobody has put forth.' I was fascinated by it ... I think it's a remarkable piece of work ... It's the first real detailed study of the existing cartographic materials." On the other side, Terry Glavin, a knowledgeable commentator on West Coast Native culture, wrote in the *Georgia Straight*: "After a close reading of all the *Vancouver Sun* coverage and after interviews with Bawlf, Hume, and 'experts' in these matters, it is not unfair to say a shadow of a doubt remains. Sadly, it is a shadow big enough to blanket the entire coast, from California to Alaska."

Others who question Bawlf's storyline point to the description of Native groups met by Drake in accounts at the time, which suggest that the Natives were from coastal California rather than Salish Indians from the Northwest. Skeptics suggest that Drake's cousin John, captured by the Spaniards, was just telling his captors what they wanted to hear about Drake's north Pacific experiences. They reserve special disdain for one of Bawlf's most controversial assertions, that the stories of Juan de Fuca were really based on Drake's secret voyages. According to Bawlf, Juan de Fuca learned of Drake's voyages via the testimony of a renegade Portugese navigator known as Morera around 1584. Morera travelled with Drake all the way up to Clarence Strait, in Alaska, before falling ill and being left somewhere on the northwest coast. In a few days, Morera recovered and started walking south. Four years later he arrived in Mexico and told Spanish authorities about Drake's travels, drawing a map for good measure. Bawlf says de Fuca saw Morera's information about Drake's supposed strait and incorporated it into his own tales.

Here is what Terry Glavin has to say about Bawlf's theory: "Some guy tells a patently fraudulent story which nevertheless contains a legitimate description of the B.C. and Alaskan coast because it comes third-hand or fourth-hand from another guy who may or may not have existed, who walked all the way from either Alaska or B.C. to Mexico, 400 years ago."

The controversy will continue late into the night, with both sides investing the considerable passion that cartographic conspiracy theories inevitably evoke. And in the end, we will likely never know whether or not the truth follows the lines on Drake's maps. They are just floating somewhere out there in the uncertain boundary between knowledge and ignorance.

4

NATION BUILDING

FOR CANADA'S FIRST BRUSH WITH civil disobedience, the events of October 11, 1869, lacked the sweeping drama of the hunger strike and sit-in campaigns of Gandhi in India or Martin Luther King in the United States. Yet as defining moments in the development of a young country, what happened on the pancake-flat prairie that day summed up what Canada was to become in the years ahead. And the flashpoint of confrontation was an iron chain sixty-six feet long.

On that October morning, Major Adam Clark Webb, a Dominion land surveyor, and his company were working on the first survey of Western Canada, running their Gunter's measuring chains over the land. Every eighty chains represented another mile of prairie defined. When they reached an obstacle that blocked their chains — a river or stream — they got out their triangulation equipment. They measured a baseline at right angles to the survey line, then picked a prominent point on the other side of the river that represented the top of their imaginary triangle (if they could find a

78

prominent point on the flat prairie). Finally, they measured the angles of the triangle from the ends of the baseline, and then the trigonometry ace in the survey party did his calculations. And on they went, dividing a landscape of rivers and tall grass into numbered, and environmentally neutered, parcels of property, six miles by six miles square.

On October 11, the surveyors arrived at the grazing "hay privilege" lands of André Nault at the rear of the river lots. They were approached by a group of Metis led by Louis Riel, Nault's cousin. Wherever the Metis congregated, there was only one topic of conversation: How would they respond to threats to Metis life that they felt the surveyors represented? Could they avoid the fate of Native groups in the American frontier? The rebels literally made their

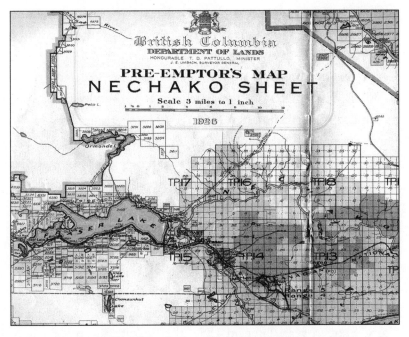

Pre-Emptor's Map/Nechako Sheet, produced by British Columbia Department of Lands in 1926. The map indicated parcels of land available for homesteading, and little else. Author collection.

stand, right on the surveyors' chains, barring them from their work. Reading the mood, Webb and his men put down their chains, packed up their equipment, and left.

The defiant act by Louis Riel and his Metis cohorts was a statement against what those chains represented: the imposition of a surveying and mapping system that threatened the Metis' very existence. Like other acts of civil disobedience, Riel's stand was not unexpected. When Webb set out with a party just east of the Winnipeg Meridian, the anchor line that governed surveys west and east on Canada's prairies, he knew the local mood was sour. Webb was part of the advance troops of the Dominion government instructed to grid and parcel out land to homesteaders. Two months earlier, Webb's boss, Lieutenant-Colonel J. S. Dennis, had warned politicians in Ottawa that trouble was brewing on the prairies. It was obvious to those surveyors in the area that the Metis were anxious, concerned that the rectangle grid system, an idea imported from the United States, would mean drastic changes to their way of life. Dennis was told to proceed with the survey as proposed.

What Dennis had not appreciated was that the Metis organized life on the basis of a different geometry. The Metis understood the imperious nature of the prairies and settled in long strip farms, like those in New France, which gave each farmer river frontage and access to irrigation. They did not understand the logic of the surveyor's geometry, with rectangular lots ill-suited to the arid land. And they realized, rightly, that the acts of surveying and making a map were basic acts of nation building. They could not see their own nation on those maps.

Just one month after Riel laid his foot on the Gunter's chain, the Metis took control of Red River country when they occupied Fort Garry. Sixteen years later, in 1885, the Saskatchewan Rebellion, again under the direction of Louis Riel, burst out, setting off a chain of events that would lead to Riel's hanging later that year.

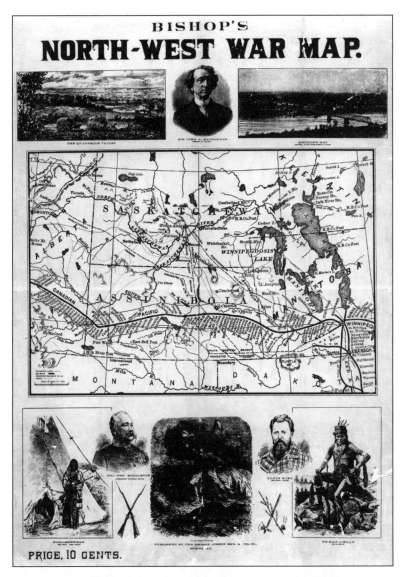

Bishop's North-West War Map, produced by the George Bishop Eng.
& Ptg. Co. of Montreal in 1885. With its crude depictions of Native
warriors, the map was intended to stoke ill will in central
Canada against the Metis and the Saskatchewan Rebellion.
National Archives of Canada (NMC-015955).

For a nation in the making, the Saskatchewan Rebellion was a sensation. News of the Indian wars in the United States captivated Central Canada; now they had their own Indian wars. To feed this interest, companies and newspapers churned out maps, the first time the mass media in Canada had participated in an event of such magnitude. One of the most decorative poster-maps produced at the time was *Bishop's North-West War Map*, published by George Bishop Eng. & Ptg. Co. in Montreal and sold for ten cents. Bishop's poster of Red River country featured a railroad map, showing all the sidings, telegraph lines and trails. The illustrations above and below the map, however, reflected the mood of the time. The illustrations on top, of Sir John A. Macdonald and the Qu'Appelle Valley, were countered by illustrations from the days of Bressani in Huron country — images of Indian "savages" shown scalping a dead soldier.

Cartography has been described as a silent arbiter of power, and the Metis would not disagree. Surveying and mapping are basic acts of statecraft; their impact is so pervasive and so basic as to be hardly discernible. Maps were certainly crucial in the jockeying in the Americas by Britain, France, Spain and Portugal from the sixteenth century on. One of the earliest-known existing maps to show the New World, the *Portolan World Chart* (c. 1500) attributed to Juan de la Cosa, staked a claim for the British based on John Cabot's 1497 voyage. Portuguese claims were made on the *Cantino Planisphere* of 1502, based on the findings of Gaspar Corte Real, who returned to Lisbon from the New World in 1501. The land, named Terra del Rey de Portuguall, is placed, conveniently, east of its actual location. That way, it lay on the Portuguese side of the arbitrary line dividing the non-Christian world into the two spheres accorded to Portugal and Spain by a papal bull issued in 1493.

There are at least three different ways in which maps are significant to building a nation. The first is that they lead to the visualization of the space of the nation, the identification of territory. In the popular imagination maps say, "These are our borders, this is the Motherland." Maps also conceive geographical space as an abstraction that is then converted into political regions of states and provinces: This land is known and comes under the jurisdiction of the Canadian state. And the third way is by mediating relations between states and societies. Maps are crucial tools in managing international relations.

Not surprisingly, maps played a large role in shaping Canada in the eighteenth century, a time when first the British and French, and then the British and Americans, settled their differences with a mixture of bellicosity and diplomacy. Like armchair generals rearranging their toy soldiers, the British and French, in particular, jockeyed for power on the vellum battlefield with maps as their proxies. The century opened with the publication in 1703 of Delisle's *La Carte du Canada,* a landmark in the history of Canadian cartography. The English felt Delisle had restricted the limits of their possessions. As the century unfolded, however, the English were most often guilty of crudely using cartography in the service of statecraft. In 1709, Samuel Thornton drew a map showing two routes to Hudson Bay: the British route through Hudson Strait and the French route overland. It showed the boundary between French and British territory running through the middle of the Labrador Peninsula, and it was intended to support the claim of the Hudson's Bay Company during peace negotiations that the whole of the Hudson Bay watershed was British, despite the fact that Fort York had been in the hands of the French since 1697.

The rivalry between England and France became ever more intense in both Europe and the New World. There was continuing dispute over Nova Scotia and the Great Lakes region, where the French were becoming more aggressive. The Treaty of Utrecht, signed by the two countries in 1713, was designed to sort out these claims. It called for a commission to be established to fix interior

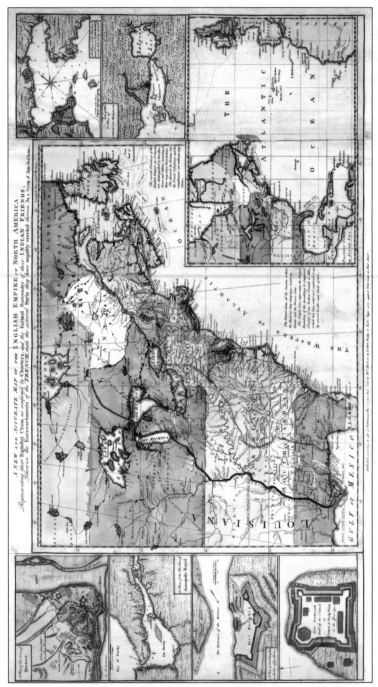

A New and Accurate Map of the English Empire in North America; Representing their Rightful Claim as confirm'd by Charters and the formal Surrender of their Indian Friends; likewise the Encroachments of the French, with the Several Forts they have unjustly Erected therein, produced by Robert Sayer and William Herbert for the Society of Anti-Gallicans in 1755. The propaganda map wildly exaggerated British claims to New France. National Archives of Canada (NMC-21053).

boundaries. The commission met for a couple of years after 1713 but came to no conclusion, then met again in the late 1750s and again failed to come to a conclusion. Between 1713 and 1756, there were no formal boundaries, just lines on maps that showed various cartographers' interpretations of where boundaries should be set. They were claims and nothing more, mere wishful thinking or pre-emptive posturing, though they were not presented so modestly.

This was Canada's Golden Age of propaganda maps. The English showed off their gifts of imagination, using official and semi-official maps to denounce the French as "intruders" and "usurpers." One of the crudest appeared in 1755, a product of a brutish organization known as the Anti-Gallican Society, a British organization devoted to promoting English interests in North America and to channelling anti-France feelings in the lead-up to the Seven Years War. The Society published a map it titled *A New and Accurate Map of the English Empire in North America: Representing their Rightful Claim as confirm'd by Charters and the formal Surrender of their Indian Friends; likewise the Encroachments of the French, with the Several Forts they have unjustly Erected therein*. Accurate it was not. According to this map, New France was but a rump between the Ottawa and Saguenay rivers, while Cape Breton was transformed into Cape Britain. Map historian Conrad Heidenreich delights in the absurdity: "The British maps are ironic in that they laid claim to a country explored and mapped by the French for over one hundred and sixty years, a country about whose geography few Englishmen would have had the slightest notion had it not been for the published French maps to which they had access."

(Not that the British were incapable of producing fine cartographic work. In 1761, Governor James Murray commissioned a map of Canada shortly after the conquest of New France. The topographical survey, in forty-four sheets, shows roads, farmland and the general lay of the land. The superlative maps were drawn only in

manuscript form, undoubtedly for military use, and were never published; in the words of Iain Taylor, former chief geographer in the
Earth Sciences Division of Natural Resources Canada, the Murray
maps were "state secrets that befitted a recently conquered land.")

Map evidence became a major issue in 1749, when England and
France established commissioners to determine the boundaries in
Nova Scotia. The Treaty of Utrecht was either sloppily written or
composed to defer the hard questions for some other time. The only
boundary settled was that Newfoundland was to go to England,
except for the north shore, where the French retained some fishing
rights. The British claimed all the way from the Atlantic Ocean west
to the Mississippi, and from the Gulf of Mexico north to the Great
Lakes. The French, on the other hand, held that British territories
ended at the ridge of the Appalachian Mountains, and that the
lands to the west — from modern Ohio to modern Louisiana —
were theirs. The most intractable problem was in Eastern Canada.
By the twelfth article of the Treaty of Utrecht, "Nova Scotia, or
Acadia, with its ancient limits," had been assigned to England.
Unfortunately, there was no agreement on what "Nova Scotia, or
Acadia, with its ancient limits" really meant, nor was there agreement on even the name of the territory — Acadia, as it was known
by the French, or Nova Scotia, as it was known by the English.

To determine what the Treaty meant, the Boundary Commission
set out to study all the charters, land grants and treaties from the first
European contact right up to 1713. In the ensuing debate, each
country produced maps to prove its point. The French claimed all
the areas they had explored, although they were prepared to give up
a thin strip of land along the southern coast of the peninsula from
Cape Canso to Cape Sable. The British claimed all of what is now
the Maritimes, right through the Gaspé region to the south shore
of the St Lawrence River. The two sides scoured the maps published
in the preceding fifty years, and then a most curious thing happened:

to buttress their case, the French submitted English maps, while the English presented French maps.

The French commissioners presented three British maps: Edmund Halley's world chart (1702), which placed the name Acadia on only the peninsula; Henry Popple's (1733) map of North America, which showed Acadia along the coastline; and Thomas Salmon's map of the English colonies in his *System of History and Geography* (1739). The British discredited Popple's map because it was too generous to the French, and they did not think much of the others either. Instead, British commissioners extolled the merits of Guillaume Delisle's *Carte de l'Amerique septentrionale* (1700) and *La Carte du Canada ou Nouvelle France* (1703), both of which extended the area of Nova Scotia, together with Jean Baptiste Bourguignon d'Anville's map *L'Amerique septentrionale* (1746) and Jacques-Nicolas Bellin's chart of Canada (1744). These maps showed New France to be north of the St Lawrence River and the limits of Acadia to stretch north beyond the isthmus and west along the mainland to the St Croix River. "These French maps . . . ought to carry extraordinary weight, especially where they support the claim of Britain," the British commissioners said. Referring to their esteemed compatriot Bellin, the French responded: "Bellin was obviously misled by English maps and ideas in assuming a New Scotland really exists distinct and independent of Acadia."

In reality, the cartographic evidence on both sides was thin. Mary Pedley, assistant curator in the map division of the University of Michigan's Clements Library, looked closely at the list of maps consulted by both commissions, and was struck by the absence of any surveys actually made in the region or any manuscript maps that were among the documents used by the commissioners.

WHILE IT WAS NOT PRESENTED AS evidence to support either the English or French, Dr John Mitchell's *A Map of the British and French*

Dominions in North America, published in 1755, loomed large over both nations and was the pivotal document to fix the Canada–United States boundary at the forty-ninth parallel. Called "the man who made the map of North America," John Mitchell was a physician and botanist living in Virginia when he began working on his map of the continent.

Mitchell was an unlikely cartographic star. Considered in his day one of the finest scientific minds in North America, he is credited with the earliest work on the principles of taxonomy to be written in the United States; Linnaeus named the partridge berry *Mitchella repens* in his honour. As a researcher, he was active in physiology, climatology and medicine, and was an authority on yellow fever. He had a lifelong interest in exploration and surveying, and while living in England, he got caught up in the anti-French mood of the day. He was indignant at the French encroachments on the English colonies.

In 1749, Mitchell began to take a deeper interest in the mechanics of map-making. Mitchell despaired of the quality of maps — few Englishmen bothered to make a large-scale map of North America, Henry Popple being the exception — and at how cartographers merely copied the mistakes of others. He collected maps, travelogues, and notes from historians and geographers, and completed his first draft in 1750. Because it was based only on publicly available sources of information, the map was rather crude, even in Mitchell's opinion. Edmund and Dorothy Smith Berkeley, his biographers, wrote, "He garnered knowledge of certain areas unknown sixteen years previously but, like Popple, his foremost interest was to point up the growing threat to British ambitions of French expansion. As a Virginian, he had long been aware of this. As many other colonials, he was fascinated by the possibilities of the vast, unexplored land to the west . . . He was unwilling that lands of such promise should go to the French by default." The best way to fight the French, Mitchell thought, was through the map. His purpose was to present to the

British public an image of all the colonies so that the true scale and extent of the French threat could be exposed. One thing his first map quickly made obvious was the lack of knowledge of boundaries, roads and precise locations.

Impressed by Mitchell's attention to detail, the Lords Commissioners of Trade and Plantations retained him in 1750, giving Mitchell access to a vast and growing storehouse of charts and surveys coming from the New World. He became a keen student of reports, claims and papers, in particular the journals kept by His Majesty's ships of war at the Admiralty Office, from which he gleaned precise information of latitude and whatever could be surmised about longitude.

On February 13, 1755, the first issue of the first edition of Mitchell's revised map was published, and over the next thirty-six years, twenty-one variations of the map appeared. The original Mitchell map incorporated the best colonial maps of the day. The Mitchell map quite credibly showed the outlines of Lower Canada and the maritime region, but it did get a few of its facts wrong. It indicated that Lake of the Woods was the easternmost of the Great Lakes, connected by a river to Lake Superior. And Mitchell believed the source of the Mississippi lay north of Lake of the Woods. Or so it seemed: Mitchell placed a large inset east of Lake of the Woods, out from under which flowed the Mississippi. On this he merely copied the information that appeared on Philippe Buache's map of 1755, the one that featured the sketch made by the Cree guide for La Vérendrye.

When negotiations opened in 1783 to set the boundary between British North America and the United States, the British were presented with two options: either the forty-fifth parallel, which would have continued the existing New York–Canada border west, or a line through the middle of the Great Lakes to Lake of the Woods and then due west to Mitchell's wrongly placed Mississippi. The

British opted for the line through the Great Lakes. (It was David Thompson's explorations for the North-West Company in 1797–1798 that established the source of the Mississippi as well south of Lake of the Woods.) The British then put the idea of the forty-ninth parallel on the table. That was the purported boundary between French America and the territory controlled by the Hudson's Bay Company. The French had rejected this line, but because the border showed up on maps published in Europe and America, such as Jean Palairet's *Map of North America* in 1765, Britain's "diplomatic assumption" gained cartographic credence and it was generally believed that agreement had been reached. The forty-ninth parallel became a fact on the ground.

More difficult to resolve was the Maine–New Brunswick boundary. The dispute dated to the Treaty of Paris in 1783, which ended the American Revolutionary War. The Treaty defined the boundary between New Brunswick and Maine as the "highlands" that separated the waters flowing into the St Lawrence from the rivers flowing into the Atlantic. Where were the "highlands"? Were they mountain ranges or watersheds? That depended on who was looking: The British considered present-day Maine towns such as Presque Isle as falling in New Brunswick; the Americans considered Edmunston and parts of Quebec as Maine territory. There was also a dispute about the location of the St Croix River — an important "due north" line was to be established at the source of the St Croix. The Mitchell map failed to help. It listed a St Croix River but inaccurately showed how rivers flowed. The issue came to a head when Maine began granting land in the disputed Aroostook Valley, which threatened British access to the St Lawrence. Even as British and American negotiators were nearing agreement on other matters, Maine's political leaders were holding firm.

As the boundary issues became more complex and as the years dragged on, it was decided that each side would submit a copy of

Mitchell's map with a line marking what it believed to be the intended territory. These maps would resolve the issue in the most unexpected way.

In 1838 Daniel Webster, the American Secretary of State, acquired one of the marked-up Mitchell maps, the copy formerly owned by Revolutionary War hero Baron Friedrich von Steuben, on which a red line said to have been placed by an earlier American negotiator marked the border turning west, not north, from the source of the St Croix. This position favoured the British, which is why it was suppressed. In 1842, American historian Jared Sparks approached Webster about a map he had recently found in the Paris archives. It was a 1746 map by d'Anville, on which, according to Sparks, no other than Benjamin Franklin had drawn "a strong red line" showing the United States borders agreed to in the 1782 peace talks with the British. The line again supported the British, not the American, interpretation of the Maine border. Sparks drew a "strong black line corresponding to the red one" onto a map of Maine, which Webster used, along with von Steuben's Mitchell map, to soften Maine's resistance to a compromise settlement. (For his troubles, Sparks received $250 from the United States Secret Contingent Fund and £2,988 from Baron Ashburton, Britain's negotiator.) Maine received the fertile Aroostook valley and Madawaska settlements south of the St John River, while Britain retained an overland route to Quebec and control of the ridge where it closely approached above the St Lawrence.

The British had their own Mitchell map surprise. Webster's British counterpart, Baron Ashburton, learned that a Mitchell map from the collection of King George III had been transferred in 1839 from the British Museum to the back rooms of the Foreign Office. A search for the map led to George Featherstonhaugh, who was in charge of assembling the cartographic evidence for the English. Featherstonhaugh had withheld the map, which just happened to have its own red lines of boundaries claimed by the Americans in Maine–New Brunswick and between Lake Superior and Lake of the Woods. On it was a handwritten inscription that read: "Boundary as described by Mr Oswald." (Richard Oswald was one of the British negotiators in 1782.) Now here was a map, hidden by the British, that seemed to be sympathetic to the American case.

In the end, it did not amount to anything. If there was no proof that the other party had actually agreed to the boundaries shown on the hidden maps, then they did not prove anything. But the maps had served a purpose: The "red line" maps finally cowed the Maine politicians into accepting the compromise, while the King George III map neutralized Lord Palmerston, one of the fiercest critics of the British North America–United States boundary, who was implicated in the cover-up.

MAPS GIVE SHAPE TO STATES both real and imagined. They provide visual identity for a country just finding its way. In the mid-nineteenth century, both on the ground and on the Mitchell maps, the lines were established that defined the geopolitical entity called Canada. But maps produced in the following decades showed just how conflicted the young country was over its self-image. Should Canadians protect their historical affiliation with Britain and its still-growing Empire? Or did they cast their lot with the United States, the vibrant and up-and-coming superpower to the south?

Making the cartographic case for ties across the Atlantic Ocean was George Parkin, the premier advocate for the British Empire and the "New Imperialism" movement that straddled the nineteenth and twentieth centuries. A New Brunswick native and secondary school teacher, Parkin had immense influence not only in Canada but in Britain as well; he wrote for the London *Times* and lectured frequently, counting Sir Winston Churchill and Rudyard Kipling among his admirers. Because of his extensive travel, Parkin was an astute observer of his own country and of broad technological trends. His message was clear and resonant: Anglo-Saxons should form a "magnificent Oceanic Empire" to further the cause of civilization and Christianity.

Parkin stood conventional thinking on its ear. Where others perceived a British Empire as a collection of scattered states isolated by oceans, Parkin believed the Empire was actually held together by those very same bodies of water. His reasoning was that modern technology — steamships and telegraph cables in particular — had shrunk the world, and that the British, owners of the vast majority of the world's submarine cable and possessors of a powerful and far-flung navy, were best placed to take advantage of what the new technology offered.

Parkin most effectively communicated his imperial ideals in his wall map, titled *The British Empire Map of the World on Mercator's Projection*, published in 1893 by map engraver John Bartholomew. A staple in classrooms across Canada and Britain, the *British Empire Map* showed the workings of the Oceanic Empire and Canada's place — and role — within it. The colouring that separated the British Empire from the rest of the world was its first striking element: Pink represented British possessions, such as Canada, India and Australia, while drab grey was reserved for the "Chinese Empire" and the "Russian Empire." Prominent blue lines showed British steamship routes; foreign routes were shown in faint dotted lines. With such colour coding, it has been said, colonies and countries appeared like detachable pieces of a jigsaw puzzle, with the British having the most impressive board.

Parkin paid particular attention to illustrating British defences. Terry Cook, who did his doctoral thesis on Parkin in the early 1980s, noted that reliable coal supplies at stations around the world were vital to sustain Britain's sea power. He said Parkin made a special effort to illustrate this fact on the famous map. "Fortified British naval stations with coal supplies are marked by large black crosses — well over twenty in all — and so prominently that the cross for Halifax blots out two-thirds of Nova Scotia," Cook wrote in the journal *Cartographica*.

In Parkin's imperial federation scheme, Canada had central importance and was therefore the most prominently featured country on the map. By strategically using the Mercator projection and showing Australia on both the right and left sides of the map, Parkin placed Canada at the map's very centre, as a land bridge between the Atlantic and Pacific oceans. The controversial Mercator projection, the most common means by which cartographers "flatten" the spherical earth to a plane surface, accurately shows land mass at the equator but distorts land as one moves farther from the equator; at the thirtieth parallel, for example, the scale increases fifteen percent. Seen on a Mercator projection, Canada appears much larger in proportion to other countries than it is in reality. Equally important, Cook pointed out, the Mercator projection is favourable for areas such as Australia and the oceans. This allowed Parkin to play up the oceanic connections he felt tied the British Empire together.

Radiating from Canada's east and west coasts were lines indicating steamship routes and telegraph cables, putting the country at the hub of the Empire's oceanic byways. "Not insignificantly," Cook wrote, "the most important part of that route — the Canadian Pacific Railway — is marked on the map in bright red, far more prominently than other imperial railways, yet another indication of Parkin's Canadianism."

(A miniature reproduction of Parkin's map was featured on the first imperial penny postage stamp, considered the world's first Christmas stamp.)

In many ways, *The British Empire Map* reflected the view from Central Canada, where the British had a two-hundred-year history and where borders were long, if crudely, established. Parkin's strong opposition to absorption into the United States was widely shared. But west of Lake Superior, where large-scale agricultural settlement was just beginning, other "nations" — defined not by surveys and international boundary markers but by states of mind or oral history — persisted in the shadows and, in time, on maps.

The Inland Empire was one such state. Centred on Spokane, Washington, the Inland Empire was a grandly named region that captured the sense of wild and unfettered possibility in the American and Canadian West between the late 1880s and the early 1910s. It loosely defined a region comprising northeastern Oregon, most of Washington State, northern Idaho, western Montana and, in the words of one pamphleteer at the time, "the best part of British Columbia," meaning the southern part.

In this Alice in Wonderland empire, the international boundary simply did not exist. What did exist was great mining potential in the Kootenays and kinship relations that overshadowed the international boundary. Travel back and forth across the border was effortless, and sometimes necessary to get between points within British Columbia because of the north-south mountain ranges and the undeveloped transportation network. Katherine Morrissey, author of *Mental Territories* (1997), quoted a young Bank of Montreal clerk who transferred from Rossland to Greenwood in 1896, and who found himself making a transborder detour. "In order to reach this Camp I travelled south on a railway newly built, connecting Rossland to Spokane. I left the train at Bossburg, in the State of Washington, and travelled by stage coach back over the border into the Kettle Valley Country [British Columbia]." The requisite maps, turned out by real estate companies, local chambers of commerce and railroad companies, served to fix the picture of the Inland Empire in the minds of westerners. According to Morrissey, the maps "labelled the various resources of the empire, highlighting the 'soon to be opened' reservations and the potential locations of 'irrigable agricultural lands,' timber, and railroad lines, along with existing farms, mines, and towns."

The sun set on the Inland Empire rather quickly. The modern and more ambitious version of the Inland Empire is now known as Cascadia, the region encompassing, on some maps, the whole of British Columbia, Washington State and Oregon, and, on other maps, represented as a circumscribed "main street" from Vancouver through to Seattle and ending in Eugene, Oregon. It has been referred to as a "mythical but geographically linked land." Professor Matthew Sparke of the University of Washington views Cascadia primarily as a geoeconomic relationship, one that treats spatial relations "with the same top-down, view-from-nowhere, visual preoccupations of classical geopolitics." The Inland Empire state of mind lives on in Cascadia: alienation from faraway central governments, a global view of trade, and environmental sensitivity.

The maps that best show the shape of this brave new globalized world of Cascadia are drawn from, appropriately enough, advertisements by transnational companies selling transnational products or services. A good example is the ad produced for Cellular One of the McCaw family, which is based in Seattle but which has significant business interests in British Columbia. Like true map-makers, the copywriters created new place names to define Cascadia's main street: "Call Anywhere From Vanseacoma To Anywhere in Portlecouver."

Maps based on such ephemeral states of mind are curios that show how western identity, like a tectonic plate, is still not a settled affair. But other maps of Native groups of the Pacific Northwest rest on the bedrock of oral history. They are much more difficult to ignore or pass off as curiosities. In place of latitude and longitude, time-tested maps of Native groups are defined by stories, songs and ancient place names.

It was not so long ago that the early European explorers used their own maps to write Native people off their own land. Now, Native groups in the Pacific Northwest are blending their own ancient stories with modern mapping technology to win back what was lost. In *Maps and Dreams*, Hugh Brody wrote about maps that showed land use and occupancy by Inuit in the Northwest Territories. These map "biographies" of how hunters, trappers, fishers and berry-pickers used their territories gave a fascinating portrait of life on the land and how the hunting culture was sustained even after European arrival and settlement. On topographical base maps, each Inuk marked everywhere he hunted, fished, trapped, picked berries and camped — lines and circles, and circles within circles. They drew the outer boundaries of the areas they used. Then the maps were aggregated to create a composite view.

In the Pacific Northwest before European exploration, relationships among Natives were between Houses — kinship — and not nations. Clans speaking different languages still shared customs. People moved with their food sources — fish and game. Boundaries, therefore, reflected such fluid movements and depended on oral traditions. The fur trade and surveyors, however, undercut these relationships by either playing one clan against the other or simply ignoring those boundaries.

Natives spent a century trying to convince politicians that they had title to land; many went to jail for destroying the equipment of surveyors trying to lay out reserves and, in the 1970s, finally began making headway. The turning point came in 1987, with the Delgamuukw case. The Gitksan and Wet'suwet'en, two Native groups in British Columbia, brought a suit against the British Columbia and federal governments over the recognition of their Native sovereignty. The name of the plaintiff came from the Gitksan chief, Ken Muldoe, who was known among his people as Delgamuukw.

The case was a huge affair: The court heard three hundred and eighteen days of evidence and another fifty-six days for closing arguments; in that time, tribal representatives presented a Native view of land use and boundary. Followers of the case learned that the Gitksan Houses have an *adaawk*, a collection of sacred oral stories about ancestors, histories and territories. They learned that the Wet'suwet'en have a *kungax*, which is a spiritual song, dance or performance that ties them to their land. And they heard of a feast hall where the Gitksan and Wet'suwet'en people tell and retell their stories and identify their territories to remind themselves of the connection they have with their lands. The feast has a ceremonial purpose but is also used for making important decisions. Witnesses from both tribes performed ceremonial songs — embedded with geographic knowledge — in court, although the songs were not considered as legitimate testimony.

Setting boundaries by stories is much different than drawing lines on maps, but that did not stop the Native groups from trying. A major part of the trial was the presentation of a collection of detailed hybrid maps showing Native fishing sites and other land uses, and the Houses that control the sites. The trial judge, B.C. Supreme Court Judge Allan McEachern, took one look at the cartographic evidence and called it "the map that roared." What he meant no one could say: It might have been a derisive put-down of the tribes' "national" aspirations. Then again, the judge might have admired the Aboriginals' efforts to remap their territory without the trap-lines, pipelines and other marks of colonial possession. "The maps served at once both to communicate in and disrupt the cartographic convention of the court," wrote Matthew Sparke of the University of Washington.

The so-called Map that Roared and other cartographic evidence were unlike the conventional maps that the court was used to seeing. In place of the familiar map of British Columbia was one that showed the density of the Houses and their approximate boundaries and names. There were at least one hundred Houses indicated on the Gitksan map alone, and the resulting map resembled a collection of

European duchies. Significantly, the maps were based on oral stories and songs performed at feasts and other tribal gatherings. The place names were based on Native words. Orientation was based on how the land was viewed from the ground rather than from the air. "North" was upriver rather than what the compass indicated.

In making such hybrid maps, the tribes took the risk that the information would be used against them or that it would not be respected because of its imprecision. Just imagine the scene: A Native from northern British Columbia trying to explain to a judge from the south about maps that are translations of traditional songs; "No, Your Honour, my map doesn't exactly match the lines of the map that you know so well." Judge McEachern assessed the maps by the standards of the state and the Cartesian mapping of the Empire, and they were found wanting. He questioned the accuracy of Native cartography; it was clearly not the kind of cartography that the court valued as accurate maps to represent property claims.

While government lawyers and the judge remained unimpressed with the maps of the Gitksan, they also cited European cartographic ignorance when it suited them. This unusual turn of events occurred over the issue of the Royal Proclamation. Declared by George III in 1763 following the Peace of Paris, the Proclamation held that British subjects in the New World could claim Aboriginal lands only after obtaining the informed consent of the Aboriginals themselves. The Gitksan and Wet'suwet'en, however, never gave their informed consent in any treaty with the Crown. The government lawyers responded that the Royal Proclamation did not apply to British Columbia because, they claimed, the Pacific Northwest was not adequately known cartographically — a dubious yet ironic claim. "Precisely because it had not been properly mapped, it was not yet a transparent space of state power," said Sparke. "The usual spatial arrogance of European imperialism assumed elsewhere by the government lawyers in arguments about extinguishing Aboriginal rights was thus displaced." In other words, if your land is not mapped, you do not exist.

The two Native tribes lost their case before Chief Justice McEachern, but the judgment was overturned in 1996 on appeal by the Supreme Court of Canada, paving the way for the use of oral traditions in equal measure in determining claims to Aboriginal territory. As a result of Delgamuukw, evidence that substantiates Aboriginal title may include oral history, Native place names, genealogical information, direct experience on the land and written records of encounters with early explorers and government and academic representatives.

The far-reaching judgment had an almost immediate effect. As Aboriginal groups became more active in pushing their claims for land, they realized that their case could be strengthened if they could translate oral history onto maps that could be presented as evidence in a language that modern Western society would understand.

The strategy worked beautifully for the Nisga'a of the Pacific Northwest. The Ayuukl Nisga'a, a code of clan law thousands of years old based on stories, songs and names, guides the Nisga'a people. The Nisga'a believe their traditional territory is defined as all the lands drained by the Nass River and its tributaries, from glacial headwaters to Pacific estuary, that everything and anything flowing into the Nass Valley is part of their territory. The Nass River flows southwest through the Coast Range mountains. As a result of negotiations throughout the 1990s, negotiations in which Native-made maps played a major role, the Nisga'a won control of some one thousand two hundred square kilometres in the lower Nass Valley, representing between five and eight percent of what they considered their territory. The agreement in principle with the provincial government was signed in 1996, and was adopted by the provincial legislature in 1999 and by the federal government in 2000.

But the map-making exercise also had an unintended conse-
quence. The Gitksan and Gitanyow (a tribe of the Gitksan nation
independent of centralized tribal organizations) charged that they,
too, had rights to the Nass Valley, above Aiyansh to its headwaters —
rights that the Nisga'a and the British Columbia government conveniently ignored in their land claim settlement. The Gitksan have
their own oral history, encoded in their *adaawk,* which describe
ancient migrations of the House and songs. Traditionally, the border
between the Gitksan and Nisga'a had been negotiated through famil-
ial ties through clan adoption or intermarriage, and reciprocal cere-
monies after battles. Once the Nisga'a agreement was approved, it
created a much less fluid, and more fixed, border. This is how Neil
Sterritt, one of the chief negotiators for the Gitksan, described the
situation to a *Globe and Mail* reporter: "The Nass River is three hundred eighty kilometres long. The Gitksan, my people, own the upper
third. The next third is owned by the Gitanyow, a remarkable people
who, since their very first contact with Europeans, decided to remain
independent. The next third is owned by the Nisga'a. What the Nisga'a did was very simple. They said they owned it all and the government believed them. The government had people who knew better
but it was a political decision to go with what the Nisga'a said."

The Nisga'a said the issue was merely a question of "overlap" and
that problems could be worked out through tribal mediation. The
Gitksan called it "an act of aggression." The Gitanyow people claim
that more than eighty-five percent of their traditional territory is
included in the agreement as Nisga'a settlement lands. Sterritt has
made the case that the Nisga'a began in the 1900s claiming only
the lower Nass below the Kinskuch River, tried in 1913 to claim the
middle Nass valley but were forced to retreat, and then in the 1980s
introduced maps claiming the lower and mid-valley once again. In
the 1990s, when negotiations with the province and federal government became serious, the Nisga'a then produced maps claiming

even more of the Nass watershed, first up to Treaty Creek, two hundred fifty-four kilometres beyond the Kinskuch, and then finally right to Nass Lake, two hundred seventy-four kilometres beyond the Kinskuch. "The amount of land claimed by the Nisga'a increased nearly fivefold in thirty years," said Sterritt.

There is a cartographic record that Sterritt marshals to support his position. He offers a flavour of the kind of oral history that makes up the geographical knowledge and claim-setting of the region. He points to the Barbeau-Benyon Northwest Coast files dating to the 1920s, dealing with "ownership" of a mountain known as Wilgax-t'aahlgibuu (unnamed on government maps), immediately north of the Kiteen River. The files include exchanges with Gitanyow and Nisga'a chiefs. Nisga'a leaders Charles and Johnny Morven acknowledged Gitanyow claims when they said:

> There is a controversy as to the ownership of portions of Tok ground, especially with the Gitwinhlkul [Gitanyow House chiefs] Wudaxhayetsxw and T'ooxens. T'ooxens in the former years had married into the Nisga'a House. The Nisga'a chief then gave as a wedding dowry to the Gitwinhlkul the privilege of using portions of his hunting grounds for the benefit of his children. The rights of the dowry ended on the death of the Gitwinhlkul man. But the Gitwinhlkul still claim the privilege claiming that the right has never been extinguished. The present T'ooxens may not claim it. But the House of Wudaxhayetsxw claim it. They are Tsetsaut people in origin.

Naming natural features of one's territory, such as mountains, rivers and lakes, and knowing the toponymic history are part and parcel of claiming territory, something that the Nisga'a agreement allows for. Sterritt also describes the provision for recording seven place names within Gitanyow and Gitksan territory in the British

Columbia Geographic Names System. The Nisga'a will record the Cranberry River as *Ksi W'iipdalks* (water/of/cranberry), a recent and literal translation of the Euro-Canadian name, as opposed to the Aboriginal name *Xsiyagasgiit*. "The purpose of this effort," said Sterritt, "appears to be to establish a Nisga'a presence in parts of the Nass watershed where it does not exist."

If the Nisga'a situation is a cautionary tale of the double-edged consequences of mapping in the service of nationhood, there is every reason to believe that similar, three-sided disagreements will arise in the coming years; Native group against Native group, and Native group against government. Most of the two hundred or so Native bands in British Columbia are engaged in the mapping of the traditional use of their territories, a similar situation in other parts of Canada. The North Slave Metis Alliance, for example, is seeking to stop the Dogrib land claim in the Northwest Territories. As reported by the CBC, the Alliance leader, Clem Paul, said the nearly completed Dogrib claim ignores his group's traditional use of the region. "We were here before the Hudson Bay," Paul said to the CBC reporter. "We were here before the Northwest Trading Company; we were here trading amongst ourselves at the north end of Marion Lake."

The Dogrib say the region's Metis will be included in their final land claim and self-government agreement. While some Metis in Rae are happy with that, Paul disdains the idea. "I'll kill myself before I become a Dogrib. I want recognition as a Metis person with Aboriginal rights."

Those words could have been spoken by Paul's not-so-distant ancestor, a man who gave his life resisting the imposition of someone else's map on his people. That man was Louis Riel.

5

PATHFINDING

The headline in London's *Daily Mail* on May 9, 1934, read:

MAP-MAKING IN CANADIAN WILDS:
Scientists Aid in Exhibition.

Below it appeared a photograph of tractors being loaded onto the Canadian Pacific freighter *Beaverburn* at Le Havre, France. The story that followed reported on a fantastic expedition.

Early in July, Mr. Charles C. Bedaux, an American living at Chateau de Cande, Monts, Indre-et-Loire, will conduct, under the name of the Bedaux Sub-Arctic Expedition, the passage of 30 people, five Caterpillar tractors and 75 horses from Edmonton, Alberta, to the Pacific Ocean by way of Fort St. John, British Columbia, Redfern Lake, Sifton Pass and Telegraph Creek.

The object of the expedition is solely a scientific one, the main purpose being to open a road in the country known as Cassiar, and

to map, with the aid of a geographer loaned by the British Columbia
Department of Lands, the new and unknown country lying between
Sifton Pass and Dease Lake.

On the surface, the story seemed bracing enough. For those living in 1934 with any appreciation for the dense forest, soggy muskeg and soaring mountains of the Cassiar, the image of tractors trying to blaze a trail was fantastic and hard to conceive, like travelling to the moon. But what the story did not report was even more tantalizing. Who was this Bedaux, who had the hubris to believe the project could succeed? Was it true that the expedition was provisioned with caviar and fine wine? And, for the really curious, what did the anonymous "geographer loaned by the British Columbia Department of Lands" think of the expedition? How in the world had he got caught up in this madness?

Frank Swannell, the anonymous geographer, was an Ontario boy, born in Hamilton in 1880. At seventeen he travelled west, first to Manitoba, working on harvest and threshing crews, and later to British Columbia, where he worked at New Denver on mining prospects. The next year, Swannell wanted to mine for gold in the Klondike, but he did not have the necessary six-hundred-dollar grubstake. Instead, he trained as a surveyor, mapping mineral claims and railway land blocks. Over the years, Swannell became particularly adept at exploratory and triangulation surveys, covering the remote parts of the province.

Swannell made his name as a surveyor who could cover huge areas quickly while labouring under difficult conditions. He did the Omineca, Ingenika and Finlay river watersheds, and the Nechako Basin in northern British Columbia, densely pockmarked with lakes. This was during a time when surveyors cut their own paths while lugging some one thousand kilograms of supplies and sensitive measuring equipment, when poles or rudimentary sails and makeshift rafts took the place of outboard motors. Mosquitoes provided a special sort of torture. And for this Swannell received fifteen dollars a day pay from the province.

Swannell had an artist's touch to go with his mapping precision. It could be seen in his deft sketch of a roiling stretch of white water on the Big Bend in the Upper Finlay River, headwaters of the Mackenzie River. The only other explorer known to have penetrated the river was Samuel Black, chief factor of Hudson's Bay Company, who ran those rapids on September 10, 1824. During rapid reconnaissance in 1914 to map the Finlay from Fort Grahame to its headwaters, Swannell and his team retraced the route, passing through the terrifying chasm on September 29. With Swannell were George Copley, his assistant; Jim Nep Yuen, the "Chinaman cook"; and James Alexander, the canoeman. Swannell recounted his experience in an article for the *Beaver* in 1956.

Swannell's diary, a section of which is printed next to his map of the rapids, tells of what greeted them. "Worst water I ever saw but we had no option. It had to be run, lining or dropping down with the pole being impossible." They had no choice but to run the rapids, since the dugout they were using was far too heavy for portaging. Copley added this note to Swannell's entry: "We had sized up this place from above and Jimmy [Alexander] wanted Nep Yuen to go ashore and walk down to where we could pick him up. Jim Nep refused point blank, said he might as well get drowned with us as see us drown and die of cold and starvation himself. He lay down in the bottom of the canoe." On his bird's-eye drawing of the rapids, Swannell offered an annotated map of how his party picked a path, indicating where they had to bail out the dugout canoe, where they were swamped by eight-metre-high waves, and how the currents played. It took Swannell and his buddies three days to get through the four-kilometre-long canyon. But he emerged with a new map in his hand.

IF SWANNELL WAS MOST COMFORTABLE running rivers and bunking down under a ceiling of stars, his new boss, Charles Bedaux, had more delicate sensibilities. His Manhattan apartment was scented daily with lilac water, while his castle in France was staffed by some thirty servants. He kept haberdashers busy on both sides of the Atlantic. Bedaux had all the acquisitive instincts and insecurities of the nouveau riche, without a great stock in scruples. The son of a French railroad labourer, Bedaux had immigrated to the United States at the age of sixteen and worked odd jobs in New York City. His break came when he developed a factory efficiency system he dubbed the B-Unit. Industrialists in the United States and Europe embraced the system, and Bedaux became fabulously wealthy.

Once he had the resources, Bedaux indulged in several odd expeditions, in particular a sixteen-thousand-kilometre drive across North Africa in 1930 and two more modest trips through British Columbia. But these earlier efforts were dwarfed by the audacity of the Bedaux Sub-Arctic Expedition. There was no questioning the ambition of the Expedition: Bedaux's itinerary would take him through one thousand eight hundred kilometres of rough and largely unknown territory, by turns marshy and densely forested, and at rarefied altitude. The plan was to set out from Edmonton and head to Fort St John in the Peace River region, and then head northwest to the summit of the Rockies. The trip, if all went well, would end at the Pacific Ocean just beyond Telegraph Creek. There were hundreds of kilometres of unmapped country between the Peace River land surveys, southeast of the Muskwa River. What charts existed were "guess maps," said Bert McCorkell of Fort St James, who spent time with Swannell mapping. If successful, the immodest Frenchman said, "it will open up a vast region that has never been explored."

The Bedaux Expedition included forty-three people, and everyone had a job. There was a Spanish maid to attend to Bedaux's wife,

Fern; an Italian countess to attend to Charles himself; a movie cameraman to record the adventure; and a Scottish gamekeeper. It was an odd and idiosyncratic cavalcade, but it also included a cracker-jack science team headed by Edmonton geologist John Bocock. Bocock hired two top geographers: Ernest Lamarque to lead the advance group that blazed a trail, and Frank Swannell to map. It is hardly surprising that when Charles Bedaux asked Bocock to recommend a mapper for his mountain expedition, the first and only person considered was Swannell, "a very able man to whom hardships are the breath of life," as Bocock wrote to his boss. Swannell had worked with Bocock on a resources survey for the railways in 1929, and his letter to his colleague, written in January 1934, clearly showed his eagerness to join the expedition. Swannell's employers had no hesitation about releasing their star mapper, since it would be a rare opportunity to map the uncharted country between Muskwa River and Dease Lake on someone else's nickel.

The expedition was well provisioned. The twenty tons of equipment were packed on five Citroen half-tracks and, when they could go no farther, on one hundred and thirty packhorses. The "equipment" included some non-essential items. The expedition team members ate pâté de foie gras and caviar, and chicken livers cooked in fine French pots, washing it all down with champagne and wine. They slept in comfortable beds, within much-noted asbestos-roofed sparkproof tents (that leaked like sieves), and washed in bathtubs they brought along. They clothed themselves in cashmere sweaters and fur parkas. They drove in two limousines; more than one hundred horses were used to carry gasoline. For the workers, Bedaux handed out cigarettes and chewing gum each evening. The cowboys got four dollars a day, a good wage since there were few jobs to be had in the Peace River area that year. (The novelty was not entirely unpleasant. Lamarque wrote: "I was amused and surprised, the next morning, when the man whose tent I shared told me not to get up too soon, for coffee would be brought to me." A couple of days later he tasted pâté de foie gras for the first time.)

Full of hope, the expedition left Edmonton in a parade on July 6. Some five hundred townspeople watched with amusement as the five shiny tractors with a roller where the bumper should be — with Bedaux driving the lead tractor — started pulling away from the Macdonald Hotel shortly after 1 P.M. The Edmonton newspaper reported approvingly on the odd vehicles. "The tractors themselves are marvels at surmounting obstacles. The . . . tracks will take the heavy burden over soft muskegs with little difficulty and up to a 40 degrees slope on low gear at one mile an hour." Rivers would be forded with the aid of special floats; steel cables and winding gear would pull the vehicles up sheer bluffs. The main party, of which

On the "road" with the Bedaux Sub-Arctic Expedition. Citroens with rollers in place of bumpers were designed to navigate rough patches; at times the cars were almost swallowed whole by dirt pathways turned into mush by record rainfall. National Archives of Canada (PA-171598).

Swannell was a member, did not actually cut trail; that was the job of two advance trail-breaking teams.

That evening, the expedition was hit by a violent rainstorm and lightning. It was a telling omen. One day they were stuck in a stream, the next day they were axle-deep in swamp. They trudged through heavy gumbo for tens of kilometres. There are photographs of tractors being pulled out of the mud by horses. Unremitting rain did not help matters. Like a captain of a sinking ship, Bedaux started tossing equipment overboard. Swannell looked on in shock when one of the tractors got stuck in mud, and Bedaux got out and "asked" Swannell to leave his twenty-kilogram Wild theodolite (used to measure horizontal and vertical angles) to lessen the load. Later, Bedaux turned Swannell's surveying assistant, A. H. Phipps, into a personal servant. Bedaux also tossed people overboard. He fired the radio operator, making matters even worse for Swannell, who relied on radio to get a Greenwich time signal, an anchoring figure in his mapping calculations. As an alternative, Swannell used the stars to chart the expedition's course.

By the time the company reached the Muskwa River, two tractors had been abandoned, their steel shoes and traction teeth no match for the morass. Beyond being overloaded and ghastly overworked, the horses had to contend with floods and wet saddle blankets that did not get a chance to dry out in the rainy weather. Countless animals dropped dead from exhaustion. Through it all, Bedaux refused to part with his luxuries and persisted in shooting a movie, staging wacky scenes of cowboys squirming on the ground as if in pain from fatigue. All this from a man who made his fortune telling others how to be efficient in their operations.

In the face of this farce, Swannell stayed focused on the task at hand. He kept scrupulous records of not only topographical information but also barometer readings, the kilometres made, temperature and weather conditions. He decorated his field book with drawings of peaks and geometrical measurements necessary for precise cartography,

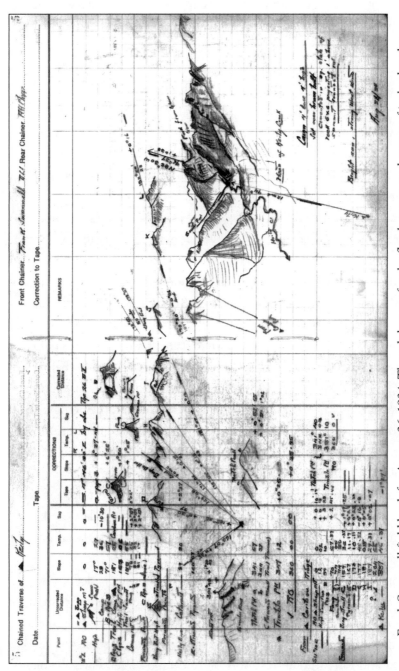

Frank Swannell field book for August 26, 1934. Though known for the flamboyance and excess of its leader, the Bedaux Expedition allowed Swannell to map crucial portions of the Rockies. British Columbia Archives (MS-0392).

and stuffed his diary with newspaper clippings chronicling the expedition's progress, adorned later by the many photographs he took. And his diary entries reveal the increasingly madcap misadventures. On July 24, he wrote: "Our trailers carrying winch and cable, 1400 pounds in all, cause of much profanity — wheels splay apart." On July 29: "Al [Phipps, the surveyor] and I requisitioned by Crosby [filmmaker] for a moving picture stunt — Balourdet [Citroen mechanic] drived through the bush with Ev [Withrow, camera assistant] and I on the running board with axes at the ready. Al on ahead afoot calls out and we all three slashed road . . . for the car. Amazed Indians witness this performance. Ditch the 2d trailer." On August 4: "In the evening a movie by flares simulating a fire in camp. I dash across in frantic haste to save my tent — this is the cue for our buckaroo cowboys to drive the pack train in front of the camera. The others dash out of the tents with dunnage and Josefina finally emerges screaming. All went well except the pack horses stampeded and wouldn't face the flames."

On September 10: "Several movie stunts with the horses pulled up — a wild stampede on camp caused by a dozen bolting before a fusillade of rifle shots stopped by Balourdet and me. In evening distribution of 9 bottles of champagne and another stampede photographed by flares and another episode of the great forest fire act." On September 28: "Horse shot along trail an awful sight as a wolf and grizzly bear had been at it." Finally, in late September, Swannell offered a picture of Bedaux as the party split up, a short distance beyond the Ospika. After an early lunch, Bedaux and his immediate circle left in a flotilla of four boats. The "Dudes Boat" had a small tent and stove erected, in which Bedaux and the two ladies "denned up," marvellously attired in fur parkas and padded trousers. "We others in nondescript sweaters and moose hide coats shiver in the open boats," Swannell recounted either ruefully or with amusement.

Bedaux decided to pull the plug on the expedition some four hundred and forty kilometres short of Telegraph Creek but still some fourteen hundred kilometres away from their starting point. Only Ernest Lamarque, trailblazer for the party, succeeded in crossing the mountains by the Bedaux route. Ironically, Lamarque was convinced that the expedition could have been successful had reconnaissance and preparation of the route been undertaken a year before the tractors rumbled out of Edmonton.

Later, there would be rumours about the true motivation of the expedition; one of the more interesting speculations was that Bedaux had used the Canadian mountains on behalf of the Germans as a testing ground for military transport trucks in alpine conditions. He dismissed all such rumours as nonsense and, for good measure, took credit for the true pathfinding labours of Lamarque and Swannell. "No, the true theory is simply that I believe Canada and the United States want an international road through there, and I want to be the first to try it. While the expedition failed to reach its final goal, I believe that I attained my objective. I feel that I have traced the route and shown it to be a practical route throughout the greater part of the distance." Eight years later, in fact, the Alaska Highway was built along much of the Bedaux route.

Swannell's diary betrays no resentment, but in a letter written in 1956 to a fact checker from *Maclean's* magazine, Swannell still seemed disillusioned about Bedaux's mixed-up priorities: "The Triangulation system of control had to be abandoned, and I did the best I could fixing positions by observations for latitude and longitude. The weight saved was negligible — two famous asbestos-roofed tents were a packhorse load each and the metal tubing poles another horse load. Phipps was put in charge of their erection and talks feelingly of the trouble erecting them — the poles battered and twisted — in a country full of timber."

Twenty-five years after the expedition, in September 1959, there was a big reunion at the home of Ernie Petersen, expedition hand, north of Fort St John, British Columbia. There was great frivolity, dancing until three in the morning in the old log store ("women to [sic] few but make up with vigor," Swannell wrote to himself). Many of the expedition members managed to attend, but the person who made it all happen, Charles Bedaux, did not. After his experience in the mountains of Western Canada, Bedaux was increasingly aligned with the Fascist forces in Europe, developing close relationships with top Nazis and acting as a go-between for the Vichy government in France and Nazi leadership in Germany. He also was said to have passed on information to the Germans. In December 1943, he was captured by American forces in the Sahara, where he was trying to build an oil pipeline. The Americans flew him back to the United States and charged him with trading with the enemy. On Valentine's Day 1944, he took an overdose of barbiturates and died at the age of fifty-six.

Swannell fought in the First and Second World Wars. He was wounded severely twice, and his eye and one side of his mouth were crooked as a result of a head wound received while serving in France. His diaries are silent on the issue, but what he thought of Bedaux's allegiance is not hard to guess.

FIFTY-NINE SUMMERS LATER, wilderness guide Hap Wilson was doing his best Frank Swannell imitation. Like the famed map-maker running the rapids on the Big Bend in British Columbia's Upper Finlay River, Wilson was doing his own river reconnaissance back in Ontario, on the fabled Missinaibi. The Missinaibi is a five-hundred-kilometre waterway that figured in the early days of the fur trade. Though it was not as remote as the Upper Finlay, stretches of the river were as wild as the Big Bend, and paddlers greatly needed a reliable map of the underlying geology and play of the river if they wanted to emerge wet but alive. As a veteran guide and river rat with the precision and artistry of a Swannell, Wilson was in the best position to produce those maps.

In June 1993, he was carefully paddling above Thunderhouse Falls; carefully because Thunderhouse Falls is an aptly named, rollicking section of the Missinaibi. The full force of the river's energy is compressed in a gorge above the falls before the river drops twelve metres. This stretch has been known to claim lives. A couple of years before, Wilson paddled over the body of a canoeist who was trapped just upstream, at Albany Rapids. And just two weeks before, Wilson had heard, two paddlers from Ohio had drowned trying to get through Thunderhouse Falls. On this sunny day, as Wilson took note of the river from his canoe, his eyes noticed the reflection of a metal object. He paddled closer to the pool above the falls and fished out a camera, the film inside still fresh with the undeveloped photographs of the two unlucky canoeists who had died two weeks before.

Wilson would later learn much about the victims. Ken Randlett, thirty-nine, and David Zenisek, twenty-three, had planned the trip to the Missinaibi the year before. Ken was planning to celebrate his fortieth birthday on the river; David had a date with the altar later that summer. The second day on the river, the four-man group stopped several kilometres above Thunderhouse Falls, planning their next move. They consulted the government-issued topographical map that indicated, via a dotted purple line, the location of a portage on the east side of the river to safely bypass the treacherous sluiceway. Portage on river right, just shy of the falls. They tracked to the east, looking for the portage marker, but found none. Nor would they, since the portage was on the west side of the river. By then they were caught by the rapids, rumbling over boulders and pillow-rocks.

Craig Zelenak, one of the four buddies on the trip, described the power of the river to a reporter for the *Toronto Star*: "Take a roller coaster off its track and put a canoe on in its place with waves three feet high on each side." The canoe Craig was paddling overturned, but he was able to reach shore. The canoe carrying Ken and David hurtled over the falls. "I didn't realize they had gone over the falls until I found a lifejacket ripped in half," Craig recalled. Four days later, Ken's body was recovered twenty-four kilometres downstream from the falls; the next day David's body was recovered.

Accidents happen, especially on wilderness rivers, but Wilson sensed a pattern, and suspected that a contributing factor was being overlooked — misleading topographical maps. He had long been concerned about the accuracy of topographical maps issued by both the provincial and federal governments, a concern shared by other veterans of the waterways. The case of Ken Randlett and David Zenisek spurred him to dig deeper.

To test his theory, Wilson decided to take a closer look at the deaths on the Missinaibi. He visited the Ontario Coroner's office in Toronto. He went through the records of about five hundred drowning deaths in the region and isolated the thirty-two that occurred on the Missinaibi over a period of seventeen years, determining the conditions under which the victims drowned. In one file was a photograph of two men in their early twenties, laid out on steel gurneys in the morgue, their faces contorted and their life jackets on. They were plucked from Thunderhouse Falls. Wilson figured that seventeen of the drownings could have been prevented had the victims known what was around the corner, what was ahead, where was the portage, what were the peculiarities in flow patterns.

The coroner's reports indicated the victims had Ontario Ministry of Natural Resources maps that had not been updated. Wilson then examined sixteen topographic maps that covered the same part of the Missinaibi route — some of them government maps but others not — and found disturbing errors on at least twelve of them. Some rapids on the maps were actually falls, some rapids and falls were not even marked. And perhaps the most glaring error: A life-saving portage before Thunderhouse Falls was identified on the east side of the river instead of the west side.

Wilson also noticed that a dozen of the victims were Americans. "The government at that time just finished spending over $100,000 on a full-page advertisement in an American magazine touting that heritage river as a waterway that can be paddled from Superior to James Bay," said Wilson. "Even the topo office was putting in ads in magazines urging, Come use these topo maps. Lots of Americans and some Europeans coming to Canada picked up these maps."

There was no way to prove that the maps were solely responsible for the string of deadly river mishaps, but the Ontario government pulled them nonetheless and ordered new ones made. The government even contributed funds for Wilson to produce a canoe guide to the river. *Missinaibi: Journey to the Northern Sky* was published in 1994, a product of six months of reconnaissance and another six months of studio work to produce the maps and drawings. The map book is good as an example of a conscientious pathfinder communicating what he has learned, only in his case the path being picked out is through a boulder-strewn waterway. In all his river maps, Wilson grades the difficulty of rapids, describes general conditions and hazards, illustrates primary and secondary running channels, details portage locations and indicates the length of runs. It is a very fluid environment to map. Consider the fickle flow patterns that affect the path you can safely take down a river. If it rains for three days on the Missinaibi, for example, the central section swells; in mere hours, water levels can rise as much as ten metres before Thunderhouse Falls, making the currents more difficult to navigate. All Wilson can do as a river cartographer is make the variables known to the paddler; it is then up to the paddler to adjust to environmental conditions. It is a fact that he acknowledges in each of his map books. In his Missinaibi book, Wilson dealt with the vagaries of charting a river from the inside out: "Rapids that round bends may be impeded by sweepers or strainers (fallen trees and log jams). Each spring freshet scours the shores and washes timber

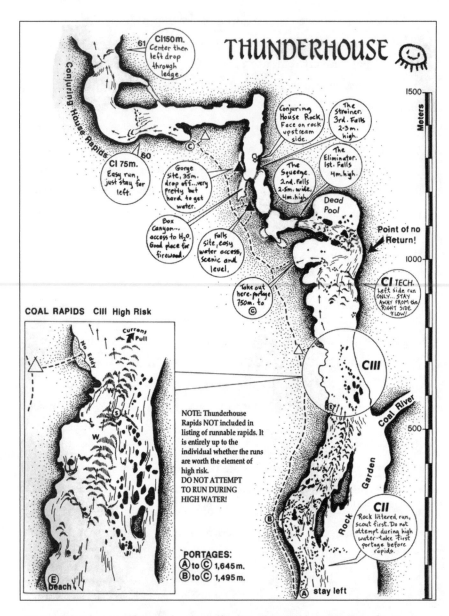

Map of rapids near Thunderhouse Falls, from Hap Wilson's *Missinaibi: Journey to the Northern Sky*. To map such a fluid and seasonal environment, Wilson tries to chart as many river variables as possible, often using symbols and place names of his own invention. Courtesy Hap Wilson.

downriver, frequently to become lodged in the most inappropriate places. Rapid diagrams are for reference only and gauged at optimum running conditions with all safety procedures in place."

Wilson's first maps, done in 1977, showed routes through about eight thousand square kilometres of the Temagami area of Northern Ontario. At the time, there was considerable pressure to open the area to logging, and the Ontario government asked Wilson to do an "inventory" of natural resources, which he did, including finding many of the old Indian trails that were overgrown. To locate the trails, he crawled on his hands and knees through thick spruce and alder, and was rewarded by uncovering old bags of beaver casters, which trappers used in the 1930s and 1940s to mark and define trails. He did similar studies of the Dumoine River in the Ottawa Valley, as well as the Black and Coulonge, all considered for hydro-electric development. By modern standards, the topographical maps were crude, at a 1:26,000 scale and with no detail, but they showed Wilson how accurate maps could encourage people to use the rivers and old trails and create an ecotourism industry as a counterweight to logging and hydroelectric development.

Over the years, Wilson has developed and refined his own carto-graphic style from hanging out in reference libraries and studying old maps. It helps that he has developed a knack for reading the charac-ter of a river, its flow levels. He has been known to travel down a river three or four times at different water levels to see what the rapids are like. He picks a particular time and studies the rocks, the visible high-water marks on rocks and boulders, the channels, the flow patterns, and the rainfall patterns, and can read and classify a rapid by looking at it one time and running it once. He tries to run a river in low and high water or, if restricted by time, will try to determine an average reading. "I'm a pen and ink artist," Wilson said. "I like the feel and look of hand-drawn maps. I don't like computer-generated maps and have fought for years against that technology. I look at hand-drawn maps as pieces of art and not just rendering of a few lines on a page. It's my interpretation.

"I'll get in a canoe, put my helmet and life jacket on, tuck everything in, and then run it. I'll play the eddies and pools and see where the current tugs are, boils or hydraulics, and then pull off into another eddy where I can get another look ahead and then just work my way down the rapid like that. Often only one run is necessary."

Wilson believes maps should relate the story of the river. He translates that story onto old-style maps annotated in hand script with advice like this: "Difficult high-volume rollers in spring . . . spray covers required (and adequate life insurance!)," "Ferry out here. Poor eddy but possible in low water," and before Thunderhouse: "Rock-littered run, scout first. Do not attempt during high water. Take first portage before rapids." He has developed his own symbols, using feathery flourishes and stipples to illustrate rapids, haystacks and shoals. And if a rapid or waterfall does not have a widely recognized name, either Native or English, Wilson will give it one. He will find something peculiar about the rapid — its aesthetics or hydrology — and tag it with a name such as Bedrock Bend.

"What I try to get across is that I like people to know that I've done the fieldwork, I've been there and I spent the time and the information I put down on paper isn't because I just derive pleasure for myself, but I'm doing something for someone else and making it pleasurable for them."

While Wilson's maps may be welcoming and heavily annotated, that does not guarantee their proper use. The fact is, he often bumps into canoeists who have maps in hand but clearly no idea where they are. Having a map does not lessen the need to look in the proverbial rear-view mirror every few minutes to stay oriented. He gets plenty of fan mail, but also letters from people complaining that a portage marked on his map was nowhere to be found. "What can I say, You can't read maps," said an unapologetic Wilson. "It was obvious they were two kilometres away from another bay where the actual portage was. As an outfitter, I spent a considerable amount of time with novices, saying, 'Here's your map. Keep this in front of you all the time and know where you are and you won't have any trouble.' That's all there is to it."

For his sixth and latest book, *Mapping Muskoka Wilds*, Wilson did the map-making during the winter months by lantern and solar energy in his cabin in Temagami. Wilson and his partner, Stephanie Ackroyd, moved to what is Central Ontario's cottage country five years ago. As is his habit, Wilson got to know the small and out-of-the-way waterways of the region, and was surprised at little pockets of secluded lakes that escaped developers. It is classic Canadian Shield country, as rugged as northern Manitoba or the interior of Quebec, regions Wilson knows well. He has also noticed the stepped-up pace of development in cottage country, the monster homes, the subdivisions, the golf courses. Many cottagers do not know what is around the bend in their lake, and tourists to the area do not venture beyond the well-known skiing and hiking spots. Wilson sees his maps as giving more options to the local outfitter and lodge owner because of the seasonality of the business.

"The more I researched Canadian rivers, the more I was convinced we needed maps," he said. "One of the things that really hit home, besides the environmental damage, was the fact that our topo map system was being used for the wrong purposes. They were developed for political reasons, for military reasons, but not for general recreation."

Wilson knows very well that producing popular and accessible maps to wilderness areas — in a sense, opening those areas to a wider audience — is a double-edged sword. Many canoeists see his work as encouraging more traffic on *their* rivers, undercutting the serenity that the maps are intended to celebrate. In fact, there were problems in the Temagami region when the Lady Evelyn-Smoothwater

Wilderness Park was established in 1983. The park's boundaries were placed on maps, which attracted legions of paddlers. In the mid-1970s, traffic was particularly bad on the Lady Evelyn River. Wilson's response: "I would rather bump gunnels with a few like-minded canoeists paddling a river than have to portage around a hydro dam." Wilson made the argument to the Ontario provincial government to expand the mapping; instead of focusing on one canoe route, he urged, let's give them twenty-four routes over a much larger area. The government agreed. Traffic on the Lady Evelyn peaked in the 1980s and is now down considerably as paddlers have been encouraged through maps to look for other rivers. (With budgetary cutbacks in Ontario, no fieldwork is being done to maintain the routes and portages, and Temagami is again seeing a smaller recreational base.)

"To me it's a straightforward issue: you either use it or lose it," Wilson said. "Having worked for the Ontario government, I know a bit about the system and how it works. It depends on the particular resource. If it looks like it's not being used for anything, then the extractors are going to get carte blanche to do what they want, whether that be Hydro or clear-cutting with minimal reserves. What changes that is if you create a recreational corridor and get more people out. Not thousands every weekend but a few dozen people a season. That's all you need to change the scope of a waterway."

Incremental differences can be hugely significant for pathfinders who make maps as well. A clear and inviting map can lead to an exhilarating run through rapids; a portage misplaced on a map can mean death. Hap Wilson can rest easy knowing there have been no fatal mishaps at Thunderhouse Falls since the publication of his map of the Missinaibi canoe route. The stakes for Charles Bedaux and Frank Swannell were more personal — how does one put a value on Bedaux's ego or Swannell's professional credibility? Swannell's legacy was the greater of the two: At least he retired with honour, and his observations and calculations added to the knowledge about the northwest corner of Canada, ushering in the Alaska Highway and all manner of development. How differently would Bedaux have lived out his final years had his expedition been a success?

Though their differences in approach are abundantly clear, Wilson's private mission in river cartography and the Bedaux Expedition's very public spectacle are welcome reminders that map-making can involve sweat, physical risk and endurance. In our digital age, you can make your own maps at the click of a computer key; a few more clicks and a satellite image of your town can be on the screen. You have to admire those map-makers who are willing to be battered in a churn of rock and water or pinched incessantly by clouds of black-flies just to show the way for others to follow. Even if they have Dom Perignon to wash away the misery.

6

EXPLOITATION

"THE LAKE IT IS SAID never gives up her dead / when the skies of November turn gloomy." In 1976, when memorializing the wreck of the *Edmund Fitzgerald*, folksinger Gordon Lightfoot conjured the powerful and enduring images of Lake Superior: deep, dark, foreboding. Perhaps because of its surface size and the fact that it is the deepest of the Great Lakes, Superior earned the respect of Aboriginals as well as modern-day mariners, and it has long been a challenge to map-makers. The Jesuits produced the most famous map of the lake's coastline, a map that stood unchallenged until the nineteenth century. And even then, it would take much longer for the central part of the lake to be charted. It was widely thought that the lake was at least three hundred metres deep in places, so mariners did not feel the need to take any special care while sailing far offshore.

But with the growth in commercial traffic early in the twentieth century came a disturbing number of cases in which substantial vessels, such as lake tankers, mysteriously disappeared. The *Edmund Fitzgerald* was the most heralded case, but the oddest was that of the French minesweepers *Inkerman, Cerisoles* and *Sebastopol*. In November 1918, they set out from Thunder Bay to France, manned by experienced sailors. *Sebastopol* arrived safely, while the other two ships were never seen or heard from again; in spite of the fact that both carried wireless equipment, no radio message was ever recorded.

In June 1929 while on a surveying mission, the United States Coast Guard vessel *Margaret* was steaming along in the middle of Superior when its echo sounder began spitting out odd readings. It went from picking up depths in the hundreds of metres to a mere fifteen metres. The ship retraced its path and confirmed the readings. It could mean only one thing — there was a mountain rising up near the surface in the middle of Lake Superior, and within the shipping lanes.

The next year, the Canadian Hydrographic Service's *Bayfield II*, on its final mission, measured the depth of Superior by lowering lead lines and confirmed that there was indeed a massive shoal rising up to within six metres of the surface. Later named Superior Shoal, it was placed on charts during the Second World War as a warning for mariners to avoid. But the *Bayfield II* found something else. In searching the area for wrecks, the crew lowered a grappling hook that caught on a tangle of fishing net. And it also spotted fishermen on a tug quickly pulling in their own fishing nets and heading back to port in Michigan.

Stories later came out that, although the shoal was not formally mapped, it was not unknown. Fishermen, particularly those working out of American ports, were well aware of the shoal because that was where large schools of fish — lake trout and ciscoes — congregated. There were tales of huge hauls, though there were also rumours put out that the fish were oddly flavoured and mutated, alarming stories that served to discourage others from exploiting the shoal.

These American fishermen had a shrewd understanding of fish and human behaviour. They knew that accurate maps were crucial to safely navigate the surface of the earth and how these maps could be powerful tools of exploitation — even when they were withheld. They knew the power of mapping and were not about to identify their treasure. Keeping their "maps" of the shoal to themselves, they were assured of bountiful catches, even at the cost of countless ships being sunk on the submarine mountain in the middle of Lake Superior.

It is a story that Brian Harley would no doubt have enjoyed. As professor of geography at the University of Wisconsin in Milwaukee, Harley was at the forefront of the map "deconstruction" movement until his sudden death in December 1991. In 1989, Harley wrote what was to become perhaps the most-cited article in geography circles, "Deconstructing the Map," published in the journal *Cartographica*. In it, he wrote that cartography is seldom what cartographers say it is — an objective, and even scientific, piece of knowledge. In reality, there are powerful forces, internal and external, swirling around maps and the people who make them. Behind most map-makers is a patron: a government making a geopolitical statement, a newspaper needing to sell copies, an oil developer looking for the next big strike. "In modern Western society, maps quickly became crucial to the maintenance of state power — to its boundaries, to its commerce, to its internal administration, to control of populations, and to its military strength," Harley wrote.

Maps are also arbiters of power because cartographers manufacture what Harley called a "spatial panopticon." To catalogue the world, he pronounced, was to appropriate it. The cartographer/cataloguer selects categories of information, establishes rules for abstracting the landscape and places elements of the landscape into hierarchies. States eagerly marshal these forces to exploit their resources to the fullest and to exploit other states as well. As a nation built on resource extraction, Canada knows this fact well.

The first piece of present-day Canada "appropriated" by European map-makers and exploited by fellow countrymen was not even land but the storied Grand Banks off Newfoundland. It is a little-noted fact that the Grand Banks and the rich cod-fishing grounds were cartographically known long before any other part of what would later become known as Canada.

The Grand Banks are a ninety-four-thousand-square-kilometre stretch of shallow water the size of France off the southeast coast of Newfoundland. They begin about one hundred sixty kilometres from Cape Race at the southeastern tip of Newfoundland and extend as far as five hundred kilometres out into the Atlantic Ocean. They are actually a series of raised submarine plateaus with a water depth ranging between thirty-six and one hundred eighty-five metres. The relative shallowness of the water creates rich and welcoming conditions for marine animal and plant life to flourish on the bottom, warmed by the waters of the Gulf Stream, which pass over the southern portion of the Banks in winter and cover almost the entire area in summer.

On his 1497 voyage to the New World, John Cabot described the Grand Banks as so "swarming with fish [that they] could be taken not only with a net but in baskets let down with a stone." News of what Cabot had found spread quickly throughout Europe. Within ten years of his voyage, hundreds of fishing ships sailed each spring to Newfoundland from France, Spain and Portugal, returning in the fall with their catch of salted codfish. Late in the sixteenth century, ships from the southwestern counties of England took their place, setting up confrontations between Britain and France late in the seventeenth century.

While the migratory fishermen from Europe had pictures in their heads of the most productive spots on the Grand Banks, the mapping

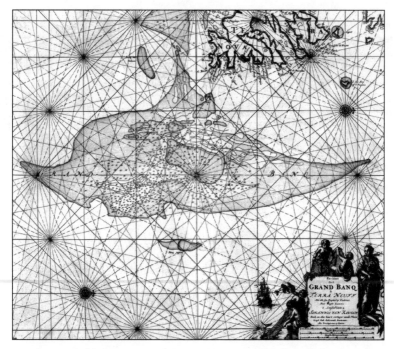

Pas-kaart van de Grand Banq by Terra Neuff . . . by Johannes van Keulen,
1687. The Grand Banks region off Newfoundland was the first part of
the New World cartographically known by Europeans.
National Archives of Canada (NMC-1867).

of the actual shape and scope of the Banks was in the eye of the
beholder. The Grand Banks appeared on sixteenth-century charts as
a narrow strip, but Champlain's map of 1613 gave them an elon-
gated triangular form. On Giacomo Gastaldi's woodcut map, *La
Nuova Francia* (1556), the Grand Banks appear in a long stippled
band that looks like a thin snake. On Joan Blaeu's 1662 *Extrema
Americae. . .Terra Nova. . .* (with a cartouche showing codfish hanging to dry on jigs), the Grand Banks look like stylized lips. On
Vincenzo Maria Coronelli's *Canada* (c. 1692), the Grand Banks
seem larger than the island of Newfoundland itself; that map's
cartouche features plump codfish with red ribbons in their mouths.
And on Gerard Van Keulen's highly elegant *Nouvelle Carte Marine*

du Grand Banq de Terra Neuff (c. 1728), the Grand Banks, with all
the latest soundings and markings, are given the unusual shading
treatment usually reserved for land masses rather than ocean floor,
making them look like wispy dun-coloured jellyfish suspended in the
North Atlantic Gulf Stream.

Like the Superior Shoal, another submarine feature of great con-
sequence, the Grand Banks were very likely known in the years
before they showed up on maps, and for the same reasons that
Michigan-based fishermen kept the Superior Shoal off the charts to
protect their rich grounds. The Basques, for example, have long
insisted that they were fishing on the Banks before Cabot, though
Basque archives have no records of any voyages to Newfoundland
before 1511.

The Portuguese also claim that they were fishing here before
Cabot arrived; the fact that the Portuguese as early as 1506 were
levying a ten percent tax on Newfoundland cod imported to the
country certainly suggests that they were exploiting the Banks for a
long period. But again, their maps would not necessarily tell that
tale. After every expedition, map-makers for Portuguese kings incorporated information from the most recent voyages of exploration. By
1502, Portuguese cartographers were well on their way to creating
master charts, synthesizing the latest knowledge of oceans and coastlines. These meta-charts were state secrets, and the only ones known
to exist were those pilfered by Italian competitors.

English ships, too, had ventured into the North Atlantic before
Cabot's voyage. The first known voyage, by John Day, an English
merchant active in the Spanish trade, occurred in 1480. The next
year, two ships sailed from Bristol in search of "a certain Isle called
the Isle of Brasile," a fabled place whose name was derived from a
Gaelic word meaning "blessed" or "fortunate." The ships carried salt,
suggesting that the purpose of the voyage had been to fish. And
there is the letter written by Day and reporting on John Cabot's

expedition of 1497; Day claimed that what Cabot discovered "is assumed and believed to be the mainland that the Bristol men found." Armed with this circumstantial evidence, some scholars suggest the pre-Cabot Bristol expeditions had actually discovered the Newfoundland fishing grounds, and that their sponsors had kept this discovery a secret for as long as possible in order not to share the fishing grounds with anyone else.

Official government surveys did not start until 1795, when the British Admiralty set up a Hydrographic Office to coordinate the production of sea charts for the Royal Navy under hydrographer Alexander Dalrymple. "It was definitely a paradigm shift to think of doing a survey and making a chart for anyone's use, including one's enemy," said Dave Gray of the Canadian Hydrographic Service.

THE ABILITY TO MAP UNDERWATER mountains took a leap forward in the wake of the *Titanic* disaster in 1912. Researchers in the United States and Europe set out to devise a method to detect large objects underwater. The result was the acoustic depth finder, or sonar, an acronym for sound navigation and ranging. As the technology improved and allowed for a continuous picture of the sea floor, sonar offered marine cartographers the satisfaction of seeing in real time the peaks and valleys of the terrain beneath their survey ships. Maps and nautical charts, generated by technological breakthroughs, have continued to play a role in how the Grand Banks have been exploited but also in how that exploitation can be checked. After the Second World War, Gray said, mariners had the ability to position themselves with radio positioning systems: Loran-A (1950–1980), Decca (1960–1985), Loran-C (1980–present), Doppler satellite navigation (1970–1995) and global positioning systems (1990–present). Positioning accuracy has grown from two hundred metres to the present ten metres. Fishermen have also been able to map the fluid masses of fish. Side-scan sonar reveals the presence of fish so accurately that, in some instances, operators can even identify the species.

Fishing boats have been deadly efficient, so much so that the vast swarms of cod that greeted Cabot are more like stragglers now. In 1977, Canada declared a two-hundred-mile exclusive economic zone and imposed strict controls on fishing inside this zone. About ten percent of the Grand Banks, known as the Nose and Tail, are beyond Canada's two-hundred-mile limit. Look at modern maps of Canada, and you will find the boundary defined by a broken line showing how Canada has appropriated the ocean real estate as a means of cartographic control and conservation.

The Canadian government had tried this before, during the 1920s, when officials began to map trapping areas in northern British Columbia and then in other areas in Northern Canada. Individuals or families were expected to purchase an annual trapping licence, which gave them the exclusive right to trap their "registered lines." The registered traplines were thought to be the best way of protecting limited wildlife resources from excessive harvesting. But they also served to bring Natives into the market economy. Registration was not designed with Indian land use in mind, Hugh Brody wrote in *Maps and Dreams*, but Indians nonetheless were urged to register lines and accept the rules of the newest colonial game. According to Brody, it was the first direct attack upon and restriction of Indian life in the region.

The establishment of the exclusive economic zone did not stop the collapse of the cod fishery, just as the registered traplines did not have an appreciable effect on the levels of wildlife harvesting. While there is still fishing life left on the Banks, there is a much more significant and powerful commercial lure: petroleum and gas reserves ready for the tapping. Oil diviners have replaced the jiggers, while ocean-bed seismic surveyors and sky-high satellites have replaced the sounders and shipboard surveyors.

The first scientific report on geological samples from the Grand Banks appeared in 1878, but it would take another century before oil would be struck. In the early 1950s the first geological survey was conducted, and in 1964 came direct geological investigation of the bedrock. That triggered extensive exploration and some twenty-three significant oil and gas discoveries in the Jeanne d'Arc basin on the Grand Banks: 2.1 billion barrels of oil, 9.3 trillion cubic feet of natural gas and 413 barrels of natural gas liquids. The most note-worthy discoveries were Hibernia in 1979, Hebron in 1981, and Terra Nova and Whiterose in 1984. Exploration has now expanded to the deeper waters of the Flemish Pass area on the eastern edge of the Grand Banks.

Getting at those massive energy reserves requires accurate and ongoing mapping. Maps of the ocean surface reveal the dynamics of the waves, the temperature fluctuations of the water, the tracking of icebergs that could jeopardize offshore oil platforms. Maps of the ocean column and floor reveal where cables are to be laid. And maps of the seabed's geology determine likely locations of deposits. The stakes are high, but so are the opportunities.

Glen Gilbert has been operating his own marine mapping business for the past seventeen years, and he has no shortage of contracts. His company, Canadian Seabed Research (CSR), does mapping for governments and fishery groups, but its most lucrative work is marine geological and geophysical mapping for the big petro-leum companies. CSR's speciality is using an array of sonar equip-ment to gain an acoustic picture of the seabed, which it turns into maps that oil companies can use to make decisions. There is stan-dard echosonar to determine water depth and seabed slopes, and the more modern side-scan sonar that gives an acoustic picture of what's on the sea bottom — bedrock outcrop, till, boulder beds, gravel, sand — and maps the location of debris on the sea floor such as pipes, wrecks and automobiles. Gilbert's company has other equipment — sub-bottom profilers, boomers, sparklers — that sends blasts of electrical current through the water column and sediments and into the bedrock to get an idea of what kinds of rock will be found. It can penetrate one and a half kilometres into the seabed. "We use an awful lot of side-scan sonar," said Gilbert from his company's home in Porter's Lake, Nova Scotia. "It's the next best thing to emptying the water and looking at what's down there. You can see the difference between sand, silt and clay, boulders, shipwrecks, pipelines. We've seen lobster pots."

Gilbert makes it sound as if the acoustic pictures are as clear as Polaroids of the kids taken at the beach, but in fact, there is considerable art to translating sonar information into maps that are usable by oil executives. It is akin to making predictions about a baby's gender and health based on an ultrasound image. The quality of the images depends on a number of factors. Have the images been collected in ideal conditions and with the right people operating the best equipment? And how experienced is the person eyeing the sonar? Experience is especially crucial when there is no "ground truth" to go by. By ground truth Gilbert means sending down a camera to take a close look at the bottom, collecting a core sample of sediment or drilling metres into the sea floor. Given that the Grand Banks can be covered in up to one hundred metres of roiling water, diving is not in the cards. "If you've done this ground truth in different regions over fifteen, twenty years, you start to have a better appreciation," he said. "You have to be a good geologist, and understand things in the context of geological history. If it were easy, it wouldn't be any fun."

It is neither easy nor without peril. You reach the Grand Banks after a good twenty-four-hour steam out of St John's, Newfoundland, travelling at ten knots. The surveys generally last anywhere from one week to one month, and during that time the surveying team prays that meteorological forces will be kind. Usually they are not. The meeting of the Gulf Stream and the Labrador Current sets up a complicated oceanographic environment. Winds are unpredictable. Icebergs are constant menaces. Heavy fog messes with the sonar mapping. Coupled with ice, the Grand Banks is a difficult environment. The capsizing of the oil platform Ocean Ranger back in 1982 is a grim yet telling illustration of the power of the Grand Banks' natural forces. Just ask Gilbert. "There was a fella I used to work with, Rick Sheppard, who was lost on the Ocean Ranger," he said. "He was a geologist who just went out for a one-week shift. Didn't come back."

What all the mapping has shown is that the topography of the Grand Banks is similar to that of the island of Newfoundland: There are plains, hills, mountains and valleys. Some areas are covered with coral trees, while others support no life. There are alternating ridges and channels that in many instances are extensions of the ridges and bays of Newfoundland. The Banks tilt east to west, and there is a sharp drop near the southern edge. There is plenty still to learn. What forces created the conditions on the Grand Banks? What are the sediment dynamics? What happens when icebergs scour the sea floor and grind away at the bedrock? The answers are coming slowly. But commercial pressure, rather than scientific curiosity or environmental need, is defining the questions asked by the marine mapmakers. "Some issues are more important than others," says Gilbert. "The problems driven by oil companies get resolved because they have to get resolved. The environmental aspects don't get treated with the same high level of intensity and funding."

GILBERT IS PERFECTLY RIGHT; as tools of commerce, maps attract money and minds to their cause. In the case of the Grand Banks, no technological effort has been spared to help oil companies learn the lay of the land beneath the waters of the North Atlantic. It may seem counterintuitive, but those maps have shown greater and greater detail of the inner workings of earth as they have moved higher in the sky and upper atmosphere. Radar, microwaves, infrared and ultraviolet light and remote sensing combined with computer technology all make possible almost-instant maps of mineral deposits and geological fault lines on the ocean floor.

From oil drilling on the Grand Banks to forestry in Central Canada, aerial maps have helped make Canada the resource juggernaut that it is. The earliest recorded photograph taken from the air in Canada was in 1882, but its use in map-making took off only after the First World War. Very early on, it was a particular boon to forestry companies. In 1919, expeditions were organized in Quebec and Labrador to experiment with techniques to take surveys of timber limits from the air; it was said that aerial reconnaissance would accomplish in six weeks what it otherwise would have taken six years to cover. The first large-scale attempt in Central Canada took place in 1921, when the Ontario Department of Lands and Forests dispatched three "flying boats" to the shores of Pelican Lake at Sioux Lookout. Standing in the forward cockpit taking the full brunt of the wind, surveyors took photographs directly forward and forty-five degrees to each side of forty thousand square kilometres of forests.

(Taking the photographs was only half the trick of making maps suitable for exploiting Canada's forests. What foresters wanted the maps to tell them was how much wood the trees would yield. Forester H. E. Seely came up with an ingenious way of measuring the height of trees or a stand of trees from the length of their shadows that appeared on the air photographs. Once the height was determined, it was fairly easy to calculate the cubic contents of uncut timber.)

The information derived from aerial mapping held great commercial, political and military significance. Canada certainly did not want to be beholden to other countries for that kind of information. Canada had a strong tradition of keeping the control of aerial photography and mapping within the country, according to L. W. Morley, the first director general of the Canada Centre for Remote Sensing. "We did not like the idea of having to purchase imagery of Canadian territory from a foreign country, nor of having a foreign country acquire imagery of Canadian territory without advance permission," he wrote in a brief history of remote sensing in Canada. "Such a concept was in violation of the Chicago International Convention, which required any state wishing to acquire air photography of another country to first get permission." In the days when aerial mapping relied on low-flying airplanes, it was not difficult to monitor whether one country was breaching another's sovereignty. But when the United States began using satellites orbiting in outer space to generate remote sensing maps of the earth, some countries, Canada chief among them, were concerned that the United States could gain information on mineral and petroleum deposits in Canadian waters and pass on the information to American companies. Canada, mindful of how maps are, in Harley's words, "silent arbiters of power," felt that was a clear breach of sovereignty. According to Morley, NASA argued that the U.N. Treaty on the Peaceful Uses of Outer Space applied, which allowed any state to conduct any activity in space provided it did no harm to other states.

As it turned out, Canada sent its own satellites into space and developed remote sensing technology that was second to none.

WHILE REMOTE SENSING SEEMS to offer petroleum companies "touchless" mapping of the Grand Banks from the silence of outer space, the most significant marine mapping done for petroleum companies is highly invasive. It is called seismic surveying, and it can map rock layers more than ten kilometres in the seabed and underwater properties without having to drill a well. But seismic surveying also has unintended consequences that make it highly controversial.

The idea is straightforward: Blast the bedrock with a huge force and record the echoes as they bounce back from beneath the ocean floor. The time for each echo to return depends on the depth and properties of the rock layers. The huge force used to be explosives; these days, it comes from an array of high-pressure air guns towed behind survey ships that deliver an explosive release of compressed air. To gain usable information, the air guns go off every dozen seconds or so as the ship follows a grid pattern several hundred square kilometres large. The echoes are captured on hydrophones; with enough hydrophones at work, a three-dimensional portrait of the rock layers can be created.

For environmentalists and fishers, seismic surveying is a controversial form of mapping. Marine animals use both infrasound and, at times, ultrasound to sense their environment and to communicate with one another. The explosive sounds produced by the air guns, therefore, can have a range of effects on marine life. It is claimed that within a few metres of the sound source, fish can be killed or injured, and since sound travels through water, marine mammals and other animals quite a distance from the mapping can have their hearing damaged or have their feeding or migrating behaviour affected. There is some thought that fish larvae would suffer as well.

Whether the seismic surveying has a lasting effect on fish stocks or just forces fish to make temporary adaptations is unclear. A study by researchers in Norway, where seismic mapping has been conducted since the 1960s, revealed that the catch rates of cod and haddock are reduced by at least fifty percent during and after seismic testing. Two studies in California, where there has been extensive experience with offshore drilling, looked at the impact of seismic surveying on the commercial hook-and-line fishery for rockfish. Comparing the catches when the air gun fired with those when it did not showed that the sound reduced the rockfish catch rate by more than fifty percent. The effects appear substantial at ranges around five kilometres from the survey vessel and seem at least detectable ten times as far away.

Research into the effect of seismic surveys on fish reproductive habits is sketchier. Similar to other fish species, male cod vocalize during their mating dance to woo the female and allow her into the male's jealously guarded territory. Air guns may very well disrupt this communication. On the other hand, the urge to reproduce could be stronger than whatever blast air guns provide. It is just not known. What is known is that seismic mapping is a basic and ongoing feature of offshore petroleum exploration and development.

The negative findings seem to be borne out by anecdotal evidence. East Coast cod and halibut fisherman Herb Nash, in an interview with a researcher from the Living Oceans Society, based in Sointula, British Columbia, said he and others have known all along that the seismic testing has been scaring the fish away, but that the oil industry has not been sympathetic. "Not only does seismic testing decrease our catch rates, it cuts our fishing time way down, too," he said. "One day we had just finished setting up our halibut gear and they pulled up next to my boat and told us to be out of there in two hours so they could start seismic testing. It takes twelve hours to haul in our gear and they wanted us out of there in two hours, no consultation, no nothing."

For a variety of reasons, the issue of seismic surveying has not become controversial on the Grand Banks. The Banks have been exploited for centuries, and besides, overfishing is an easier target than surveying techniques in the controversy over the collapse of the cod fishery. And with the Newfoundland economy perpetually struggling, the offshore oil and gas industry is welcome. Similar developments are less welcome among Cape Bretoners, who are forced to contemplate oil and gas rigs off the Cape Breton coast and near the entrance of Bras d'Or Lake. In January 2002, just before hearings were to begin on whether two companies should be allowed to explore for oil and gas offshore, a report by the federal Department of Fisheries and Oceans raised concerns about the impact of seismic testing on populations of right whales and leatherback turtles that frequent the area.

Similar controversy rages on the Pacific coast. Developers there have long been anxious to map the geological characteristics of Hecate Strait, between the Queen Charlotte Islands and the British Columbia mainland, to discover a Pacific version of Hibernia. Their hands have been tied since 1959, when the Province of British Columbia imposed a moratorium on exploration drilling on the coastal waters—a ban that was lifted for six years to allow for the drilling of fourteen exploratory wells before being re-established. In 1998, the matter came up again when the Geological Survey of Canada produced a report estimating that oil reserves in the Queen Charlotte Basin alone could be 9.8 billion barrels, five times the estimate for the Grand Banks.

Developers would dearly love to know how accurate those estimates are, but that would require extensive seismic mapping. The Living Oceans Society offers a taste of just how extensive that mapping would be. The Society says one oil company proposed in 1985 to use up to thirty-six high-pressured air guns to perform seismic testing in the Hecate Strait. "Spread over an area one hundred and fifty metres wide by one hundred metres long, the guns would have fired every fifteen seconds and covered a total area of five thousand two hundred kilometres."

The provincial government, awash in deficits, is considering its options.

FROM COD TO CONSUMER. In the world of mapping, there is little difference. Using maps to identify your pool of prospects and then to reel them in works as well with the marketplace as on the Grand Banks. Businesses ask: Where do our customers live? How far are they willing to drive to reach our store? Where should we put our warehouse to most efficiently service our outlets? For answers, they turn to maps generated by geographic information systems (GIS).

GIS essentially is using computers to ask questions of maps, which necessitates that the maps be in digital form. The primary require-ment for the source data is that the locations for the variables are known; the location may be the coordinates of longitude or latitude, or postal code, home address, telephone number, or highway kilo-metre marker. Applied to the high-stakes world of business, GIS is a treasured tool. Marketing experts plumb the depths of databases of information on store locations, customer and client lists, and tele-phone records. Retailers such as Sears and Shoppers Drug Mart maintain a customer database made up of information from each transaction, from private label credit cards and loyalty programs to area codes and licence plate numbers; in short, any information that can be linked to a location and "geocoded." The sales transactions are then tied to the store where the purchase was made, creating a spatial pattern of where customers are clustered. Customer data can also be tied to additional data, such as lifestyle clusters, to determine the buying behaviour of a specific demographic — women over age fifty, for example — based on those patterns. The retailers can then send out highly targeted information to specific groups of consumers or tailor the product mix of individual stores.

It is not just retailers who use GIS. Agricorp, a Crown corporation based in Guelph, Ontario, administers crop insurance for the province's farmers using a form of GIS mapping. A big part of Agri-corp's business is determining which claims are genuine and which are fraudulent. To do that it maintains a database of client informa-tion, in particular the client's average annual yield, which deter-mines insurance premiums. Agricorp links that data to general information on farm yields in various parts of Ontario: climate con-ditions, soil, trends in yield. It then combines all the information in a map that quickly illustrates if a particular farmer's production claim is appreciably higher or lower than that of his neighbours, or what the history of the area would suggest.

The first public use of the term "geographic information system" was in the movie *Data for Decision*, a National Film Board documentary on the making of the Canada Geographic Information System (CGIS). One of the stars of the show, and someone closely associated with the development of GIS, was Roger Tomlinson, a British national who adopted Canada in 1957. The story goes that in 1962, while flying to Toronto from Ottawa, Tomlinson met Lee Pratt, the recently named head of the Canada Land Inventory (CLI). The CLI was a wildly ambitious project to produce a land use and planning map of the country's uninhabited, marginally "unproductive" land — some three million square kilometres — that could be converted to other uses, such as forest plantations or recreational areas. As chief of the computer mapping division at the Ottawa-based Spartan Air Services, Tomlinson was intrigued by the challenge and became an important part of a team that would bring cartography fully into the digital age, at the leading edge of what the prevailing technology could produce. The team had to invent a scanner that would be able to digitize the maps, for example, while Tomlinson was crunching numbers on an IBM 360/65 computer with what seems today to be a flimsy 256K of memory.

At first, geographers did not know what to make of CGIS. It is only in the past twenty-five years that businesses figured out how to use GIS to monitor and control consumers and gain an edge on competitors. One of those in the fray early was Tony Lea, a Torontonian well trained in the worlds of geography and statistics. Lea is a former academic who has taught both spatial analysis and GIS at the University of Minnesota, University of Toronto and Ryerson Polytechnic University. He has been using geodemographic analysis for businesses since the mid-1970s, when he began working at the market analysis consultancy Compusearch, so he can rightfully be considered a pioneer in trying to divine commercial intelligence from the confluence of geography and demographics.

The vast majority of GIS business applications focus on a number of straightforward tasks. Lea offers the market mappers' tool kit: "geocoding" customer addresses with street maps; mapping customers in a market as dots; creating a "geodemographic profile" of customers "based on age, gender, family income, or the neighbourhood in which they live." Sounds impressive, but Lea says standard GIS and geodemographics are not exactly laser-guided weapons. A good way to describe geodemographics is mapping by inference: ABC Inc. does not know my income or level of education, but it does know where I live, so it will draw inferences on my tastes — the automobile I drive, what I put on toast in the morning — based on the attributes of the neighbourhood in which I live. It requires the best possible data and a whole lot of faith. It is far from perfect — though I live in a neighbourhood dominated by families with infants and young children, I do not own a minivan and I skip breakfast — but it is better than nothing and a lot less expensive than a citywide or national promotional mailing.

Lea's bread and butter is helping clients study their "circular trade area." They want to know how upscale a business neighbourhood is and if potential customers living or working in the area are more or less likely to patronize their business or a competitor's. On a map of the area, the store is placed at the bull's eye of a circle. The radius of the circle — its distance from the store — depends on the type of retail operation. "It's a mile or half a mile for a convenience store, one and a half miles for a drugstore, three miles for a hardware or grocery store, and for a department store seven miles, except if you're in North Bay and it would be forty-two miles," said Lea. The analyst then takes the demographic information of people living in the neighbourhoods within the circle.

This type of circular trade area analysis can be useful to see at a glance, say, which are the four most upscale stores in your network. But it is crude: It doesn't account for breaks in that circle, such as

2002 Customer Spending Potential map of Metropolitan Toronto, produced by MapInfo Canada. Such maps, based on geographic information systems, help marketers identify promising areas for their businesses. Courtesy MapInfo Canada.

rivers, railroads or ethnic divides. Other variations include "gravity models," which define a trade area based on its attractiveness relative to other trade areas, and "drive time" or "drive distance" models to determine how easy it is to use a vehicle to get to an outlet. The attraction of all these models for businesses is obvious: The maps that are generated appear easy to understand. They give the businessperson the illusion of being a jet pilot, studying the terrain far below with the help of aeronautic charts.

"The principle of GIS, of using an attribute of an area and assigning it to a person, is an age-old principle of ecological inference but it's been made easier by GIS software and it's been promoted because people can see it visually," said Lea. Lea himself adores maps, but at heart he is a statistics geek; to him, numbers lined up in columns on a page are almost always more revealing than those visualized on a map. Many of his clients do not want to talk statistics or variables. They see the map that is generated as an analytical tool in itself. "So in understanding what type of people patronize your store, retailers who don't have a lot of statistical skills would haul out a big file folder of maps with coloured dots representing each of their stores," said Lea. "Store number 213 has blue dots, you can see customers are mainly east of the tracks. Compared to a person who has never looked at a map, that's a huge, huge lift in understanding a problem. But the map doesn't answer the question, 'If we put another store halfway between these two stores, what proportion of the new store's volume would be cannibalized from the existing stores?' And it may be counterproductive."

Lea is excited over an even higher order of GIS intelligence. He recently led a project for Bank One of Columbus, Ohio, where he and his team built a set of sophisticated models for six product lines, predicting their exact volumes. "The model we developed answered the question, 'If we put a bank here what would be the loan volume, the GIC volume?' . . . [We also asked,] 'If you want to put seventeen Bank One branches as opposed to twenty-seven in Cleveland, where are the seventeen optimal locations for a systems approach?'" He does similar high-level geostatistical analysis for major Canadian banks, such as Toronto Dominion, Desjardins and Caisse Populaire, and for retailers such as Shoppers Drug Mart.

In maps used for exploitation of natural resources or an individual's consumer habits, the issue of privacy is never far away. In the case of the Superior Shoal or the Grand Banks, for example, maps and knowledge of key zones were withheld to gain a competitive advantage. In the case of digital maps plotted by corporations, governments or even malicious stalkers, the maps produced with ever-greater sophistication threaten to undercut the privacy of individuals. They may reveal, for example, patterns of movement or even location at a particular time. Roger Tomlinson and the CGIS team sensed the potential back in the 1960s. As Tomlinson told one interviewer: "When we were designing the GIS in CGIS back in the 1960s, we had discussions amongst ourselves. There we were, designing a system with a theoretical resolution of plus or minus a quarter of an inch on the face of Canada. And we said, 'Well if we had adequate sensors, we could keep track of when someone went to the washroom and went back again.'"

Those "sensors" did not exist in Tomlinson's day. They do now. Certainly, the trajectory of GIS is heading in that direction. One of the most feverish areas of development in the field, says Lea, is wireless communications. Cellular telephone companies can already track where customers are located when they place a call. It raises the possibility of marketing to people based on their location at any moment in time. Lea offers one scenario: A cellphone user can subscribe to a service that would tell him or her the location of the nearest restaurant. "I'm interested in Italian foods, you know my coordinates, show me the closest Italian restaurant. And here's the map to get you there. Bang. Or show me where the traffic is slow." Another scenario, more likely to raise eyebrows, is to send an unsolicited sales message to a cellphone user in transit. Say you are driving along Bank Street in downtown Ottawa with your cellphone on. An alert or a coupon offering a special on muffins and coffee can be sent to your phone and can offer directions to a Tim Hortons outlet that is just a few blocks away.

Certainly the idea that geocoordinates and financial transactions are recorded simultaneously every time an individual uses a credit card is unsettling enough. But it goes further: Credit card transactions can be linked to public records, such as deeds or court documents, census data and other personal information that can strip away the anonymity of an individual and his or her neighbour. That suggests that the greatest potential dangers of abuse of information will not be among retailers but rather insurance companies looking to deny individual coverage or a claim, or technologically savvy swindlers. New legislation in Canada does put limits on how geo-demographic information that is collected is used. Charities, for example, can no longer trade prospects' names among themselves. People now have to give their permission for their names and other information to be traded away.

If it sounds like the number crunchers and wireless experts have taken over the map-makers in the business intelligence world, Lea is quick to insist that maps will always have an important role. "If people who can run PetroCanada stations look at a map of people who buy six hundred dollars or more of gas a month, it's an amazing insight to see the dot map show all the houses in Forest Hill or a blue collar neighbourhood with taxi drivers," said Lea. "It's extremely pregnant [with possibility]. Pregnant is important because if executives can't be excited about something, they aren't going to spend any money on it. To sell our projects, we arrive with some sexy maps to get buy-in, and then we go back to our office and do the project. Maps are increasingly important in this way."

Lea has taken those "sexy maps" all over the world, seeking and getting business from corporations wanting the latest geodemographic intelligence. And nowhere is the eagerness to embrace maps greater than in Canada. "Canada is such a vast country and somehow people take pride in knowing where Portage la Prairie is, or Moosonee, or Sudbury or Swastika. Canadians are much more appreciative of maps than Americans, much more inclined to rely on them.

"You know, I spend a great deal of time on business in the U.S. and it's quite clear when you go into a meeting that they're thrilled to have Canadians talking to them about geography and location. The other consultants just don't get it. American consultants do spatial if they have to; it doesn't come naturally to them. They don't have good jokes about it."

7

SEDUCTION

CARTOGRAPHERS LOVE TO TELL the famous story by Jorge Luis Borges that appeared in his book *Dreamtigers* (1964). Borges imagined an Empire in which cartographers' guilds attained such perfection that they were able to draw up a map "whose size was that of the Empire, and which coincided point for point with it." So great and lifelike was it that the citizens of the Empire related more to the map than the real territory that it covered. Over time, as the map frayed and disintegrated, the citizens became alienated from the real territory and nostalgic for the map.

Borges was poking fun at self-important map-makers and their sponsors, but French intellectual Jean Baudrillard took the satire to heart. In 1983, Baudrillard developed a provocative philosophical argument: Typically perceived as cut-and-dried representations of reality, Baudrillard argued, maps actually generate reality themselves. "The territory no longer precedes the maps, nor survives it," he wrote with a flourish. "Henceforth it is the map that precedes the territory."

The idea that a map could actually precede the territory it purports to represent is not far-fetched. After all, the names New France, New England and New Spain were created long before the New World was settled in earnest, yet those names alone carried little weight until they were placed on the maps being drawn of the New World. At that point, the newly colonized territories truly became extensions of their "mother" countries. Academics refer to this phenomenon as "anticipatory geography." It could easily be called cartographic seduction.

The dance of a thousand latitudes was practised in the settlement of Western Canada, a period in Canadian development during which maps played a large role in shaping destiny. Even before the end of the Hudson's Bay Company's rule of the North-western Territory in 1870 and the transferring of its lands to Canada, movers and shakers in the new Dominion were anxious to take stock of the land now under their control. Two mapping expeditions were dispatched, one British and one Canadian. Adventurer and officer John Palliser led the British expedition, while geology professor Henry Youle Hind and civil engineer and surveyor Simon Dawson took charge of the Canadian mission. Both expeditions took a scientific measure of the land and mapped their findings. Between 1857 and 1869, Palliser and his party travelled from the Red River Settlement to the Pacific coast and from the North Saskatchewan River to the forty-ninth parallel. Dawson and Hind probed essentially the southern plains of present-day Manitoba and Saskatchewan. Both expeditions identified the prairies as ripe for agricultural development, but it was Palliser's attractive and colourful map that caught the imagination of Canada's politicians. Palliser identified two zones: one a fertile belt along the North Saskatchewan River, spanning the Red River Settlement to the Rocky Mountains, and a second region south of this arc, which Palliser said was suitable only for cattle grazing. As pictured on his map, the region had an unmistakable shape and was subsequently called Palliser's Triangle.

Once it had an inventory of land on file, the central government began step two: to survey and parcel up the undulating prairie. It appointed Dominion Land Surveyors to take readings from sextant and compass, lay out distances with measuring chains and install physical markers — posts supported by cairns or mounds of earth — to define boundaries. Whereas Palliser's colourful map intimated patterns of fertility and rainfall, the new maps depicted the prairies as a convenient backdrop to a grid, where parcels of land, bounded by lines of latitude and longitude, were divided into townships six miles by six miles in size, subdivided into thirty-six sections of one square mile apiece. These were divided into smaller and smaller units, into half sections, quarter sections and even quarter-quarters, imposing the checkerboard appearance we see today. The surveyors did not concern themselves with the course of rivers, the nature of landforms, the quality of soil or the record of rainfall. The maps that resulted from their work spoke nothing of the topography on the ground, but the maps were convenient templates, "a sort of artist's frame," in the words of Rod Bantjes, of the department of sociology and anthropology at Nova Scotia's St Francis Xavier University. "In 1873 the Department of the Interior began publishing land descriptions 'frame by frame,' each frame being a six-mile square 'township,'" Bantjes said. As an example, Bantjes pointed to the work of W. F. King, Inspector of Surveys, as typical of the time. In 1882, King described Township 19, Range 5, west of the 2nd meridian as: "Rolling prairie, with a number of small swamps and clumps of poplar and willow. Soil — generally second class."

Now it was time for step three. Officials in charge of populating the prairies with European homesteaders turned these artists' "frames" into full-blown works of map art. The Dominion government produced a simple atlas series that provided general information on immigration to Canada and prairie homesteading. The atlases, thirty to sixty pages long and printed on inexpensive newsprint, were distributed free of charge throughout Western Europe and the United States. Rand McNally produced the maps, and they served as basic guides to the western provinces. The maps and accompanying imagery awakened European pastoral instincts and were a powerful means of imagining a history — and future — for the new West. "The pastoral was the landscape of [European] collective desire," said Bantjes. "By invoking it, writers offered the prairies not so much for what they were as what they could become."

Produced between 1900 and the early 1920s, the immigration atlases appeared in fifteen languages. Special attention was paid to editions aimed at the British and Americans. Jeffrey Murray, archivist at the National Archives, has spent countless hours studying the atlases and is struck by the heavy Victorian iconography that they feature and by the small, yet significant, differences in the British and American versions. "Same edition done in same year," he said.

On the U.K. version in the middle of the homestead is a flagpole with the Union Jack. On the American version, the British flag is removed. The figure that is pictured is of a young, golden-haired woman dressed in white robes as the personification of the British Empire, Britannia. They are still appealing to Americans with English background; they certainly don't want black Americans.

Murray approaches these immigration atlases and maps as a sort of social archaeologist, trying to discern the past in shards of printed artifacts. After graduating with a degree in archaeology, he spent eleven years with Parks Canada and worked on excavations at Fort Walsh and the Chilcoot Trail. "What I liked about archaeology was to be able to use everyday material culture to investigate social affairs," he said.

> *Things that aren't written down, what people at the time took for granted. When I came to the Archives in 1985, I realized that the things we call maps are artifacts; they can tell us about time and place. That's the main reason why we keep them. A lot of people, when they look at old maps, are putting it in a framework like, "Where was such and such a place? Where was the highway that they used to get from point A to point B?" What's more important to ask is, "What does this item tell us about the society that produced it? What was going on at the time? Why was the item produced?" As soon as you start thinking in those terms, you can immediately spot the little white lies that people put into a product in order to meet their objectives.*

The objective of the Department of the Interior was clearly to change people's perceptions of what the Canadian Northwest was like. In Britain at the turn of the twentieth century there was still a perception that the Northwest was cold, wild and uninhabitable. Not surprisingly, the immigration atlases featured no pictures of snow and very few pictures of urban Canada. But there were an awful lot of pictures of ample harvests and modern farmsteads. To be sure the message got out, the Department of the Interior distributed the atlases to schoolchildren, who took them home and showed their parents. Canada's immigration office in England also sponsored an essay-writing competition on immigrating to Canada, with the winning family receiving free tickets to the country. The efforts were hugely successful but also had unintended consequences. In an interesting twist, Murray pointed out, schoolteachers in various parts of Canada found out about the atlases and wrote to the Department asking for copies that they could distribute in Canadian classrooms.

"At the time, there was nothing available for Canadian public school students that told them about the geography of Canada," said Murray. "So Canadian schoolteachers were using these things as class textbooks to give information about Canada."

Private landholders had maps of their own. Promotional items produced by the private sector focused almost entirely on privately owned interests, and the major services — transportation networks, grain elevators, telegraph stations and RCMP stations — in their proximity. "The maps accompanying the immigration literature were usually accurate but poor in quality, while the textual descriptions and illustrations were garish and sensational, almost bordering along the lines of propaganda," Murray said. "An 1882 map of the North West Land Company's holdings in Manitoba not only makes extravagant claims about the climate and soil but also the short period in which a well-established farm could be developed. The accompanying illustrations show countryside more reminiscent of rural Ontario than the prairies."

Among the most sophisticated and aggressive settlement maps were those produced by the railway companies, which were anxious to sell their own land parcels as well as to encourage traffic on the lines. In 1885, the Canadian Pacific Railway (CPR) had only one line laid down through part of the prairies, but that did not stop the company from showing a number of spur lines to service future or imagined communities. "If you notice in the key, they say they are proposed," said Murray. "It would take twenty or thirty more years before some of those lines were actually put down on the ground." The attempt is to show people that it is not an isolated region. They have a way of getting there, and once there, they have a way of communicating with the rest of the world. Railway maps showed station stops — such as Swift Current — that at the time were not even built. One railway map boasted "Great Wheat Region of the Continent" and focused on Winnipeg; it was produced before the main railway line was even completed and homesteaders arrived. Anticipatory geography indeed.

Land developers who were anxious to lure settlers to their holdings also used immigration and railway maps as templates. A map produced in 1910 by the Department of the Interior was particularly useful. It showed railway lines — Canadian Northern (CN), the Grand Trunk Pacific, the Great Northern — and grain elevators along the way. Beside each elevator icon is a number indicating the capacity of the grain elevator. Private companies used the government map to make their own maps and to deliver a hardball message to potential homesteaders: Even if you pick a homestead on the best farmland anywhere, it seemed to say, it won't mean anything if you cannot get your product to market. Make sure you buy land close to transportation and grain elevators.

One of Murray's favourites is a 1910 railway map called the *Triangle Tour Map of Western Canada*. The points on the triangle are Edmonton, Jasper National Park and Vancouver; the railway line leads down from Jasper to Vancouver, by boat to Prince Rupert and back to Jasper. The map-maker cleverly used two different scales to put the Canadian Northern line in the best possible light. The scale on the right side, showing Jasper National Park, is huge, leaving little room for any other feature. By contrast, the scale on the left side is much smaller, allowing the map to take in all of southern British Columbia, from Prince Rupert down to Vancouver, including the forty-ninth parallel. "What they are attempting to do in this case is to show people that if you can take the Canadian Northern line, you've got the fantastic tour through the mountainous regions," Murray explained. "But by putting two different scales together, they can pretend that Canadian Pacific [Canadian Northern's competitor] doesn't exist. We put this in an exhibition called *Summer Times* about five years ago, and the curator of the exhibition didn't notice the discrepancy. Certainly no one visiting the exhibition noticed the discrepancy. That's what's so wonderful: They're so subtle. Maps sit on the edge between myth and reality, and we're taught they are an actual representation and certainly most map-makers try to make them a legitimate representation. But there's another side in which you can manipulate an image and come up with something very different."

In *The Last Spike*, Pierre Berton offered his own amusing anecdote about the competition between two railroads, the Canadian Pacific and the Grand Trunk, and two egos — those of William Cornelius Van Horne, cp's general manager, and Joseph Hickson, his counterpart at the Grand Trunk:

> When the Grand Trunk played down the cpr's route on its own folders, Van Horne instructed Alexander Begg, the company's general emigration agent, to strike back with a map of his own. He told Begg to show the gtr's [Grand Trunk Railway's] Toronto-Montreal road as a faint line and to drop out its Toronto-Chicago line entirely. In the matter of cartography, the general manager was quite prepared to smite his rival. . . .

While the immigration atlases and privately published maps effectively lured homesteaders to the Northwest, once on the ground, settlers learned the hard way how misleading the maps and associated material were. To make matters worse, when groups of settlers arrived with maps of their own in their heads — in effect, trying to buck the grid imposed by the Dominion Land Surveyors — they ended up isolated in the midst of large blocks of land. This was particularly so for prospective settlers from the steppes of Eastern Europe, who were the most eager to give the Canadian West a try. Gallicians, Mennonites, Doukhobors and Hutterites, in particular, brought with them very different visions of land settlement than that embodied in the Dominion Lands Act, said Rod Bantjes. "They opposed the constraints of individuated settlement, demanding to be located in contiguous 'blocks,' as well as in residentially compact agricultural villages... Their efforts to 'play outside the lines' and at cross purposes to the 'checkerboard' grid help to reveal its logic as well as some of its unresolved internal contradictions." While the quarter section legally had to be the property of only one member of the community, Bantjes said, some village communities, with varying degrees of success, attempted to redraw the lines of fields by pooling land holdings and to reapportion ownership in a way that was "spatially coherent for collective living."

The grid of the Dominion Land Survey mapped and circumscribed Native reserves as well, causing problems in northerly regions that had a resource-based, rather than agricultural-based, economy. Straight lines and squares are not conducive to an economy built on fishing, hunting and setting traplines. Such activities are tied to natural features. But the type of pattern for settlement envisioned for the Northwest Territories did not allow for the natural courses to be followed, Jeffrey Murray said. The grid established for the prairies eventually extended into forested regions of the West. Native groups had limited say in how boundaries were established. Surveyors would ask, "Where do you want your reserve located?" Then they would stake out the four corners centred on that area. The treaty Native bands at the time signed with the central government stipulated how many acres would be set aside per family of five. "So one of the things the surveyor would have to do was take a census and figure out how many people were in the band and establish a piece of land based on the size stipulated in the treaty and the number of people in a band, and their desire to be located within a certain area," said Murray. "But beyond that, if someone wanted to follow a particular watercourse that meandered, obviously it was a lot more difficult to figure things out."

Once the land surveyors had done their job, land speculators and developers took over. They played a high-stakes game of trying to anticipate where the great development train would next stop. A can't-lose town of choice was Dunvegan, some six hundred fifty kilometres north of Edmonton. Dunvegan had long been a hub of Native trails in Peace River Country and throughout the nineteenth century saw a regular parade of explorers and map-makers: In 1793, Alexander Mackenzie happened upon a band of Indians camping there on the north side of the Peace River; in 1804, David Thompson took note of the two creeks coming into the flats. Years later, a fort built on the site was a haven for missionaries, settlers travelling overland and surveyors preparing the North for settlement. So special and magical was the name Dunvegan that it was adopted by the builders of the first railroad to the Peace River — the Edmonton-Dunvegan and British Columbia Railroad, which started construction in 1913. One year later, real-estate operators began subdividing quarter sections into town lots and selling the parcels to the unsuspecting in Eastern Canada and England, who were led to believe that the railway was already at Dunvegan's door.

The developers drew maps of the land for kilometres on both sides of the river. One promotional piece for Dunvegan Terrace prominently featured a map of the subdivision with the quarter sections neatly laid out ready for claiming. Other pieces showed wharves and railways. In his history of the Peace River Country written in 1952, J. G. MacGregor wrote: "Citizens of Edmonton bought them, the young and the hopeful, as well as the old and cautious. Dunvegan was to be the metropolis of the north, and caution was thrown to the winds. Canny bankers in Scotland bought them. The lots were even sold in far away Italy." What the maps did not indicate, wrote MacGregor, was that some lots were on steep hillsides "rising in some places at an angle of seventy degrees from the horizontal." The railway never did get to Dunvegan. The growth went to other towns — Peace River, Grande Prairie — and the name of the railroad itself was shortened to the Northern Alberta Railway. Not one lot was built upon.

Ontario and Quebec had their own versions of homesteading boom and bust. The Great Clay Belt, situated directly south of James Bay in the districts of Cochrane in Ontario and Abitibi in Quebec, was touted as having great promise. In Ontario, the Liberal government called its swath of sixty-four thousand square kilometres of clay loam "New Ontario" and used it as a focus of hope for Depression-era southerners. In Quebec, the Roman Catholic Church saw the Great Clay Belt as the prime inducement to get Quebecers to stay on the land and develop an agrarian society. The Ontario Colonization Branch distributed ninety thousand maps in 1908 alone. The promotional maps and settlement brochures did their job: Between 1900 and 1931, the Cochrane District of the Clay Belt experienced the fastest growth in Northern Ontario, doubling in population between 1911 and 1921, and again between 1921 and 1931. By 1931, the region had more than fifty thousand settlers on almost twelve thousand farms. The maps and other promotional material, however, did not say anything about the early and harsh frosts, the poorly drained clay soils and the scarcity of nearby markets. Within thirty years, more than half of the farms that were established had been abandoned.

By the early 1880s, a good deal of the surveying on the prairies was completed, and the surveyors then turned their attention to the challenge of exploratory traverses in the more northerly regions. There was much speculation about the mineral wealth — in particular the gold reserves — of northern British Columbia and the Yukon District, but it was only speculation. Those in the know were beginning to filter into the region with the help of a map published in 1858 by Alexander Anderson, the Hudson's Bay Company agent based in Kamloops. The Company had asked Anderson to explore routes between his station and Fort Langley and, good soldier that he was, Anderson crossed the mountains on foot from the Thompson

River to the lower Fraser Valley and consequently discovered the principal route into the interior.

But what lay on and beneath the land? The rumour-mongers had their stories, but it was the dispassionate narrative of one of the country's most respected geologists that really lit the fires of the Klondike imagination. As the assistant director of the Geological Survey of Canada, George Mercer Dawson had the proper heft and credibility to lead the Survey's Yukon Expedition. The Expedition's goal, as defined by Dawson, was to gain "information on the vast and hitherto almost unknown tract of country which forms the extreme north-westerly portion of the North-west Territory . . . referred to as the Yukon district." The maps produced by Dawson, William Ogilvie and Richard McConnell, who came back with the first geological maps and notes from the interior of the Yukon, played a major role in directing attention to that region.

In 1887, Dawson's report on the painstaking work of the Yukon Expedition, complete with maps, was published. For the first time, the world had an accurate picture of the region's natural history, its geographical and geological features, and its prospects for mining. Though he had the circumspection of a scientist, Dawson knew that it was only a matter of time before the Klondike would be transformed. His bold prediction of a golden future in the Yukon was just what prospectors wanted to hear. In his report, Dawson spoke of the great gold finds in the Cassiar region farther south, which yielded $2 million worth of gold in 1874 and 1875. "Discoveries similar to these [in the Cassiar] may be expected to occur at any time in the Yukon district," he wrote. In 1896, Dawson's prediction of a big strike came true when prospector George Carmack, a friend of William Ogilvie, discovered placer gold on Rabbit Creek. The rush to the Klondike goldfields was in full swing, and Dawson's report had become a bestseller.

Between 1850 and 1930, there were gold rushes in many parts of the world, most notably in South Africa and California. And there were gold finds in Nova Scotia, Alaska and other parts of British Columbia. Of all the rushes, the Klondike stampede is the one that holds a special place in the imagination, although experts are unsure why that is so. The fact that a worldwide economic depression was just ending and that the Klondike represented the last vestiges of the frontier in North America were likely good reasons. Author Douglas Fetherling, who studied the gold rushes during this period, says the Klondike benefited from a number of factors. There were "engines of publicity" that had not been available before, and the remoteness of the goldfields and streams fed into the popular imagination. "A young generation that had been reared in industrialized society was drawn to it as easily as older people, whose memories gave them the basis for a better-informed, more empirical sort of hopefulness," Fetherling wrote in *The Gold Crusades*. "The fact that it proved to be an individualistic affair, inflaming the imaginations of clerks and mechanics as well as of the floating subculture of hardened prospectors, made it irresistible."

By that time, of course, neither the government nor private map-makers could turn out enough products to satisfy the voracious appetite of the public. The Department of the Interior, the federal agency responsible for surveying and mapping, was caught without up-to-date maps for the region. "The Geological Survey of Canada [the GSC] had ten years earlier produced a geological map based on George Dawson's exploration," said Jeffrey Murray. "In the archive files, we have requests from all sorts of people for maps of the interior. Very quickly, the GSC ran out of the maps. Rather than reprint it, they wanted to update it." The Department of the Interior immediately directed its chief geographer, a man named John Johnston, to create a revised geological map of the Northwest. He apparently took his instructions a little too seriously, working day and night on the project; he died before it was completed.

The government might have been caught without maps, but enterprising private companies were only too happy to oblige, flooding the market with all sorts of Klondike guides. If the gold rush was like a runaway train, maps were the shovels of coal stoking the engine. One Vancouver newspaper printed a staggering one hundred thousand Klondike maps in three separate editions. Outfitters, transportation companies and enterprising boards of trade in Edmonton, Calgary, Prince Albert, Kamloops, Victoria, Vancouver and Seattle all turned out their own maps as promotional lures to claim their stake in the Klondike madness. Each town used maps to show itself as the centre of the Klondike trade. The maps, based on the government geological survey, hydrographic charts of the coastline, hearsay from returning travellers and plain guesses, were not exactly useful in helping overlanders navigate the jumble of creeks, bogs and rivers of the Athabasca and Mackenzie watersheds.

Edmonton, for example, called itself The Back Door to the Yukon and published maps showing all railways leading to its northern terminus. Like similar efforts by other communities, Edmonton's guides were crude and hastily done affairs, produced by the local board of trade. The maps did not tell the gold seekers that the fields were thousands of kilometres of muskeg and misery away, along a wagon road to the Athabasca, down the Mackenzie and over a brutal stretch to the Yukon. Poor James Shand found out the hard way. In 1897, Shand set out for the Klondike from Edmonton with three friends. Whenever he reached a Hudson's Bay fort, he sent back a letter to the *Edmonton Bulletin* relating his experiences. In one letter, he wrote about the difficulty of finding his way down the Mackenzie River, chock full of channels, using a map. "On looking at a map it seems the easiest job possible to follow the right course, but in fact it is rather more difficult than it looks."

Archivist Murray related another story of three buddies in southern Alberta who decided to try their luck in the Yukon, and made their way up to Edmonton. They met a group in front of a hotel studying a map of the route to Dawson City. One of the friends realized the group was going to the Klondike and asked how long the journey would take. "Two or three days," was the answer. "We just have to go up this waterway, then this waterway, then we're there." In reality, it took gold seekers on the Edmonton route at least one year, and up to three years, to get into the Klondike.

Many of the maps were designed to foster the very illusion of effortless travel. Murray pulled out a map that was obviously produced by backers of the Lake Bennett route, although there is no date or authorship printed on the map itself. It is simply titled *Sketch Map Shewing Advantages of the Lake Bennett Route*. Lake Bennett was where the Chilcoot and White passes merged on the route to Dawson City. Above the map is a bold headline: "5,000 miners went by this route last year and it is expected that over 40,000 people will travel by this same route this season." The only major cities shown are Victoria and Vancouver; it doesn't show Seattle, a competing staging site. Below the map the authors list three routes to the goldfields, with the "best" route highlighted in red, boasting that it took only twelve days to reach Dawson City. The other two routes, the map claimed, took six weeks and twenty-five days to get to the Klondike. "What they've done with this map is use a conical projection," said Murray. "As a result, this looks like a strange map. But if they had chosen a Mercator projection [the standard projection in atlases of the day], it would have brought Alaska down this way and this other route would have looked shorter." The Lake Bennett route was indeed a fast route, but only if the traveller was well equipped and had plenty of cash. That's because gold seekers would arrive at Dyea with one thousand kilograms of gear that had to be carried over a daunting Chilkoot Pass to the headwaters of Lake Bennett, where a steamer would take them the rest of the way. Most people could not afford the exorbitant shipping rates that were being

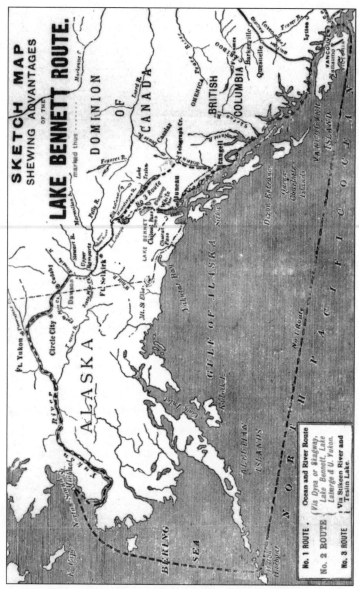

Sketch Map Shewing Advantages of the Lake Bennett Route (authorship and date produced unknown). Trying to attract gold-mad overlanders en route to the Klondike, map-makers chose an unusual projection and conveniently ignored mentioning the daunting Chilkoot Pass in order to make the Lake Bennett route most appealing. National Archives of Canada (NMC-13295).

charged. That meant carrying the equipment themselves, taking thirty or forty trips over the pass and back. Twelve days could become six months, depending on the time of year.

To get the point across, Murray produced a map created by Seattle outfitters Macdougall and Southwick. The most obvious feature is the colouring of the map: yellow prevails. Yellow is not a colour usually used by cartographers, certainly not for a whole region. But yellow was always selected for gold-mining maps. On the reverse side of the outfitter's map is a list of how travellers should be outfitted. The intent of this mapping is not so much to deceive as to persuade. There is a fine line. They want you at least to buy their outfit, but they would rather you not die wearing it. The information that Macdougall and Southwick shows is accurate enough without scaring you away from the trail. There are subliminal suggestions about the making of a gold strike, reminders of the many goldfields in the region and of endless possibilities. The Klondike is one river in a region of thousands and thousands of rivers, the map seems to whisper. If you can make your fortune off the Klondike, just think of the possibilities at all these other rivers.

WHAT IS A PAVED ROAD but another river to explore, another network of possibilities? As the Klondike gold rush petered out in 1898, another opportunity for untold riches beckoned. In the first years of the twentieth century, there were some two hundred automobiles registered in Canada; while railway building had priority over highway building, the automobile boosters clearly felt they had the future in their grasp. What better way to hasten that future than to show, through maps, the joys and speed of motorized travel within a young and promising country?

In the eyes of some social commentators, the reds and blues of most highway maps convey ever so subliminally the vital arteries of the body. Some map historians will even argue that the stringing together of local roads on the map to form what looked like high-ways meant the actual roads had to be improved to match the map images. Road maps promote the use of roads and make it necessary to build ever more roads, they say, requiring more maps. A Canadian example may well be the famed Trans-Canada Highway, which appeared on maps long before the route was completed around the north shore of Lake Superior. A map produced in 1945, for example, shows the highway, complete with the link over the top of Superior. It was only in 1949, when the federal government passed the Trans-Canada Highway Act, that work began, and not until 1962 that the east-west highway was officially opened. While it took a lot longer to build a nation of drivers than it did a nation of gold seekers, ulti-mately the automobile manufacturers and, in particular, petroleum companies, were richly rewarded.

Americans like to claim that the road map, like the quilt, is a uniquely American invention but, in fact, in the third century CE the Romans produced a map showing about eighty thousand kilo-metres of roads in their vast Empire. Now known as the *Peutinger Table* and stored in a Viennese museum, the map was in the form of a roll more than six metres long, showing roads in straight lines with distances between certain points.

The advent of modern road maps is, however, largely an Ameri-can phenomenon directly traceable to the arrival of the bicycle. Near the end of the nineteenth century, bicycling was a popular pas-time in the United States, and bicyclists joined clubs to enjoy their new activity en masse. More than one hundred thousand of them formed the League of American Wheelmen to lobby for paved roads. As better roads appeared, the League produced maps to help mem-bers find them. When the automobile came along, it fit snugly into the campaign for better roads and maps.

Cartography played a major role in the selling of highways begin-ning with the "good roads" movement in the 1880s, said James R.

Akerman, curator at the Newberry Library in Chicago. Like the roads they depicted, the earliest road maps were both liberating and constrictive. "In an era of unmarked and poorly engineered roads, guidebooks and maps made it possible for adventurous motorists to reach formerly inaccessible sites and to follow the itineraries and timetables of their own choosing," Akerman wrote in the journal *Cartographica*. "But the road map was also a promotional tool, bankrolled either by oil and automobile interests or commercial map publishers betting that auto touring would become a mass phenomenon. It was a good bet, although won at the price of bringing crowds to the road and recasting the highway adventurer into the highway consumer."

The highway system in Canada developed at a much slower pace than that in the United States. According to sociologist Rod Bantjes, in 1925 thirty-three percent of roads in American states in the north-central region were paved with gravel or better surfacing, a level of road improvement not reached in Saskatchewan until 1960. By 1930, about twenty-two percent of the roads in midwestern states were gravel surfaced, compared with three percent in Saskatchewan. "Alberta's road system was similarly underdeveloped until the oil boom of the 1950s when it began to outstrip those of both of the other prairie provinces," he said. "Manitoba had until this time been better able to finance road construction and its rural roads were comparable in quality to those of midwestern states."

Car travel remained at average speeds below thirty kilometres per hour until after the Depression, during which time most people still drove cars built in the late 1920s, said Bantjes. "Even in 1939 a sociologist, in an effort to impress his readers with the convenience of modern travel on all-weather gravel highways (four percent of all roads at the time), cites an average speed of only thirty-five miles per hour."

Ontario drivers had their own problems to contend with: dangerous jogs in the roads as a result of the original survey lines of one township not exactly meeting the survey lines of the neighbouring township. Map historian Lou Sebert explained what that meant for drivers.

> In the days of the horse and wagon, it did not really matter if the lines of one township did not meet up with the lines of another. A jog of a few hundred yards would put things right. But with the advent of the automobile these right-angle turns caused many accidents, and yet the authorities were remarkably slow to expropriate enough farmland to straighten out these hazards, even on the main highways. The older residents of Toronto can remember that right up to the opening of Queen Elizabeth Way in 1938, the simple journey from Toronto and Buffalo around the end of Lake Ontario meant the negotiating of at least four of these "hazards to navigation."

But the road maps of the time did not reflect such idiosyncrasies or the fact that Canada was not exactly in the fast lane of highway construction. From the beginning, road maps of the northern United States produced by such American companies as Rand McNally included the southern strip of Canada. One of Canada's first road maps was the *Ontario Automobile Road Map*, produced by Rand McNally & Company in 1918. The Ontario Department of Highways issued its first road map in 1923, when there were 2,935 kilometres of hard-surfaced highways. (In all of Canada at the time, there were 186,678 kilometres of improved earth highways and 80,465 kilometres of hard-surfaced roads.) What map owners saw were impressive lines connecting towns and cities, and with each passing year, more lines were added to the network.

In the United States, few "highways" were marked before the end of the First World War. It was easy to lose the trail of even the most improved routes without a detailed route book. As James R. Akerman pointed out, Rand McNally started out in the mid-1910s by repackaging general or railroad maps for motorist use but then developed its own idiom: an inexpensive and less bulky alternative to route books, marking the best intercity routes clearly in thick, clean lines with very little topography and very few railway lines shown. "The success of this new idiom depended in large measure on route marking, a feature that the earlier road maps and route books could not depend on," said Akerman. The company even provided local automobile clubs and state highway departments with financial assistance to install route signs.

Looking at the early road maps of Canada with today's eyes, it is easy to notice how road maps were used to deliver more than merely wayfaring information. A 1929 Eaton's map of Ontario showed that all roads led to the great Toronto department store and offered a special focus on the new Ferguson Highway between North Bay and Cochrane ("North Bay is reached via Bracebridge and the Muskoka Lakes highway which begins in Yonge Street, Toronto, on which Eaton's is situated."). A 1937 Imperial Oil map of Vancouver and vicinity offered whimsical and delicate icons of city life, including totem poles at Stanley Park, bathing beauties at Point Grey Bathing Beach and the Imperial Oil refinery at the town of Ioco ("You are invited to drive out and inspect the modern plant and town. A cordial welcome awaits you."). A 1939 Shell map of Quebec and the Maritime provinces announced the speed limit in New Brunswick and Prince Edward Island as "reasonable and proper," with the Shell logo appearing twenty-two times, including within a bull's eye in the middle of the compass rose. A 1954 Ontario government highway map sported a delightful picture on the cover of a happy family having lunch at a picnic table a few metres next to the highway and had exhortations sure to please a modern-day Toronto Transit Commission rider: TAKE CARE NOT CHANCES and SLOW DOWN

Cover, *Official Ontario Road Map,*
Ontario Department of Highways, 1954.
Author collection.

AFTER SUNDOWN and DO NOT THROW LIGHTED CIGARETTE OR CIGAR BUTTS FROM CAR WINDOWS. A 1972 map produced by Brewers Retail in Ontario showed the location of each of its beer stores in the province — today a politically incorrect use of cartography.

For modern collectors, early road maps have a seductive charm of their own. Click onto eBay on any day and you'll see scores of road maps for sale, most for well under ten U.S. dollars. There is a decent chance you will also see the e-mail address of Ron Whistance-Smith, for twenty-nine years a map curator at University of Waterloo and University of Alberta before he retired.

As a map curator, Whistance-Smith was well placed to indulge his interest. For his library he made a point of acquiring official road maps for each province and state, usual practice for university libraries. "Many, however, discarded the older map when the new map arrived while I, and some others, kept the older maps to create a time sequence illustrating the changes in the road networks," he said. When he retired in 1994, he began collecting as a serious hobby. He has road maps back as far as the early to mid-1920s for parts of Canada and a motor road map of the Western United States from 1915. He collects other maps as well: maps of wars (Crimea, Franco-Prussian, Russo-Japanese, Boer, First and Second World Wars, Korean, Vietnam and Gulf); maps of Western Canada's exploration and settlement; maps of Canadian cities. By counting the number of maps stored in boxes and then measuring the linear footage of the boxes and shelving in which they are stored, Whistance-Smith figures he owns four thousand six hundred road maps. They are stuffed in individual polyethylene bags and kept in his basement study.

Much of Whistance-Smith's life has involved maps in one way or the other. He used maps in the Air Force and in a Reserve Army Survey Regiment in Toronto, plotted weather maps for two years and briefed aircrew on in-flight weather conditions for another nine years. He learned more about the usefulness of maps as an undergraduate and graduate student in geography. During his many years as map curator, Whistance-Smith was fascinated by how road maps could be used, quite apart from their role as wayfinders. They show the development of the road and highway networks, the connectedness of isolated rural communities to markets, the movements of characters in fictional and non-fictional books, the location of places or roads that no longer exist. "They even show up in stage plays, movies

Cover, Official *Ontario Road Map*, Ontario Department of Highways, 1957. Author collection.

and television," he said. "I've provided road maps to a Saskatchewan production company shooting a story that took place in Minnesota in the mid-20s, and a 1937 Saskatchewan Official along with a Neilson's Chocolate Bar wall map of Canada for the *Jake and the Kid* series." Whistance Smith added:

> *I collect them because of the cultural, economic and historical content. Each map, of whatever type, records a portion of our cultural, economic and even political history. Each map is a selection of the total truth. The cartographer, when he or she sets out to design a map, must decide who and what it is intended for, and from a very great array of data, decide what they need in order to make a clear and easily understood presentation. By the same token, each map is a snapshot in time, recording what was there at the time the data was recorded.*

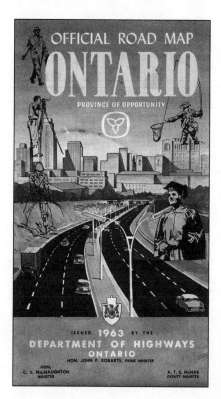

The on-line auction site eBay has done wonders for the map-collecting trade, if for no other reason than to show that the supply of old road maps in good condition is more plentiful than earlier thought. Of course, prior to eBay, prices were higher. Now, a road map may sell for more than one hundred dollars U.S. but most

Cover, *Official Road Map Ontario*, Ontario Department of Highways, 1963. Author collection.

sell for under ten dollars. The eBay bonanza has enabled Whistance-Smith to build up his collection of maps put out by regional motor associations, such as the vaunted Automobile Club of Southern California and the Alberta Motor Association, and to feed his esoteric interests. To a certain extent, he could just as well collect bottle caps or baseball cards, although such cultural flotsam is not nearly so revealing or delightful to look at as road maps. Though it is hard to see someone with four thousand six hundred maps stowed away in his basement as a picky collector, Whistance-Smith has his standards, usually based on design.

A favourite is a 1930 British American Oil Company map of Ontario, which has a cover that reads Welcome Shriners in exotic script, accompanied by a scimitar and a star between the points of an upside-down crescent. At the highest point of the crescent is a turbaned and bearded figure. Inside is a map of Toronto showing the location of Tent City, the local Masonic Hall, and the location of the BA refinery. Other favourites include a 1930 road map of the northeast States and Ontario, titled *Road Map to Canadian National Exhibition*. The art deco cover design shows five streaking automobiles approaching a cluster of pennanted and domed buildings symbolic of the CNE. "Another one I really love are three cartoons by Jimmy Frise related to BA service and products that appear on my Quebec map of the same period," he said. "I used to be a great fan of Jimmy Frise's cartoon, which accompanied weekly pieces by Greg Clark in the *Toronto Telegram* of my youth.

"Another one is a map of Southern Ontario only nine-and-a-half centimetres high by fifty-five centimetres wide, extending from Detroit and Flint in Michigan, to Montreal and St Jerome in Quebec. On the back of the map are the Canadian Ensign and the Stars and Stripes flanking the bold words VISITING CANADA. There are instructions at one end that say, 'Don't moisten until ready to apply. Have glass clean.' It appears that the map was to be applied to the upper inside surface of the windshield with the map facing the driver, or navigator, and the flag side facing out. It was copyrighted in 1927 by J. C. Liggett, and I have both 1929 and 1934–35 editions."

If you let him, Whistance-Smith will enthusiastically inventory his favourites among the four thousand six hundred candidates well into the night. And you will probably enjoy your visit, if you are in the right frame of mind. As seductive as maps undeniably are, offering an alluring picture of a new land with bountiful potential, of sparkling gold rivers in forbidding corners, of youthful memories, each one needs an owner willing to be seduced.

8

IDENTITY

BACK IN THE LATE 1980s, when he was band councillor for the Peigan Nation in Brocket, Alberta, Stan Knowlton conducted research with about twenty Blackfoot elders. The band was preparing to file a statement of claim against the federal government based on treaty rights over the construction of the Oldman River dam. After consulting with the Peigan elders, Knowlton found that the boundaries of the treaty reserve were identified, based on a report by George Mercer Dawson of the Geological Survey of Canada, as being much smaller than the Indian Act reserve the Peigan ended up with. "After looking over the appendix of George Dawson's report, I informally interviewed four elders from the Peigan reserve and two from Blood reserve to see how accurate Dawson's report was," Knowlton recalled. "Although the Blackfoot parts of George Dawson's report were consistent with the Blackfoot elders' memory, the English translations were not." To reconcile the discrepancy, Knowlton took a modern map of Alberta and removed all its place names. Then, he circulated the blank map to the elders and asked them to identify the ancient Blackfoot names for significant places of their territory. The fifty or so "place names" of mountains, rivers, plains and other features that the elders revealed to Knowlton were actually terms for body parts — foot, arm, stomach, head, eyebrow. Calgary, for example, was where the head was located. Following his instincts, Knowlton oriented the body parts on the map and, like a ghostly apparition, a figure appeared, feet to the south.

Knowlton asked the elders for an explanation, and they told him that by assembling the body-part place names, he had formed Napi, a central figure in Blackfoot cosmology. Not only that, the elders said, but if Knowlton had continued with his place names farther north or east, he would have formed a woman and a child as well, as visual markers of ancient alliances with other tribes.

The Blackfoot consider their traditional territory in southwest Alberta and northern Montana as the land of Old Woman and Old Man, Knowlton learned. The Rocky Mountains of Alberta are said to represent the backbone of the Old Man. The Nose Hill in Calgary is the centre of his face, the Elbow River a part of his arm. There was Heart River, Belly River, Thighs River, Knees River. The Old Woman's body parts are mapped out in the area around Medicine Hat, the Cypress Hills and the Milk River region. By using traditional Blackfoot place names, Knowlton had recreated the Old Man and Old Woman map.

What the Blackfoot elders showed Knowlton was a way in which the body itself could be the map of a territory. As writing was impractical among the early Blackfoot people, Knowlton said, it appears the land was used as the preferred medium to store information. Mapping with names of body parts was a manifestation of the relationship between the Blackfoot tribes and the rest of the universe, "a reflection of a greater relationship that originates in the stars and returns to the stars."

This cartographic cosmology lives on among Blackfoot artists. "For Blackfoot, our territory is the imprint of Napi," Amethyst First Rider, creator of the Trickster Theatre in Calgary, told a conference in 1999. "So in our stories, Napi puts his body imprint on the land, and that's where our landscape comes from in Blackfoot. All his body parts; we know our territory through the body parts of Napi. So, you have to go and renew these relationships, and that's what literature, storytelling, is about, because you have stories where things happen: you renew those stories, you renew those relationships."

Non-Natives do not have as intimate a relationship with maps of the territories in which they live and move, but much of their communal identity is still bound up in the cartography of their lands. This shows up most obviously in the names that we attach to places on the map. The names on Canada's earliest "maps," those existing long before the arrival of Europeans and carried in the heads of travellers, were often forms of storytelling and identity, as well as navigational aids. European contact brought an entirely new identity, to be imposed on the land. While the body-part names of the Blackfoot or the expressive names of the Inuit lived on in their oral traditions, new names were planted as flags of imperial identity.

The bestowing of place names was often a very considered affair with the intent to fashion the land that it named. Historian Daniel Clayton has written about how Captain George Vancouver, who mapped the north Pacific coast between 1792 and 1794, was instructed to put a British image on the Pacific colony. "He was the representative of George the Third and was meant to stamp his geography 'British' and describe its main features," Clayton wrote. Vancouver named many of his discoveries after royal, aristocratic, military and political figures and, though he had many cordial meetings with local Native groups, he stayed true to his mission and disregarded their place names. While he generally recognized names given by previous explorers, Vancouver exercised some cartographic realpolitik early in his travels along the Pacific coast. He named "The Gulph of Georgia" — changed in 1859 to the Strait of Georgia — for the king, and "Possession Sound," at the opening of Puget Sound, to signify the place where he claimed formal possession of the Gulf of Georgia region for Britain. As Clayton noted, when Vancouver discovered later in his voyages that a Spaniard had already named the gulf, he imperiously relocated that name to a narrow strait nearby, so that Britain could impose its claim to the strategic entrance.

More often than not, however, place naming was an act of personal identity and vanity. In Alberta, surveyors were notorious for their self-indulgent whimsy when conferring place names. There are stories of some surveyors naming major landmarks for their wives or dogs. Though not a surveyor, and likely not a dog lover, even the eminent Otto Klotz was swept by the rush of naming land. Klotz was a major figure in the history of mapping Canada; he was appointed Dominion of Canada Chief of the Astronomical Observations in British Columbia and the North West in 1885. In the summer of 1886, he surveyed three mountains, only one of which was already known by a name. He named one of the other two mountains after himself, although in his diary he sounded rather defensive about it. "It is probably a delicate matter to name a mountain or lake after oneself but when I ask myself candidly who has the first right, the appropriate one to claim the name, it certainly is the explorer, the man who measures them, locates them, climbs them," Klotz wrote to himself. "My eyes are not the first to gaze upon these mountains, but they have been nameless, and I am the first to give them their geographical and topographical position." His superiors in Ottawa clearly did not think much of his suggestion. It was not until 1945 that Klotz got his mountain in the Yukon, and in 1957 a second peak, in British Columbia's southern mountain chain, was christened Mount Klotz.

That same year, geologist Andrew Lawson was doing fieldwork in the Rainy Lake region of northwestern Ontario. The work involved extensive topographical mapping and the naming of geological features. Working on the Rainy River near the Couchiching Rapids and a feature known as Pither's Point, Lawson stopped in from time to time at the home of Mr Pither, who worked as a Native agent for the Canadian government. His wife, Rebecca, always made Lawson's surveying party feel at home. In return, Lawson named three islands near Rainy Lake above Pither's Point "Rebecca," "Cheery" and "Hostess."

The American credited with bestowing the largest number of geographical names on Canadian features is Lieutenant Frederick Schwatka of the United States Army. In 1883, Schwatka led a small and secret military expedition of five soldiers across the Chilkoot Pass and traversed the length of the Yukon River. The goal was to produce a topographical map of the region for possible future military use, and the Canadian government was not notified of the expedition. Schwatka dispensed names like a conquering general, ignoring existing names given by miners or Natives, claiming they were difficult to pronounce. There was Lindeman Lake for the secretary of the Breman Geographical Society, Bennett Lake for the founder of the *New York Herald* and patron of exploration, and Watson River for a professor at Harvard University. Wearing the mantle of the Ugly American, Schwatka was quite boastful of his exploits in books and speeches.

When the colourful poet-geologist George Mercer Dawson followed in Schwatka's footsteps on behalf of the Geological Survey of Canada, he became less and less impressed with Schwatka's boasts and, in his own report, downplayed the American's achievements. Dawson was particularly unimpressed with Schwatka's disregard of existing place names. In his report of 1887 of his own explorations in the Yukon District, Dawson wrote: "He has completely ignored the names of many places already well-known to the miners, throughout the country, substituting others of his own invention, one of which even differs in the different versions of the map of his route which he has published." If there was any justice, Dawson concluded, the place names would be struck, but because of the "eminence of some of the names" Schwatka's toponymy stood.

The rancour, however, lingered, and in 1888 Dawson proposed that an official board for Canada be established to rule on the naming of places and geographical features. The Surveyor General took a step in that direction when an officer was assigned to review the nomenclature in the North-West Territory, at that time defined as the land between the Great Lakes and the Rocky Mountains, north of the sixtieth parallel. In 1890, the United States established its Board on Geographical Nomenclature, which showed a distinct enthusiasm for naming features in Canada as well, a move the Canadians considered alarming. As Alan Rayburn, an authority on place names, has written, "In asserting the need for a similar body in Canada, the Surveyor General pointed out in 1896 that the United States was making decisions on Canadian names and that these were being used by other countries." The next year, the Geographic Board of Canada was founded, later renamed Canadian Permanent Committee on Geographical Names and, still later, the Geographical Names Board of Canada.

The presence of a Canadian board might have slowed down the appearance of American names but did not stop it. The names of some twelve former presidents are commemorated on major geographical features in Canada's north — Lincoln Bay, Mount Grant, Roosevelt Peak — although not without some resistance. In the mid-1960s, proposals to rename a community in New Brunswick and a prominent mountain in Alberta Mount Kennedy were vigorously fought off (the name Mount Kennedy was finally bestowed on a peak in the Yukon).

The Arctic is especially dotted with American names. In a paper published in the journal *Names*, Alan Rayburn isolated a block of a topographical map of the Arctic archipelago to show how hardly any name was derived from Canadian sources. Most commemorate American explorers and scientists and were given by Adolphus Greeley, who explored the area between 1881 and 1884, and Elmer Ekblaw, who was there between 1914 and 1917. Neil Peninsula and Elmerson Peninsula were named for Ekblaw's sons Neil and Elmer. "The most northerly point of Canada is Cape Columbia, [a name] given by George Nares in 1876 in honour of the poetical name of the United States," Rayburn wrote.

At some point, no one is sure precisely when, the origins of place names themselves became something to study and regulate. It probably began when a state realized how place names could form a historical narrative as well as appease the vainglorious: in this way, a place name reveals the past and puts a stamp on the future. In Canada, toponymy was likely born in the period between 1905 and 1909, when James White, Canada's first Chief Geographer, sent out a survey to postmasters throughout the Dominion asking them about the origins of their post office names. At the time, postmasters were in the position of naming areas to facilitate mail delivery.

These days, the Geographical Names Board of Canada has the ultimate responsibility for coordinating and directing the correct usage of Canadian place names, with the provinces having authority within their own boundaries. While their main role is to approve names for features of the Canadian landscape, these bodies spend much of their time revisiting place names that are well established, in some cases reasserting identities that have been lost over time. "Reconstituting" maps to ensure minority groups are properly acknowledged and to remove names that are considered discriminatory to modern ears is not an easy task. In the 1980s, Canadian mapmakers began to adapt the official map to local usage by replacing some European-derived place names with those of local usage, though for some Indian groups the religious significance of special names prohibits their publication on maps. In 1987, Frobisher Bay became Iqaluit, a move at the time considered controversial. Since then, twelve other community names have been changed: Eskimo Point is now Arviat, Coppermine is Kugluktuk, Fort Norman is Tulita and Pelly Bay, Kugaaruk.

Some name changes are freighted with irony. Late in 2001, Saskatchewan renamed Highway 11, which connects Regina with Prince Albert three hundred sixy-four kilometres away, the Louis Riel Trail, for the Metis leader hanged for treason in Regina in November 1885. There will be one hundred trail markers stamped with Red River carts — icons of the Metis — along the newly named highway. "Today we are making history by recognizing and honouring our collective past," Highways Minister Pat Atkinson said while announcing the decision. The fiery Riel was the force behind the Red River Rebellion in 1869 and headed the Northwest Rebellion in 1884 and 1885. He fought against the surveyors who established a grid on the prairies as a first step to colonization. One test of the suitability of a reconstituted place name is to imagine what the honouree would think of the decision. It is hard to imagine Louis Riel being delighted with his name gracing a high-speed highway so emblematic of white settlement.

It is not only Native names that are reappearing on the map of Canada. In 1998, Alberta changed the name of Chinaman's Mountain near Canmore to Ha Ling Peak in response to complaints from Chinese Canadians. In December 2000, British Columbia joined Saskatchewan, Alberta, Prince Edward Island and the Yukon in removing the term "squaw" from provincial maps ("squaw" shows up in eighty-six other place names in Canada, most frequently in Ontario and Quebec). The Cree pronunciation of woman is "esquoio," which missionaries translated as "squaw," and which eventually became a slur referring to female genitalia. For some reason, squaw was an irresistible place name for surveyors and explorers. It was used to name eleven creeks, lakes and mountains in British Columbia alone.

Prime Minister Jean Chrétien had much less success when he tried to use political muscle to rename Mount Logan, Canada's highest mountain, Mount Trudeau. Sir William Edmond Logan was the first director of the Geological Survey of Canada, and creator of Canada's first major geological map, which earned rave reviews around the world. Faced with a storm of complaints and a threatened lawsuit by descendants of Sir William, Chrétien backed down and settled for the naming of a secondary peak. Every Canadian prime minister has a mountain named after him, except John Diefenbaker; he had to settle for a lake in Saskatchewan.

But it is in Quebec that place names are employed most fervently to set and reinforce social identity. Quebec's distinct identity has long been on display in its place names; the sheer number of place names beginning with St or Ste confirms the historical religious influences that prevailed in the province. Emerging from the Quiet Revolution in the 1960s, Quebec's thinkers took a long hard look at the English face of the province. In time, their hard look settled on the toponymy of Quebec, which they felt whitewashed or bastardized French and Aboriginal history. The English had turned Ouestmont into Westmount. Coaticouc became Coaticook. Chaouinigane became Shawinigan. Témiscamingue became Timiskaming. "In toponymy, as in commerce and industry (except for agriculture), the initiative [to respect the French fact] escaped him," wrote commentator René Bonin in an *Action Nationale* polemic in 1969. "The new Anglo-Saxon boss modified cartography to suit his own interests." Bonin added:

How many of us remember the place names used during the French regime: Grandes-Fourches, Tracadièche, Chaudières, Cataracoui,

Rouillé, Pointe-Sainte-Anne, Népisigouit, Chipody, Fort-la-Jolie, Pisicouide, Cobécouide, Port-Dauphin, Beaubassin, Chibouctou, Port-Royal, Mistigouèche, Cap Fourchu? . . . From the Laurentian mountains to the eastern shore of Gaspésie, the Anglophone survey-ors based their place names on those from England. Out of national pride, who will transform them into our own image?

Who would defend French pride? The answer was the Commis-sion de toponymie du Québec, today the most activist and contro-versial place-naming body in the land. In a province where both the French and English are sensitive to language slights and subtle humiliations, the Commission's decisions regularly make news. The naming of a bridge or a change in the name of a school board are matters of heated debate, and the Commission's decisions are regu-larly parsed for political overtones. A classic case occurred in 1997. With the twentieth anniversary of the controversial language legis-lation Bill 101 looming, the Commission announced that one hun-dred and one Quebec authors would have deserted islands in a northern Quebec archipelago named after their works. The islands were to be called Le Désert Mauve from a book by Nicole Brossard, La Chambre Fermée from a book by Anne Hébert, La Fleur de Lyse from a song by Félix Leclerc. The project was to be called *Le Jardin au Bout du Monde* (the Garden at the End of the Earth) from a work by Gabrielle Roy. Quebec's Anglophones looked down the list and found only three English-language writers: novelist Neil Bissoon-dath and poets Stephen Morrissey and D. G. Jones. No Mordecai Richler, no Leonard Cohen, no Mavis Gallant; in short, very little acknowledgement of English creativity. They wondered, Whose gar-den? And on what earth?

It turned out that there was yet another layer to the story. The islands that were to be named were located in a huge reservoir south of Kuujjuaq and represented the tops of hills and mountains flooded for the James Bay hydroelectric development. To the Cree, who long fought against the James Bay flooding of land they considered traditional territory, the place naming was considered a crude act of appropriation. They said that the land already had long-standing Cree names — Rabbit Mountain, Beaver Mountain, Our Grandfather Mountain. In its defence, the Commission said it had consulted a survey of Cree place names conducted in the 1970s during the construction of hydroelectric projects along La Grande River, or the Chisasibi River as it is known among the Cree, and that Quebec likely has more Native place names on its maps than any other province in Canada. The Commission's efforts have led to the granting of legal status and the publication on maps of thousands of Aboriginal toponyms, raising the total number of official Aboriginal toponyms from 1560 in 1969 to nearly 12,000 today.

Bill Namagoose, executive director of the Grand Council of the Cree, said the islands will always be the tops of mountains on land flooded for the James Bay hydroelectric development. "We have our people buried under that reservoir," Namagoose told reporters. "Naming these islands is the same as naming tombstones after people. It's totally inappropriate. This is a political move, an attempt to occupy our territory and rename it, rather than adopt local names. When you fight over territory or sovereignty, one of the important things is to have title to the names."

AFTER A CENTURY OF INTENSE settlement and the beginnings of prosperity, a pride of place was starting to take shape in Canada in the late nineteenth century. With pride came the desire among townspeople and entire cities to show the larger world just how well they were doing. Maps were the tangible way to illustrate these new stirrings of identity, and private operators were only too happy to oblige. As N. L. Nicholson and Lou Sebert point out in *The Maps of Canada*, there was no money in colonial coffers to underwrite general-purpose mapping. At the same time, the development of lithography and the transfer process cut out the need for a skilled engraver to draw images directly on copper — opening the way to quick and less expensive printing. That job was left to small map companies and private individuals, who answered the call by churning out two types of maps. For citizens of young and thriving urban centres, the bird's-eye view was the map of choice; for the still great number of Canadians living in smaller towns and rural communities of Ontario, the county atlas found a ready market.

The bird's-eye view was a thing of beauty. It remains so. Even if the town was dusty and reeking of manure, the oblique view showed order, harmony, progress and industry, a self-portrait of which anyone would be proud. Views usually showed a busy, ship-choked harbour in the foreground. The factories were pumping smoke. Even today, spoiled as we are by views from outer space, the bird's-eye view makes us want to touch down and explore, which is the best of what a map offers.

Bird's-eye views, also known as panoramics, perspectives or aero views, were scale drawings showing street patterns, individual buildings and major landscape features in higher-than-street-level perspective. They were among the most labour-intensive maps produced. As a start, artists could have been given a plan of the town by the local board of trade, but that would form merely the base of information. Artists had to walk each street and produce a perspective grid of the town layout. They then made perspective drawings of each of the buildings, trees and other features in order to present a complete and accurate landscape as though seen from an elevation of six hundred to nine hundred metres. The drawings were then amalgamated.

In the days before airplanes, trying to picture a town as seen from six hundred metres up was not simple, particularly if the artist did not have the benefit of looking down on the city from a mountain,

The City of Halifax, Nova Scotia produced by Duncan Currie in 1890. Bird's-eye views offered a welcome opportunity to display civic pride and commercial success. This map is bordered by fifty-seven illustrations of commercial, industrial and public buildings. National Archives of Canada (NMC-034241).

cliff or promontory. As John Reps, author of the comprehensive study *Views and Viewmakers of Urban America*, wrote, the artist/map-maker had to use his imagination "to render what he could see as if he were in a tower or steeple or ship's mast." He first would decide the orientation of his view, and then would face that direction when sketching houses, buildings and other elements of the landscape. It required a vast amount of detail work. The artist had an easier job if the city was laid out in an orderly grid of straight lines intersecting at right angles, such as Toronto, rather than older cities, such as Quebec, that were more haphazard and that developed at staggered stages.

The artists also had to clearly show as many businesses and features as possible. The basic principle of linear perspective, however, worked against this goal. Using this principle, one or two vanishing points are selected at the horizon at which parallel lines appear to be converging. This technique creates the most realistic setting. But applied to a panoramic map, linear perspective made buildings in the middle and the background too small to be noticed. Owners would not even be able to identify their businesses, which would certainly discourage potential subscribers. The artists solved this problem by locating their vanishing points far beyond the horizon, wrote Reps. As a result, the streets, if extended off the map, would meet beyond the horizon and somewhere in the sky. Buildings could be drawn larger but still appear smaller than those in the foreground. The widespread use of this technique explains why so many views look like a map drawn on a plane sloping upward to the sky, Reps wrote. "It is not that the artists were ignorant of the rules of perspective. What they did was bend the rules in the interest of commerce."

Not only bend the rules but break them as well. Reps wrote that if a business were located beyond the planned border of the lithograph, the artist would "move" the factories to where it could be seen, or compress on the sides to include more of the city. And because many of these towns were in rapid development, the artist had to imagine how certain buildings would look once they had been completed.

Between 1870 and 1910, the artists, almost all of them American, developed a large and admiring audience. A noted American artist, Albert Ruger, visited a number of provinces in Eastern Canada in 1878 and drew views that, according to Reps, impressed local newspaper editors. One noted that Ruger "with unwearied patience . . . has drawn every building in outline on a scale small enough to show the whole city; has located every building so exactly that every citizen can pick out his own place." Herman Brosius was another American map artist who spent considerable time sketching Canadian cities. Between 1872 and 1876, he made frequent forays to Ontario, producing fifteen lithographs of towns in the province. His works are noted for their very high angle and accuracy. A Canadian artist of note was Robert Auchmuty Sproule, who came to Canada from Ireland in 1826 at the age of twenty-seven. Late in 1829, he began to produce views of Montreal, creating fourteen in all.

Being products of commercial map-makers, the panoramics were heavily marketed items that followed a common business strategy. Salesmen would arrive in town and try to drum up support for early sales even before the "fieldwork" had been undertaken. When speaking with residents, they appealed to civic pride. When pitching to businesses, they encouraged the purchase of multiple copies by offering to list the enterprise in an accompanying legend or business directory. And when talking with town officials, the salespeople would extol the value of bird's-eye maps as a way to fix an image of the town in the minds of the locals, as well as possible tourists and businesspeople from other parts of the country.

Newspapers were one of the first businesses the salespeople approached to whip up interest in their works of cartographic art. Here is how the *Daily Times*, the St Thomas, Ontario, newspaper,

began its report on October 14, 1886, on plans for a "pictorial map"
of the community:

J. B. Young, publisher of Toronto, has decided to publish a Pictorial
Map of St. Thomas and will call on our business men to solicit their
support. We have no doubt but he will meet with success in the
undertaking. The following is a description of the proposed work of
art; The buildings will be sketched with a pencil by a first class artist,
so distinct that the stone, brick, and frame buildings can be distin-
guished from each other, and as nearly as possible the color of the
paint on the house will be shown. This work of art must be classed
with "Bird Eye Views." It will be a genuine work of art; engraved
and lithographed in a number of colors. The natural scenery, land-
scape, and green foliage, will lend a charm to the picture which will
represent the city as it really appears, near as art can imitate nature,
and will be fit to hang in a parlor, drawing room or office.

A small geographical map will occupy the position on the right
of the map, just above the vanishing line, and will show the location
of St. Thomas and its relation to other centers of commerce, the rail-
ways and their connections. Around the margin of the picture will
appear the prominent public buildings, business blocks and private
residences, forming a border in diamonds and rings, also representa-
tions in symbols of different industries, etc., will be set forth in
pleasing taste. At the bottom will be printed on the outer margin the
names and addresses of the principal business and professional men,
arranged alphabetically and classified according to their business or
profession. A number opposite to the name and address correspon-
ding with a number marked on the street or on the building.

In fact, such stories were a well-established facet of the sales
approach, according to Reps. The artist's agent, working as an
advance man for the boss, drummed up interest. This story almost

surely would have been followed a week or two later by a second newspaper story stating that the artist was now at work in town sketching the buildings and would soon show a preliminary drawing to ensure accuracy. A third article would note the completion of the drawing and urge subscribers to make sufficient orders to justify the expense of printing. Several days later, the newspaper would report on the departure of the artist and that arrangements were underway for the printing of the panoramic. Most, if not all, accounts would say that the resulting lithograph would be "a splendid addition to the walls of every drawing room and business office."

For the vanity map purveyors, an important source of income lay in the sale of images appearing as vignettes in the border of the map, the Halifax bird's-eye map of 1890 being a prime example. The vignettes showed mansions, churches, principal public buildings, industrial plants, office blocks, and a variety of retail and wholesale businesses," Reps wrote. "A person wishing to be given such special prominence was expected to pay a fee or at least to subscribe for many copies of the view."

While the view might have been different, there were many similarities between the bird's-eye view maps produced for city dwellers and county maps and atlases for the great many rural residents of Ontario, Quebec and the Maritime provinces of New Brunswick, Nova Scotia and Prince Edward Island. Of the fifty-eight maps known to have been made, thirty-two were of Ontario counties. For one thing, that was where substantial population growth in the late nineteenth century occurred. There was also an eagerness to attach community pride to something tangible, such as a map. This hunger for identity was actually born in the early days of Upper Canada, when, in the late eighteenth century, Lieutenant-Governor John Graves Simcoe established counties to promote loyalty to the Crown and to act as a vehicle for development of a democratic system. Instead of using numbers to identify counties, Simcoe enthusiastically plucked names from local sources — Leeds, Stormont, Glengarry — as well as from English counties — Lincoln County, Northumberland County.

Detailed and annotated maps showing these counties in their finest light began appearing in Canada in 1856, just when bird's-eye views were starting to be put up in the parlours of the cities of the northeast United States and Eastern Canada. New York State–born George C. Tremaine and his two nephews are generally credited with the first Canadian county land ownership map of Norfolk County, Canada West. The business model and salesmanship of the county map were strikingly familiar. Silver-tongued salesmen fanned out in the rural communities, going from farm door to farm door to get villagers and businesses to sign up in advance for their map. The maps were sold by subscription before they were printed. Each of the county atlases consisted of a historical text, township and town maps, portraits, views and patrons' directory, and business cards.

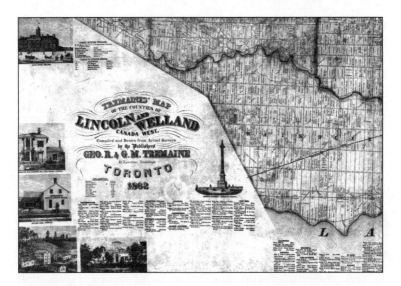

Tremaine's Map of the counties of Lincoln and Welland Canada West, produced by Geo. R. and G. M. Tremaine, 1862. For genealogists, county maps hold such enduring interest that they are regularly republished. National Archives of Canada (NMC-019014-1 to 4)

For their money, subscribers got recognition on the map by having their names in prominent type on their farm lot or beside their place of business. For an additional fee, drawings of the subscriber's farmhouse, factory or store were included in the margin. The more money paid, the more information on your family and property would be included. According to former University of Western Ontario map librarian Edward Phelps, the basic Lambton County atlas of 1880 sold for $12.75, and for that the buyer had his name printed on the map and in the subscribers' directory, with four lines of biographical detail. Portraits, more developed biography and real estate views were extras. The personal and business profiles were written by either the subscribers or by freelancing teachers looking to make an extra dollar writing a family biography.

Jeffrey Murray, archivist at the National Archives, said the mapmakers played on a newly developed identity. "It flattered their customers' vanity by offering them a chance to associate their name with neighbours and with the leading members of their community," Murray has written. "For rural residents, the maps compiled by these salesmen . . . were not just a geographical reference tool but also visual evidence of their success as pioneers."

The next logical step in county vanity was the county atlas, a shrewd packaging of the county maps that commanded larger sums. The origins of the county atlas are murky, but Lou Sebert offers a possible story. According to legend, he said, one of the American mapping companies found that some of the purchasers of their maps had cut up the map, township by township, and pasted the pieces into an album together with handwritten notes on the size, population and business activity of each township. "The sales advantage of having a product that would fit into the drawing-room desk and at the same time be a handy business reference was at once apparent," Sebert said, "and the county atlas trade was on its way." As early coffee table books, the atlases were generally well produced in large format and with gold leaf on the embossed cover in a style, Edward Phelps has written, "which may be called 'Victorian optimistic' . . . The paying biographies make their subjects to be uniformly respectable beyond reproach."

Not that the maps were shabby knock-offs of township survey plans. They often had more accurate and up-to-date information, since salesmen visited each landowner and collected basic information and sketched in details of land use. In some cases, itinerant map-makers went from county to county measuring distances, using wheel odometers. The Surveyor General eased the way by making available the official plans to private map-makers. Original surveys were often not very accurately done, so landowners were also motivated to know the exact dimensions of their land, Sebert said. "Many had privately remeasured their property to see if there would be a tax advantage in claiming less land than that shown on the official plan. Thus the country farmers knew the measurements of their land and were able to provide the county atlas representatives with data to make a more accurate map of the county than any previously available."

As records of land ownership, county maps were undoubtedly valuable, and they have an enduring attraction for historians and genealogists. They were not much good to land use planners and the captains of industry building the infrastructure of the young country; they did not indicate relief, so were of no value to railway planners. (Such information required topographical maps, which the Canadian Army began producing in 1904.) Even as historical documents, they must be seen through several filters. Map-makers were not above tidying up their drawings by placing trees where they were not, adding picket fences for a touch of gentility and having the requisite horses milling about. As Murray pointed out, the map-makers were heavily self-censored and certainly did not present a community picture of any nuance. "Families that lived outside the dominant society — Chinese and Native people, for example — were usually not represented."

As a measure of their enduring attraction, many of the county atlases have been reprinted on a regular basis, particularly in the 1970s and again in the past few years, and are selling for eighty dollars each in the big box bookstores of modern suburbia. They are treasured not only for the view they offer of a more bucolic time, but also for their genealogical and historical value. In the words of Edward Phelps, county maps were "a seminal contribution to the 'warp and woof' of the historical texture of local Ontario."

To this day, a good measure of civic pride is derived from a town's presence on road maps and atlases. That is especially true if you reside in a smaller town that lies in the shadow of a metropolis and which is teased for its lack of nightlife. Cartographic existence is important. It is easy to take this for granted until something upsets the normal order of the universe. What happens if one day you are on the map and the next day you are not? Pictou is one town that found out.

It may only have five thousand citizens, but Pictou is a major tourist destination in Nova Scotia. It is known as the birthplace of "New Scotland," and the first map of the Maritime provinces was published here in 1854. Its beaches attract travellers from far and wide, though for a while, back in 2000, they might have had some trouble finding the town because it was left off the latest provincial road map due to a computer error. It was just one of some two dozen towns inadvertently left off the road maps, though the reaction was most anguished in Pictou. The provincial Ministry of Tourism and Culture promised to fix the error, but that was little comfort. The mayor of the town, Lawrence LeBlanc, captured how the residents felt when he spoke with the *National Post*: "The damage is done. The darn things have already been sent out. [Residents are] just throwing

their hands up in disgust and they can't believe the stupidity of it."
LeBlanc went on to say that a television crew sent to Pictou to cover
the story, as well as a group of tour operators, took the wrong turnoff
because Pictou was missing from their maps.

In the cartographic world, there are always unintended consequences. After the crisis had passed, LeBlanc said that while he did
not want to be left off the map again, the national news reports on
the gaffe gave Pictou a much bigger profile than any map reference
could have. "And it didn't cost us anything," he said. The map flap
conveniently overlapped festivities surrounding the launch of the
Hector — a historical reconstruction of a merchant ship that
brought Scottish settlers to Pictou in the eighteenth century.
Thanks in part to the publicity, a Web site advertising the town and
the festival received 767,000 hits in six months, and telephone calls
came from as far away as Tucson, Arizona. "It worked so well for us
that New Glasgow wants to do it next year," LeBlanc joked.

It is bad enough if your town is left off the map due to a printing
error. The civic bruising is all the greater when your town is deemed
no longer large enough to warrant a dot on the map. In Ontario,
there are a number of towns with holes where their dots used to be.
Since 1990, fine and well-established villages such as Atherton,
Gunter and Millbridge have been excised from the Ontario highway
maps. It used to be that as long as your town had six houses, a grocery store, a restaurant or a gas station, and a motel, it would qualify
for its place on the provincial map. In the 1990s, the Ontario Ministry of Transportation ruled that a town had to be recognized by the
Ontario Geographic Names Board and have an official blue highway
sign granted by a regional municipality to be placed in the map.
Allen Abel, a writer for *Canadian Geographic*, visited the town of
Latta, on the Moira River just north of Belleville, to find out how
the burghers felt about their town being removed from the latest
Official Road Map of Ontario. Admittedly, there were not a lot of

Lattans drowning their sorrows, since the town only has one hundred residents. Some tried to find the bright side. "Since we don't exist, does this mean we don't have to pay taxes anymore?" asked one shopkeeper. Abel also stopped in at Housey's Rapids, just east of Gravenhurst, where members of the local women's club were sufficiently upset about their town's omission starting with the 1984 issue of the provincial map that they hounded provincial and municipal politicians until a blue sign, and their place on the map, were established.

Of course, if you can find a province breaking civic hearts by erasing towns from maps, you are just as likely to find a province taking the opposite approach. That province would surely be Saskatchewan. Given the vagaries of the province's wheat-based economy, it has more than its share of towns-that-used-to-be; more than half of all towns that existed in Saskatchewan are now largely abandoned. Recognizing that citizens might want to visit their ancestral home, even if that home is in a ghost town, Saskatchewan's bureaucrats decided years ago to return some of these forgotten communities to the map. Bill Barry, an author, is a booster of all things Saskatchewan, and the lay authority on place names and civic history. You would think he would welcome the resurrection of old place names. Surprisingly, he is not so sure he likes the idea of names of long-forgotten towns reappearing on maps. "It implies that there's something there to see," he said. "The net value isn't so obvious if it's misleading. On special historical maps maybe, but I'd be reluctant to see them on modern maps. That's going overboard, don't you think?"

9

REIMAGININGS

"WALLACE STEGNER WROTE IN HIS BOOK *Wolf Willow*, 'I may not know who I am, but I know where I am from.' I would say: 'I may know who I am, but I do not know where I am from.'"

Marlene Creates stands Stegner's words upside down for the sake of clarity — just as an Inuk travelling on the land would rearrange stones in order to create another coordinate on an imaginary map. Creates is an artist, not a traditional hunter, but the comparison is apt. To better understand the feeling of rootlessness that informs her work, Creates has been on her own migration throughout Canada and Britain since the 1970s. She has been searching for, in her words, "a zone of belonging." She caught a glimpse of that comfort zone in what some would call crude maps born of memory and imagination, and drawn for her by elders she has met on her travels.

Just as Creates rewrites Stegner to gain a measure of personal truth, so, too, does she rewrite the rules of cartography to explore the strange alchemy of geography and identity.

"I may know who I am, but I do not know where I am from."

Creates is originally from Montreal, where she was born in 1952, but the city holds no emotional resonance for her. Part of her is still back in Eastern Ontario; she studied visual arts at Queen's University in Kingston and lived for twelve years in Ottawa. But now living in St John's, Newfoundland, she is as close to home, that soulful home, as she will ever get. Creates moved to St John's in 1985, a deliberate decision to live close to where her maternal ancestors lived; some of them were involved in the fishery on Fogo Island off Newfoundland's northeast coast. It was also a good place from which to create maps of meaning, for fewer places have such a gulf between what is seen on a map and what is experienced on the ground.

In slide-show presentations for university and art gallery audiences, Creates's first images depict her green-faced home looking out to Signal Hill and The Narrows, the entrance to St John's Harbour. She notes the irony that the newest province of Canada is also the oldest settled land. "The conventional published map of Labrador shows the interior as mostly 'wilderness,' but it has actually been inhabited for more than seven thousand years," she said. "But very few of the Native place names are on the map."

Creates looks at maps with an artist's eye, something honed by her years on the road and observing. In the early 1980s, she spent several summers travelling slowly through England, Wales, Ireland and Scotland on a blue Vespa motor scooter, visiting ancient standing stones and stone circles in remote places. Once she neared a destination, she would stop and knock on a villager's door and ask directions. Invariably, she would meet elderly people — the young had moved to the cities — many of whom had lived in the same place their entire lives. Her hosts would use a scrap of paper or the back of Creates's road map to draw a little sketch map. "Not only were these maps practical, because they helped me find my way, but they also fascinated me because of the kinds of things that were drawn as landmarks," Creates said. "I was on the moors — not a featureless landscape, but it's pretty close — and yet people were able to pick out things in this environment to help me find my way. Wonderful drawings, unself-conscious, functional, beautiful."

During the school year, Creates was teaching visual arts in Ottawa at Algonquin College and then at the University of Ottawa. She made a point of having all her students draw a map of Ottawa as a way of allowing them to look at their subjective perceptions of the same place. The results were more interesting to the teacher than to the students. "All these people drawing a map of the same place, everybody with a completely different sense of scale and proportion, the things they remembered and the things they didn't remember, and where things were in relation to each other — it made for very interesting drawings," Creates said.

A key event in her development as an artist occurred in July 1985 when Creates was on a field trip on Baffin Island in the eastern Arctic. While she was in Pond Inlet, she wanted to explore outside the community; to walk alone over terrain that was not mapped in enough detail on the topographical chart she had with her. One day she asked Craig d'Entremont, who was born in Southern Canada but had lived in Pond Inlet for some twenty years, how she should approach her tundra "hike." Like the moors in Britain, the tundra seemed to Creates to be stark and undifferentiated. D'Entremont drew a map, on which he placed a gully, but also suggested that Creates talk with Paul Idlout, an Inuk who had lived in Pond Inlet all his life. "There's a risk of polar bears," d'Entremont said. "Paul will tell you if it's safe to go." Creates tracked down Idlout, who drew a map of the same area of the tundra, including the gully. D'Entremont's and Idlout's maps, however, could not have been more different from one another. The one d'Entremont drew had words written all over it. It was angular, with simple, smooth lines and written explanations. The one Idlout drew had complex, flowing lines.

"You could see, as he was drawing it, that he was imagining the actual topography, the shape of the terrain, and he was trying to mark it on this flat piece of paper with pencil lines," Creates said. "Not a word was written on it, just these descriptive flowing lines."

That same fall of 1985, Creates moved to St John's. In 1988, she set out to paint a picture of Labrador as a place other than *terra incognita*. It would not be a traditional artistic rendering, and it would not even be by her own hand. She headed first to Nain, the northernmost community in Labrador. She started spreading the word that she would be interested in meeting elders who would be willing to talk about the places where they had grown up. Most of them had lived in single-family groups in the bays along the coast of northern Labrador. These bays are named after the families who had lived there: Webb's Bay, Voisey's Bay, Flowers Bay. During the interviews, Creates gave all the elders acid-free paper and pencils and asked them to draw maps of the places of their youth while they told her about their memories. She also photographed the map-makers in their domestic settings in the communities where they now lived. Using their drawings, which Creates called "memory maps," she visited the abandoned place each elder had described, took a photograph of a landmark that had been drawn on the map and, where appropriate to the story, collected an object from the landscape: a piece of blackberry sod, a small pile of sand, some buttercups, a stone, a bundle of saltwater grass, a log with a bolt. She combined the map, photograph, found item, and story each person had told her into an assemblage; altogether there are eighteen assemblages in the series titled *The Distance Between Two Points Is Measured in Memories*, Labrador 1988.

In all these cases, the Labrador maps involved people picturing themselves in a place. The stories they told, more often than not, revealed sadness at something lost as a result of having moved from traditional areas to fixed communities. "I had no expectations of

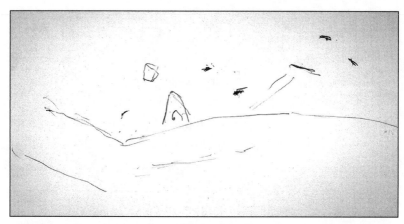

Memory map drawn by Rosie Webb (pencil on paper, 8.5 x 11 inches/
22 x 28 cm). An excerpt from the assemblage by Marlene Creates titled
Rosie Webb, from the series *The Distance Between Two Points Is Measured
in Memories* ©CARCC (assemblage of two black-and-white photographs
and one story panel, selenium-toned silver prints; memory map
drawn by Rosie Webb, pencil on paper; and a piece of blackberry sod).
Collection of The Canada Council Art Bank, Ottawa. Marlene Creates.

what they would draw," Creates said. "Any minimal mark was satis-
factory to me." Some of the maps were indeed minimal, with the
gentle outlines of islands or bays. Others were like town plans, with
homes or tent sites lined up. On a few of the maps, some place
names or other words in English, Inuktitut or Innu-aimun appeared.

Creates was not entirely without an agenda. She knew that in
northern Labrador there were three groups with historic connections to the land: the Inuit who lived on the coast; the Naskapi
Innu, who had traditionally lived inland most of the year hunting
caribou; and the Euro-Canadians, known locally as Settlers, who
had most of their contact with the Inuit. Because of the experience
she'd had on Baffin Island with Craig d'Entremont and Paul Idlout
and their divergent perceptions of the same landscape, Creates made
sure to visit Nain and Hopedale, which are mainly Inuit communities, and Davis Inlet, an Innu community. She wanted to see if the

maps the elders drew mirrored any cultural differences. But none revealed themselves. What the memory maps did show, dramatically and poignantly, were the differences between the experiences of the men and the women.

Among Creates's favourites are the maps made by Rosie Webb and her husband, Chesley Webb. Rosie's map is dominated by a tri-angular form squatting right in the middle of the page, astride a path with a few marks on the periphery. "This pointy shape on her map is the smokehouse," said Creates. "It was the foremost feature when she described the place, and these little marks are where the houses were. She's describing the territory around the smokehouse." This is the text panel in the assemblage, which is what Rosie Webb told Marlene Creates as she drew the map:

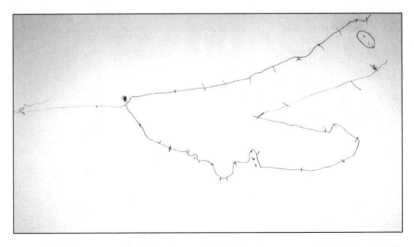

Memory map drawn by Chesley Webb (pencil on paper, 8.5 x 11 inches/ 22 x 28 cm). An excerpt from the assemblage by Marlene Creates titled Chesley Webb, from the series *The Distance Between Two Points Is Measured in Memories* ©CARCC (assemblage of two black-and-white photographs and one story panel, selenium-toned silver prints; memory map drawn by Chesley Webb, pencil on paper; and sand from Webb's Bay). Collection of the MacKenzie Art Gallery, Regina. Marlene Creates.

I had ten boys and one girl. I had fifteen altogether. Some of them is dead. I don't know how many grandchildren. I never counted. I stayed up there in Webb's Bay ever since I got married. When we got married there was only one house, his father's house. That old house is still up. Log house. Smokehouse and everything up there. Smokes char. Use what they call blackberry leaves. Cuts out square pieces of sod. It was a boat, half a boat. Just the top of a boat put on the ground. Old man's house here. Path up to our house. And Jim's house up here. Our house. And Ronald's. And Henry's little old house there. It's old that smokehouse. Way over a hundred years it must be now. Still uses it. Still good.

Rosie's map describes the cluster of one family's dwellings — the only family living near this bay — while Chesley's map is more of an aerial view showing the entire bay and many kilometres of coast-line, reflecting his hunting, trapping and fishing territory. On Ches-ley's map, the area of their home is but a dark dot at the bottom of the bay. "Rosie's whole territory, everything in her map, is con-tained in that dot on Chesley's map," Creates said. "His sense of his territory is the whole bay." These are Chesley's words as he drew the map for Creates:

That's where the house is, in The Bay. Webb's Bay they call it. Starting around here, close to it anyway, all that shore was all traps. All around there was full of traps. You'd place them so far apart. Couldn't do it all in one day. We'd do this shore one day, then the next day you'd do the other shore. And then the next day up this way, across the land. Then it would be time to see the others again. That used to be hard too. You'd leave, dark in the morning, get back at ten o'clock at night. Walking all day. Foxes and mink. Start fishing after break-up. It's all sand. You wouldn't believe how deep that harbour was. The tide takes it. It fills up every deep place. Now

you can't anchor a boat there low tide. It's all sand. Now it's hard
for me to get the boat in.

Time and again that is how things came out with the men and
the women. "This is an amazing drawing; this is Clara Voisey's,"
said Creates, showing the map of seemingly haphazard lines, almost
like doodles. "This is just the area around the Voisey house — the
shore and the vegetable gardens. This next map, by her brother Jim,
contains hundreds of square miles of the Labrador coast on the
same size piece of paper. And he names off every little island, river
and bay. It's perfectly logical: The women were at home doing all
the domestic work and looking after children — Rosie Webb said
she had fifteen children! — and the men were covering a lot of
territory hunting and fishing."

In the series, there are two exceptions to the gender differences.
Bert Saunders, a Settler raised in Old Davis Inlet, had polio when
he was a boy, and he told Creates how he was unable to go out
with the rest of the men fishing. He was restricted in his movement, and that came out in his map, which is a closely circumscribed view of the Hudson's Bay post at Old Davis Inlet. The
other exception was Hilda Dickers, whose map outlines an entire
bay. Hilda and her husband, John, just the two of them, lived for
forty years at the bottom of a bay in northern Labrador. Being
childless, she spent a lot of her time hunting. The territory she
drew is the entire bay and the nearby hills.

Creates was clearly happy with the results with the Labrador
experience. In 1989, she decided to extend the memory map project
by focusing on her relatives in Newfoundland, concentrating on
three "bits of landscape" in Lewisporte and Joe Batt's Arm on Fogo
Island: the places where her grandmother, grandfather and great-
grandmother were born. The resulting maps reveal the subtle dynamics
associated with the pattern of land use in rural Newfoundland, in

which land has traditionally been passed down from generation to generation, ever smaller pieces inherited through paternal lineage by sons and nephews and, only rarely, by daughters. To see what such memory maps are able to show, the viewer must suspend all belief in the cartographic presumption of accuracy and precision. "The maps are neither detailed nor accurate," wrote Joan M. Schwartz, chief of the Photography Acquisition and Research Section of the National Archives of Canada, in the publication accompanying the exhibit. "The spatial relations they communicate are more idiosyncratic than cartographic. The maps reveal more about dynamics than distances, more about the geographical imagination than topographical reality, more about identity than genealogy, more about the character of memory than the nature of land."

In some respects the resulting artworks, *Places of Presence: Newfoundland Kin and Ancestral Land, Newfoundland 1989–1991*, were even more revealing than *The Distance Between Two Points Is Measured in Memories*. With the artist as part of the storyline, Creates herself sketched three memory maps. In her first map, of the part of Lewisporte where her grandmother, Mary Turner, lived, Creates drew trim and tidy lines and annotated blocks — Glenna's and Jennie's houses, the potato garden — all in a row, separated from the gas station by what appears to be a thicket or meadow labelled "wild." There is the "old cemetery" and, most significantly, "great-grandmother Tamar's rose bush" still clinging on the rocky shoreline that defines the top edge of the sheet. There is a certain intimacy to the map, even though by all accounts Creates was an outsider. The memory maps of the same place, drawn by her relatives, took different approaches and reflected different memories: One showed the sweep of the harbour; another was dominated by a rail line that did not show up in other maps; another had the shoreline along the bottom; and still others gave no clue that there is a harbour or waterway. The cemetery was the one landmark that most often appeared on the maps. The viewer is well advised not to try to reconcile the inconsistencies in topographical features or spatial relationships. It would feel like a superfluous exercise.

The series of memory maps relating to where Creates's grand-father, George Layte, was born in Lewisporte exposed an entirely different set of tension points and contradictions over land owner-ship. The memory maps sketched by four of her cousins, Harold, Carl, Fred and Gilbert, all showed how the land was divided by her great-grandfather, James Layte. These were the most precisely drawn maps; Harold Layte even got out his ruler to draw his map, though for some reason he indicated strips of land for four of the brothers, not five. All the maps drawn for Creates have only men's names on the land.

Creates filled in the detail not evident on the maps: "This one is really graphic," she said of Carl Layte's. "It shows this block of land that says 'James Layte,' that's my great-grandfather. He took up this block of land in Lewisporte, and he's the one who split the land between his five sons: Albert, George, John, Alfred, Arthur. Then Arthur split his strip between his sons, so it says 'Fred, Harold, Carl and Gilbert.' That's the traditional land pattern in Newfoundland — the land is inherited by sons. Where my grandmother was born, that land has actually passed to four generations of women. I asked my cousin Joan Freake why. She said the reason that the land has passed to women is that there wasn't anyone else to give it to, only women. The assumption is that had there been a man, it would have gone to him."

Gender differences again showed up in the most subtle of ways: Generally, the maps drawn by women showed the shoreline at the top of the map, while on the maps made by men the shoreline was at the bottom of the page. The female map-maker imagined her feet on the land, with her eyes looking out to sea; the men perceived the territory from the water, looking towards the land. The memory maps showed clearly how people place themselves by the way they picture their world.

Creates had one more map that she was eager to point out. It was perhaps the most idiosyncratic map of them all. Drawn by Effie Kavli *née* Layte, the map sheet was almost entirely blank but for a series of very closely drawn lines and what looked like three tepees, almost at the very top in the left-hand corner. It was hard not to meet this map with a blank stare, but there was much more to it than met the eye. The accompanying text panel by Effie offered a clue. Hers is a story about another of Creates's great-grandmothers:

> *Old Grandmother Layte, she used to live with my mother. My dear, what a job we used to have to keep her, she used to run away from us. She'd go down the big long lane from our house, right back where Carl has his house now. The poor soul. She'd look back to see if we were watching her, and when she'd get out to the road, my dear, go. She could go like the wind . . . As far as I'm concerned, she wanted to get away, to get free. She was old, but she was smart. . .*
>
> *There was our house there, see. That's the only house that was there then, in that long lane. There was nobody else. . .*

"To me that's a very interesting drawing," said Creates. "The little triangular shapes are the houses, and this is the laneway. So strong in her mind is the laneway that she went over it again and again with her pencil."

Marlene Creates the artist has moved on from memory maps to create meditations on everyday public signage in the landscape, both urban and rural. She is no longer searching for her way home. But these maps and stories remain with her every day. They are part and parcel of her personal geography. Their lines have been drawn from the heart, conforming to their own geometric rule: that at the intersection of place and memory lies a truth that shapes generations.

WHILE CARTOGRAPHY IS considered a science and the map as clinically accurate as an EEG readout, the artist has long had an honoured and important role beside the map-maker. It was the artist who rendered the fear, excitement and expectation that swirled in the imagination of Old World royalty, investors and expedition leaders. All too often, artists were encouraged to embellish the information about what lay behind the western horizon, making the popular maps of the day like anticipatory memory maps. *The Map of the North Atlantic Coast of the New World*, taken from an anonymous Portuguese atlas and dated to c. 1540, is one the earliest maps of the New World; it is adorned with pictures by a French artist who clearly had never set eyes on the mysterious lands beyond the European horizon. The map shows unicorns, elephants and lions on the prowl. To give artists their due, some of the art accompanying maps was based on first-hand observation of the flora and fauna and daily life. The Spanish and Portuguese explorers, in particular, usually had a painter on their expeditions, whose primary role was to draw or paint maps from the rough charts made by navigators. Occasionally, though, the artist would also paint what he saw of the land and Native people, and add some monsters in unknown waters for good measure. Some maps, for example, carried elaborate woodcuts in panels illustrating the techniques of catching and flensing whales and of hunting polar bears and walrus. According to historian D. B. Quinn, the French eventually made the most use of artists. "The systematic use of a painter to record the natural products and peoples of North America begins with the French in 1564 when Jacques Le Moyne de Morgues was sent to make a survey of Florida; a selection of his drawings appeared in the form of engravings in 1591," Quinn wrote in *The Discovery of North America.*

Once the New World was settled, however, maps rarely showed an artistic flourish. Cartography was left to cartographers, art to artists. Maps that were a pleasure to behold, those by John Tallis being fine examples, were decorative creations rather than story-telling vehicles. In past decades, however, it has been popular to deconstruct maps and see in them the exercise of power. Artists, in particular, have seen the rich possibilities of incorporating mapping conventions and map artifacts into their creations. The phenomenon has been strong in Canada but is now showing up in other parts of the world. An eclectic exhibition in London, England, in the summer of 2001 showcased the works of more than thirty artists in Europe who use maps both literally and conceptually. Titled *The Map Is Not the Territory*, the exhibition provided ample proof that many artists are cartographers busting to break free. On display was a *Fetish Map of London*, text-maps of Venice, a map of objects on a desktop. An artist based in Italy engraved zinc wall-sculptures with maps inspired by archaeology, while another reconfigured islands and towns using data from population statistics to set the geographical spaces against each other in imaginary conflicts. Artist and filmmaker Peter Greenaway exhibited four works from his *A Walk Through H* series, in which "the traveller created the territory as he walked through it."

In Canada, artists such as Bhat Boy, Linda Cronin, Carol Rowland-Ulmann, and Sara Graham have all been inspired by maps and map-making. Many create art by recreating the map, a specialty of Calgary artist Sara Graham, who cuts up the ubiquitous road map, reconstructs it into sheets showing neighbourhoods and binds the result in a book format. But no visual artist can match Landon Mackenzie for sheer knowledge of historical cartography and the subtle context of map-making. Far from obliterating conventional maps, Mackenzie's apochryphal paintings start with facsimiles of significant maps from Canada's past that the artist then layers with her own stories and impressions. What results is still a map, but you are not quite sure where it takes you.

Mackenzie's commitment to understanding Canada through its maps and map-makers is easy to understand in light of her upbringing. Both her parents studied history at university, and her great-uncle, George Douglas, was an accomplished Arctic explorer; he led an expedition up the Coppermine River in 1911 as the first white explorer to use the map sketched by Samuel Hearne. Mackenzie has memories of her great-uncle telling her stories of the North, though he died when she was still young. "The little red line on the fold-out map at the back of his book *Lands Forlorn*, published in 1914, became a calling to the imagination," Mackenzie said. But it was Douglas's wife who would have the most enduring impact. "My arm-chair travelling techniques were learned at the skirt of my great-aunt Frances Mackenzie Douglas, at Stony Lake and Lakefield, Ontario, until she died in the mid-1990s," said Mackenzie, who was brought up in Toronto. "She organized my memory of his trips. What food was taken, what materials, what instruments, what ammunition, tents, everything. I revelled in her knowledge of the 'North' and she had a keen listener in me. Though her famous explorer husband, George Douglas, died when I was about ten, Frances, who I called Aunt Chinka, kept his stories and treks alive for me."

Mackenzie finally did go north, to the Yukon, in 1976. After studying at the Nova Scotia College of Art and Design, she worked for the Yukon government through the spring and summer in a job that she would later regard as filled with irony: She was a sign painter who converted road signs from miles to kilometres. The Yukon continued to cast a spell over her, even when she was back south attending graduate school at Concordia University in Montreal. She returned to the Yukon and tried to experience it as others had before her. She ran the rivers, climbed the mountains and obsessed over the migration of caribou.

As an artist, Mackenzie first attracted attention in 1981, when she won first prize at the Quebec Biennale of Painting for her *Lost*

River Series. The paintings, sprawling 1.8 by 2.1 metres, featured dark images populated by wolf-caribou hybrid creatures prowling in silhouette. Her next body of work, named the *Cluny Series*, again borrowed from her Yukon experiences, with strange creatures stalking the land of the midnight sun. Always in Mackenzie's mind were the circumstances under which the great maps of the day were assembled and the far-reaching effects they had on Canada's development. "These guys were trekking through the bush with their instruments, keeping their guides in line, keeping themselves in line," she said. "Then they would go back to London or Ottawa and have their notes transcribed by a printing house, tidy up the maps so that the person paying for the trek would be pleased. Somebody's got a grubstake somewhere. These tidy red lines. That's what fascinates me."

Over time, Mackenzie decided to approach her painting in a way similar to how her friend Canadian novelist Jane Urquhart approaches her writing. Urquhart uses pieces of documented history and extrapolates a fantasy. Though maps do not have the same linear progression as a novel, they are still storytelling vehicles, so Mackenzie set out to create a different sort of historical fiction. Before putting brush to canvas, though, she felt she had to immerse herself in historical cartography. Beginning in 1993, she became a regular at map archives in Canada and visited the map room at the Scott Polar Institute in Cambridge. She chummed with the archivists, so that they would allow her extra time and access to the material and opportunities to photograph precious maps of such notables as Samuel Hearne, Peter Fidler and David Thompson. ("I get so excited when I see some of these maps," she said. "You have to pull me off the ceiling.") But knowing from her own experience that there was always more to a map than met the eye, she searched the records and accounts for clues to what the maps served to obscure.

Mackenzie wondered how women viewed the same space and their role in exploration, which at the time was mainly a male privilege.

And she noted that while explorers were almost totally dependent on Aboriginals to move overland, their contribution and sensibility were rarely acknowledged. "There's quite a lot of Aboriginal collaboration in the colonial mapping. No matter what their mapping tradition has been, whether drawn on rock or in sand or sung, they've got their traditions on how to say 'beyond that mountain is this bay, in that bay is this river, and along that river is a very dangerous part which has a lot of white water,'" she said. "They obviously had it down, how to handle these enormous distances."

Archivists in Saskatchewan were particularly accommodating, which was one reason why, in the early 1990s, Mackenzie decided to begin a series of paintings — a novelette, as she calls it — in that province. It was in *The Saskatchewan Paintings (1993–1997)* that she started making use of maps, mining information and other archival records, blending them with her own observations and travelogues within the layers of the pictures. She explored how maps and language served to establish colonial claims and to displace Native inhabitants. On maps of her own design she wanted to trace the trajectory of exploration, to untangle the stories caught in the thatch of official maps, treaties and explorer accounts.

As the *Saskatchewan* series was wrapping up, Mackenzie began looking for material dating from when John Palliser did his 1857 scientific study of the prairies. As a result of Palliser's map and commentary, political pressures arose to make the prairies "productive," giving rise to new forms of maps by geologists and railway titans. Mackenzie now had a new use for the piles of information she had collected over the years on the districts of Saskatchewan and Assiniboia. Her next project uncovered the mental and historical territory of Athabasca. "What interests me in looking at historic maps is how the notations and calculations every five years change the truth about the representation of that space," she said. "If you take Lake Athabasca as a hit point, you can see how many different ways it's spelled, different ways it's drawn, different shapes it has. It's like a hub; who goes in and out. Also, Athabasca was a fantasy of British exploration of space: I'm going *into* the Athabasca."

As an artist-cartographer, Mackenzie does not obliterate the recognizable maps of the past. Instead, she invites the viewer to acknowledge that past and the way the stories of that time were told, and then to see the uncharted maps and to hear the disembodied voices. In her approach to the works in the *Tracking Athabasca* series, she started with several maps of Athabasca, looking at the region from different vantage points and working with a scale of one inch on the map to one foot on her pictures. "It goes from being a piece of linen to the beginning of my territory," she said. To disorient the viewer, she sometimes flips north and south or east and west and the scale of different entries. Viewers are immersed in

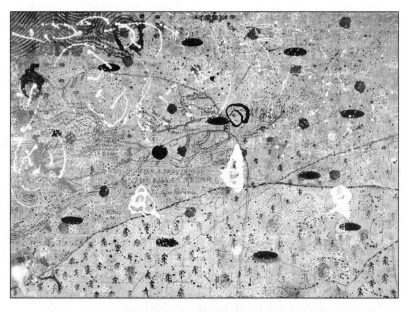

Macke it to Thy Other Side (Land of Little Sticks) (acrylic on canvas, 89 x 122 inches/228.6 x 312.4 cm), from Landon Mackenzie's *Tracking Athabasca* series, 1999. Chris Gergley.

the pieces, by design. They are all 2.3 high by 3.1 metres wide and densely configured. Mackenzie works within this format by laying the canvas on the ground and stepping onto it to fill it up. "The dimensions work so that I can make sense of this one inch to one foot grid, it makes sense of the body being lost in the space as opposed to a nice large-sized painting," she said. "We've become too accustomed on how to negotiate a picture. I want people to fall off the periphery. And I want to seduce them from forty feet away and four inches away. That's really deliberate on my part. In some places, as you walk closer to them, they develop into a precarious balance of chaos and order, and for others, as you walk toward them, they develop into more clarity and detail. You have to use your body to get the most from them."

A good example of the shifting focus that Mackenzie speaks of shows up in *Macke it to Thy Other Side (Land of Little Sticks)*, completed in 1999. Stand thirty metres away and the eye immediately zones in on acid yellow splotches, which, if she offered a legend to her map, would indicate abstract warning signs for deposits of uranium tailings. Black disks, frozen ponds or core sample holes from mining strikes hover like unidentified flying objects. Lines transect the terrain with the seeming logic of a map. Snowflakes lie suspended over fur country. Green dots, seen from the side, appear like pompoms from Mackenzie's childlike imagination. Take four steps forward and you will notice the makings of the boreal forest and the treeline. Step closer still and you will begin to make out words and phrases: "After a draught of Nelson & Hayes Rivers," "Deer hedge where the French had places of worship." South of the treeline, it is easy to make out the red grid of the map; north of the treeline, the grid is but a shadow.

Elements of the painting were initially laid down in collaboration with a friend from Fort Chipewyan, a remote community on Lake Athabasca. Doris Whitehead, of Cree, Chipewyan and Scottish ancestry, talked to Mackenzie about her complex and sometimes tragic childhood while drawing a diagram of her northern village on the linen stapled to Mackenzie's studio floor. During the all-day visit, Whitehead said, "I'm also a descendant of Governor Simpson. It's rumoured that he fathered over two hundred children when he was factor at Fort Chipewyan." Mackenzie recalled the shock of the insight: "I went, Ding! These guys left their genetic code all across the North . . . this other world that they were also sexually exploring. There was this tension, certainly in Hudson's Bay memoirs, about what to do with the men, because they were not military men used to holding in their libido. They were ordinary guys way out there in the cold."

Mackenzie had invited her Cree friend to draw a map of Fort Chipewyan to help explain the social, economic and religious conditions of her life. Whitehead's contemporary map begins the story of *Macke it to Thy Other Side (Land of Little Sticks)*; it was first drawn in Magic Marker and then overwritten by Mackenzie in her signature icing-tube paint. The map was oriented with the north facing down and had places marked, such as Safety (grandmother's place) and Danger. If you look closely, you can make out the map in places, Safety peeking out in a bit of appliqué encrusted in layers of acrylic. There are sprays of white blobs, which could be snowfalls or stand-ins for sexual spoor left by European explorers.

There are seven other maps in Mackenzie's *Tracking Athabasca* series, including *Winter Road, Diamond Mines*, where the effect is much cooler than *Macke it to Thy Other Side*; its surface is layered with beads, lace doilies and stones. In *Space Station (Falls Said to Be the Largest in the Known World so Far)*, Mackenzie offers a view of Athabasca from a satellite beyond the pull of gravity.

The pieces in *Tracking Athabasca* are unmistakably Canadian meditations. Mackenzie, after all, has lived in Newfoundland, Nova Scotia, Prince Edward Island, Quebec, Ontario, British Columbia

Space Station (Falls Said to Be the Largest in the Known World so Far)
(acrylic on canvas, 89 x 122 inches/228.6 x 312.4 cm), from
Landon Mackenzie's *Tracking Athabasca* series, 1999. Chris Gergley.

and the Yukon, and was spoonfed on the exploits of her great-uncle.
She has been out on the land and understands the folds of rock and
the smells of the forest and tundra, much like the explorers and fur
traders of the Athabasca region. But unlike those men, Mackenzie
does not draw her maps in the field. She told writer Robin Laurence
years ago that she refuses to sketch while on the land. "I don't want
to work outdoors," she said. "I've always made landscape from looking into imaginative space." Her sanctuary is the Vancouver warehouse studio where she has worked for the past fifteen years, a cross
between a laboratory and an urban wilderness. It has high ceilings
and smells like an old factory; a row of windows open to the North
Shore mountains and the squawks of seagulls. Inside is the debris of
paints, maps, books, doilies, sequins, working clothes, slides, camp
kitchen, cot, old photographs and piles of notes.

In the studio are four large paintings, unfinished but well along. They are the first works from Mackenzie's next series, titled *Houbarts Hope*, the third part of her trilogy. The title was inspired by a 1636 map of Hudson Bay; "Hope" is a safe harbour for Hudson's Bay traders who find themselves in a harsh, unfamiliar environment. Houbart is a friendly ghostly force in Mackenzie's imagination. "The title also fits the idea of the brain as a new frontier with its own hemispheres and veins like rivers and layers of water like oceans," she said. "A sequence of water roads eventually leading into the interior, penetrating the imaginative space." For this body of work, Mackenzie is researching a variety scientific imaging tools — MRI and CT scans among them. No doubt they will show up somewhere in *Houbarts Hope*, pointing the way to deeper ground.

IN MANY WAYS, THE MAPS THAT give shape to our world are inherited images. They are given to us by professionals schooled in the conventions and rules of cartography, guided by the belief in empirical science and a confidence in the nature of reality. Marlene Creates and Landon Mackenzie have both staked a claim to laying down lines on a page, and in the process, have reinvented map-making to express their imaginative wanderings and observations of cultural and community change. Their "maps" define different shapes, different realities.

Communities, too, are taking charge of their own maps, with equally intriguing results. These maps have the ineffable ability to synchronize with the emotional currents of individuals and communities, and to give visual expression to hard-to-get-at impulses. One of the most ambitious community mapping projects in recent years was *Our Own Backyard: Mapping the Grandview-Woodland Community*, initiated by the Institute for the Humanities at Simon Fraser University. Grandview-Woodland is located in Vancouver, centred on Commercial Drive. The project kicked off in September 1996 when residents were asked, "What do you value about Grandview-Woodland: What is important, unique or interesting about it?" It immediately caught on because of the quirky view of what constituted a map. Residents were encouraged to define the "shape" of the community through paintings, photographs, quilts and even story-telling. Adults made facsimiles of their favourite places in clay tiles. An artist mapped the locations and nature of celebrations in the community. High-school students spent a year taking photographs of special places and then created a collage, with the resulting images on a large map of Grandview-Woodland that they created. The "maps" were eventually compiled into an "atlas" that served not only to mirror a pride of home, but also to aid in community planning.

Across the Strait of Georgia, British Columbia artist and geographer Briony Penn initiated a similar project involving grassroots cartography. Penn created a lush and detailed map in watercolour of natural and cultural features of Fulford Harbour, her Salt Spring Island community. While she created the map with her brush, the information was based on reminiscences of several Fulford Harbour elders and observations from children. The result was an elegant hybrid that mixed natural history with local lore. There were stands of Himalayan blackberry and purple honeysuckle bushes, soaring bald eagles and breaching Dalls' porpoises. And there were annotations of environmental change: "Herring used to spawn in Fulford Harbour every spring, sometimes in such number that the roe would carpet the harbour. The last spawn was in 1983." There was the legend of the Indian reserve haunted by the ghost of Indian Charlie, and little digs that only locals would understand: "There are differences between those growing up on Beaver Point and those on Isabella Point. Maybe it's to do with whether you woke up facing east or west!"

Conventional maps have done much to channel exploratory urges, to expose the riches beneath the ground and sea, to seduce the

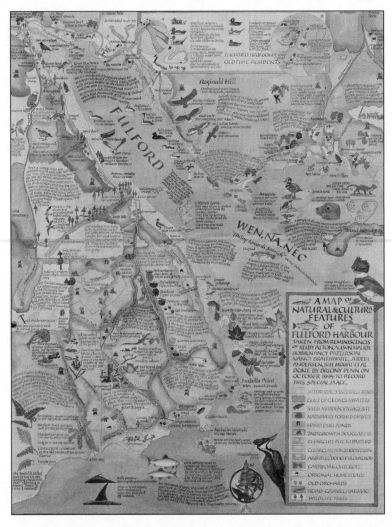

A Map of Natural & Cultural Features of Fulford Harbour/taken from reminiscences of Ruby Alton, Alison Maude, Bob & Nancy Patterson, Nancy Braithwaite, Judith Anderson, Sue Mouat et al. done by Briony Penn on October 1994 to record this special place, Briony Penn, 1994. Courtesy Briony Penn.

willing. But they have generally been created by those on the outside, looking in, around and over. Now, maps are being made from
the inside out, proving equally adept at teasing out the emotion of
memory and place. These ideas are what Landon Mackenzie plays
with every working day. In a performance script that accompanied
the Saskatchewan series, she spoke about how "language and pre-
scription organize the spaces of land and the heart and how we
internalize their forces":

> *My desk is covered with fragments of photographs from the archives,
> . . . trail maps of the Districts of Saskatchewan and Assiniboia of
> the old North West Territories. It's a place I'm from and not from.
> Though I'm from Canada, I'm not from all of its parts. Though I'm
> not from the prairie, it's a part of my identity by its absence.*
>
> *I remember hearing a quote from Stephen Leacock on a CBC
> radio show: "I've never been to Hudson Bay but I'm homesick for
> it." This is me and Saskatchewan. I chose it and it chose me back. I
> went there seeking visibility, but only internally. I'm playing with
> crossing emotional territory with historical and geographical space.
> I've become familiar with dual mapping.*

10

SURVIVAL REDUX

IT WAS A HOLLYWOOD MOMENT, and it came at the most inopportune time. I was traipsing on the Oak Ridges Moraine, somewhere in Uxbridge, Ontario. It was day one of the 2001 Ontario Orienteering Championships, and as part of a delightful homespun tradition of this oddball sport, rank amateurs can "run" the course alongside the pros. Actually, seeing the course, feeling the course, is as important as the running of it. You have a compass, a specially designed and lovingly assembled map, a whistle, a punch card and your natural wits. Easily qualifying as a rank amateur and with a fairly low supply of wits, I had three-quarters of the course behind me and a whole mess of burrs to show for the effort. I had kept fairly close to the trails, unlike the true competitors who avoid trails like deer skirt open ground. Juniors barely able to spell their names had sped by me. As I tried to discern my position while on a meadowy ridge, tried yet again to reconcile what I thought I saw on the map with where I actually stood, my epiphanous moment arrived. A scrawny lad came out of nowhere, walked calmly across my path as if I did not exist, and continued straight into a head-high stand of goldenrod. A little rustle, a mysterious breeze, and he was gone. Vaporized. At that moment I was Ray, looking out on my Field of Dreams, and there in front of me was my mentor, Terence Mann, offering a nervous giggle before walking into the ineffable otherworld.

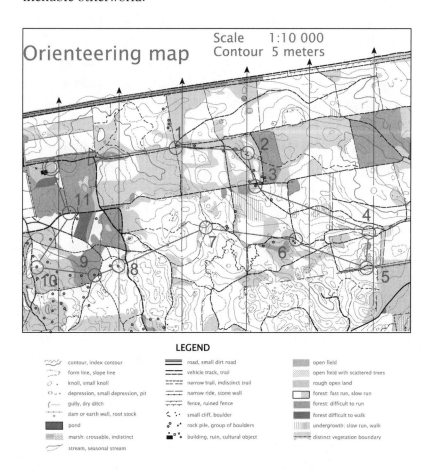

Glen Major orienteering map, one of the courses created for the 2001 Ontario Orienteering Championships. Orienteering athletes must travel between control points, reading map cues as quickly as possible.
Courtesy Toronto Orienteering Club.

The frustration that had built up over my cartographic ignorance dissolved. I had only two thoughts: "There goes a young man who can see between the contours," and "Boy, I'd like to follow him into the goldenrod." I didn't, of course. I found the next control point in my clumsy, inefficient way, and then the next, before finishing after one hour and forty-five minutes. That epiphanous moment showed me how utterly unprepared I was to survive out in the wilds, but also how supremely confident some people still are in moving on and through unfamiliar terrain.

I arrived at the orienteering event in October 2001 with the barest of knowledge of the sport. I knew it involved cross-country running between control points scattered over natural terrain, such as a park or forest, with nothing but a map and compass to guide competitors. I knew, too, that it had deep roots in Scandinavian countries, going back to the late nineteenth century, that the first competition had been held in 1897 in Norway, and that orienteering was just a few participating countries short of qualifying as an Olympic sport. Since hearing of orienteering years ago, I was curious to experience it first-hand but also surprised that it was not more popular in North America. There are perhaps five thousand orienteering regulars in Canada.

"Yeah, it is kind of surprising that it's not bigger than it is," said Annette Van Tyghem, whom I met soon after arriving at the Ontario Championships. "But it's now on the Ontario educational curriculum and we do attract a great variety of people, young and old. Blue-collar people enjoy the competition, and the educated like the physical activity and mental challenge." Van Tyghem lives in Campbellville, Ontario, and is a member of the Gators Orienteering club in Guelph. She did not get into the sport until she was thirty years old but has made up for lost time. She and her family are orienteering enthusiasts and she works with high schools to develop orienteering programs for students. She has also helped make maps for competitions.

As we stood behind her minivan and she prepared for the race, Van Tyghem offered a few pointers. The idea is to identify each control site in order; each site is circled on the map and flagged on the ground. To verify a visit, she said, the competitor uses a punch hanging next to the flag to mark his or her control card. In orienteering, the map is almost everything. For one thing, it dictates how fast the competitor runs. "The golden rule of orienteering is, 'Never run faster than you know exactly where you are on the map,'" she said. The pros will study short sections of the map, quickly sizing up the best route from the contour spacing and natural and manmade features. They formulate a plan to get from one point to the next and then set off quickly, looking to identify features that they expect to see and to identify the next features they expect to encounter, all the while stealing glances at the ground to avoid exposed roots, boulders or, the orienteer's bane, poison ivy. Amateurs like me follow simpler courses and spend time learning the idiosyncrasies of an orienteering map.

Orienteering maps are specially produced for the sport, and they are often the prime subject of discussion at the trailhead after the race is over. Inevitably, there is some grumbling that the map failed to show one feature or another. But you rarely hear complaints from competitors who are aware of what goes into making an orienteering map. Typically, it can take a year and a half to prepare a map for an orienteering event such as the Ontario championships, and costs five to six thousand dollars. If you scan the legend of an orienteering map you will know why. As well as the standard features of a topographical map, orienteering maps show small knolls, gullies, earth walls or rootstocks, indistinct marsh or trails, rock piles or groups of boulders, building ruins, forest that is a fast run or a slow run.

To capture that kind of detail is not an easy task. At the championships, I met Mark Adams, an orienteering champion who has helped make countless maps. Adams told me he had been in the sport since he was ten years old, dragged by his parents to "wayfaring" group activities. He has competed in the World Cup circuit and in one World Championships. "I learned how to make maps from my dad, and made a meagre but interesting living from orienteering map-making for four or five years," he said. "My dad has been mapping quite a bit since retiring."

Adams gave me the rundown on how the maps are put together. The first step is to find an aerial photograph of the course being mapped at the right height and scale. The photograph has to be taken in the spring, after the snow has melted but before tree leaves are out. That way, the photogrammetrist who uses the photographs can get a clear view of the ground and capture precise height and shape of landforms to build a base map. Precision is key: Contours must be accurate and vegetation lines — changes in type or height of vegetation — must be clear.

"With the base map in hand, a qualified field checker then goes into the field and covers every square metre of the land in question, verifying the information present on the base map and adding everything that can only be seen from the ground," said Adams. The field checker also "makes sense" of the base-map data; for example, the base map may indicate myriad vegetation changes, but not all will be visible from the ground. The field checker will add to and remove from the base-map detail. "In the end, any feature will be added to the map that can be of use to someone passing by and trying to keep track of their precise location," he said, "right down to one-metre-high boulders, small depressions and rises in the ground, one-metre and higher rock faces and cliffs, and so on." Finally, the field-checked data are drafted using a computer graphics or cartography software program before being printed out.

Being both a mapper and a runner, Adams is in the best position to differentiate between an accurate and less helpful map, and competitors tend to value his opinion when they are doing a post-mortem of the race. As far as he is concerned, a good orienteering map provides a consistent and accurate representation of the terrain. If the mapper has added small rock piles in one part of the map, for example, the orienteer would expect to find similar features of the same size pictured in the same way in another part of the map. Likewise, if forest of a particular runnability — density — is marked with a particular symbol in one area, say as "open forest," an orienteer will be frustrated if, in another area, similar vegetation is marked differently, say as "difficult to run."

"It takes patience, more patience and still more patience to make a good orienteering map, along with a good eye for the shapes of landforms," Adams said.

Some features are fairly objective in nature, and therefore easier to map. Laying down a fenceline or trail, for example, involves sighting with compass and measuring distance by careful pace counting. But vegetation changes and landform shapes, for example, are mappable only by eye, using the subjective judgment of the mapper, and this takes more art and practice.

The orienteering maps contain another useful feature for competitors — north lines. They are parallel lines that run from magnetic north to magnetic south rather than from true north to true south, making it easier to quickly take a bearing using a compass. Sometimes not even the north lines are any help. I was about halfway through the course, heading for control point number five, looking for a stream that I identified on the map. Maybe I wanted to see it too much, but I looked at a dry gully that I thought could very well be a stream, at least in the springtime. I later learned that I was "bending the map," making reality conform to my expectations of what I wanted to see rather than seeing what was there. Adams assured me that bending the map happens to the best of them. "This is what one tends to do when one is tired especially, but it's a common human weakness," he said. "It's gotta be the map that's wrong, it couldn't be me."

Adams did not admit to having bent the map himself. The fact that he has such experience making maps himself helps him when he runs a course. "Making maps teaches you that a map is a subjective interpretation, not ever a perfectly clear and orderly representation of the terrain," he said. "From this you learn to allow the mapper some latitude, and also that each map has to be learned anew; how did *this* mapper interpret *this* terrain?" Another advantage is being able to appreciate subtle variations in shape and height of landforms. "Contours are a very abstract way to show the shape of the land," he said. "Having practice in drawing the contours yourself makes you better at interpreting the contours on another mapper's map."

I asked Adams if he had ever been laid low by a faulty map in the heat of a race. He said it is more a matter of misinterpretation, offering as an example the time he was in France participating in a World Championships qualification race. He lost several minutes, and a chance at qualifying for the final, when he came out on a track on a hillside looking out over an area of very low but very thick undergrowth, bushes about knee-high. Adams picked up the story: "The mapper had chosen to represent this area by 'runnability' and had therefore coloured the area as dark green on the map. In my mind, dark green meant thick forest and I expected the area in front of me to be mapped according to visibility, which would have made it a shade of yellow, probably with green diagonal lines to represent the thick bushes along the ground. To make a long story short, I was in the right place, along my chosen route, but I thought I must have gone wrong. I turned and ran the wrong way looking for the 'right place,' and only later realized my mistake. Was it badly mapped? Perhaps. But the point is that I had been too rigid in my expectations of how the vegetation in that area should be mapped."

Of course, the orienteer's job would be a lot easier if he or she had a Global Positioning System (GPS) receiver in hand. Lock into a satellite orbiting high overhead, pick up your latitude and longitude, and leave the finest Norwegian wayfarer in your dust. Orienteering enthusiasts are at turns scornful of and curious about the new wave of navigational technology that allows them to pinpoint a location in an instant. They are quick to point out, rightly, that GPS readings cannot necessarily get you from point A to point B, that you still need some orienteering or map smarts to do that.

Still, GPS technology is improving by the day. The backbone of the system is an array of twenty-four satellites that orbit earth every twelve hours, communicating with ground stations. Developed by the American military, the system in its commercial incarnation was for years nothing but a curiosity. Even though anyone with a GPS receiver could capture his or her coordinates, the signal was intentionally degraded by the military to limit its effectiveness to outsiders. That changed on May 1, 2000, when the United States government decided to drop the interference. Overnight, GPS accuracy improved to some five metres from more than one hundred metres. The GPS boom began. Two short years later, slick GPS marketers have created a whole new industry — designer cartography. Case in point: Garmin, one of the prime manufacturers of receivers, now offers its eTrex receiver–map-makers in six colours. The basic comes in yellow. The "sea foam green" Venture model has a built-in database of cities and accepts uploadable points of interest. The "ocean blue" Legend adds an electronic map. The Summit packs sensors for barometric altimeter and electronic compass functions. The top-of-the-line Vista boasts a built-in map of North and South America, street maps of three major cities, twenty hiking routes, a digital compass and altimeter. It will give an accurate reading within three metres. Looks good on the coffee table, next to the picture book on the Rockies.

Two days after President Bill Clinton signed the order to free up
the full power of GPS, Dave Ulmer, an American engineering con-
sultant, filled a Tupperware container with some tacky treasures,
buried it in an out-of-the-way location, and then posted the location's precise coordinates of latitude and longitude to an Internet
mailing list for GPS fans, challenging them to use their GPS receivers
to find the container. The idea caught on like a pop fad; Ulmer had
unwittingly fathered a new pastime: geocaching, an ingenious
hybrid of orienteering and a scavenger hunt.

Consider the elegance of the geocaching model. Get a small
waterproof box or bucket, filll it with intriguing items to share or
give away — a map, music, games — and a logbook for visitors to
sign, and bury it in a secret location. Get a precise fix on the location of the box, go to the Web site *www.geocaching.com* and post
the latitude and longitude. And the scavenger hunt is on. Or
become a player by looking for a cache in your neck of the woods,
and when you discover the cache, leave something of your own in
the bucket. Caches could be on a rocky ledge in a wilderness area.
They could be in a subway station of a big city. On February 17,
2002, there were 12,426 active caches in 106 countries, and 631
caches in Canada alone.

It is interesting to speculate what Norman Hallendy's Inuit mentors would make of geocaching or competitive orienteering. Or, for
that matter, Bart Campbell's hobo grandfather, or the seafaring
fishermen of long ago singing their way up and down the coast of
Newfoundland and Labrador. To lay your head down each night, safe
and sound, was the reward for another day of survival. The Inuit's,
hoboes' and fishermen's maps — *inuksuit*, chalk drawings, songs —
were beacons that lit up the "dread frontier populated by the heated
imagination." To see map-reading turn into a game would be a rather
foreign concept to understand. Then again, they probably would be
the most enthusiastic and skilled orienteers on the planet.

For the Inuit in particular, modern topographical maps have long supplanted the most traditional forms of way-finding, such as *inuksuit*, although Inuktitut place names and the pride in Native knowledge persist. John MacDonald, who manages the Igloolik Research Centre for the Nunavut Research Institute, has written how topographical maps have affected the traditional way-finding practices of older Inuit. In *The Arctic Sky: Inuit Astronomy, Star Lore, and Legend*, MacDonald quoted one leader, Mark Ijjangiaq, on his experiences with modern maps. "When I first started reading maps I would travel to places by routes that were not frequented. I started to take routes that looked good on the map, which I found to be much better. The route passing through Qukiutitalik, that used to be taken by my father and others, is no longer the route I would take. I had found a better one." Ijjangiaq continued:

> The time Kupaaq and I took Atata Lursuu [Father Larson, a Roman Catholic priest] over to Mittimatalik [Pond Inlet] I did not believe in maps. There was a good trail that we could have followed easily, but Atata Lursuu insisted that we follow the trail that was marked on the map . . . So we ended up following what was shown on the map and sure enough it was the right trail to follow. From that moment on I started to believe in maps. I started to take maps seriously and was able to read them consistently. When one is travelling by dog-team we usually travel at a steady pace, so I am now able to determine how long it would take to reach a certain point on the map . . . even if I have never been to that place before. I am now convinced that maps are as accurate as they can be, but there was a time I did not believe in them.

Maybe Ijjangiaq and Mark Adams have more in common than one would think. Fathers Bressani and Petitot, the Delisle boys, John Mitchell, Hap Wilson, Ron Whistance-Smith, Marlene Creates and

Landon Mackenzie, yes, even that crypto-Nazi Charles Bedaux. They all had that riddle ringing in their ear, the quintessentially Canadian question mirrored in the maps of our lives: Where is here?

Here is where we are.

AFTERWORD

I FIRST TOOK THE MEASURE OF Digital Earth in August 2000. I
was in Ottawa at an international gathering of cartography's leading lights, and everywhere I turned — at plenary and poster ses-
sions, during keynote speeches, in the commercial hall — I heard
the rumbles of revolution. It seemed everyone wanted to stake a
claim to Digital Earth, a paradigm articulated two years earlier by
then former U.S. vice-president Al Gore. Gore had described a
vision of a multi-resolution, three-dimensional representation of
the planet that contained vast quantities of "geo-referenced data"
— bytes of information pegged to location. Children and adults
alike would navigate this immersive world through a head-
mounted display that would show earth from space, then use a
"data glove" to zoom in on regions, countries, even individual
houses. They would hyperlink to environmental, political or cultural
information, and take a magic carpet ride over a three-dimensional
picture of terrain, creating new maps infused with newsreel
footage, oral history and newspaper accounts.

At the Ottawa conference, the outlines of Digital Earth could be discerned. On display was a virtual globe that animated the planet with sound and movement. In another room was the first large holographic map, showing the Austrian Alps in three-dimensional brilliance on wafer-thin material. Researchers reported how some forty million maps were customized and distributed on the World Wide Web every day, via Yahoo and other portals. Real-time mapping, such as the monitoring of Alberta forest fires offered by the Canada Centre for Remote Sensing, would soon be freely available on the Internet. "Farmers with access to the technology of precision agriculture," said conference keynote speaker Michael Goodchild of the University of California, Santa Barbara, "can build maps of their fields... at much higher resolution than traditional soil maps, and can capture and compile detailed spatial information using devices attached to their harvesters and tractors."

In the years since, what I observed at the Ottawa conference has spread to the outside world. Technology has brought us ever closer to the do-it-yourself cartography of Digital Earth in ways not fully anticipated by Al Gore. You can already download customized maps to your Palm Pilot or other mobile device, as well as upload to the Internet information you collect from the field for others to use. The most far-reaching applications are being realized through Global Positioning Systems (GPS), which enable precise coordinates to be fed from satellites to hand-held receivers or even computer chips. For a number of years, police forces in North America have outfitted parolees with GPS bracelets to monitor their movements. Now a bracelet has been developed that combines GPS and wireless technology, allowing parents to track their children's movements via the Internet. There is even talk of implanting a dime-sized biosensor and GPS receiver in diabetics and other ailing patients, which would relay the patients' coordinates to doctors in case of a medical emergency. You would have to go back to the Renaissance for a similar period of map-making frenzy. At that time, one in five technologists was engaged in cartography, although the maps were tools of exploration and colonization and were meant for the political elite. In the future, maps will be tools of surveillance, and the map-makers will be the consumer elite.

All this merely creates a picture of where mapping technology is leading us. Are we willing to follow? Some of us may be, others not. People in the eastern Arctic lead more perilous lives than most Canadians. They are three times more likely to die from accidental death — drowning or dying from exposure while travelling at sea or over land. Of anyone, Northerners should be the most welcoming of technology that aids safe wayfaring. In fact, the Nunavut government a number of years ago tried to reduce the number of avoidable deaths by distributing seventy personal locator beacons to thirteen communities. The beacons were to be used by travellers to alert search-and-rescue operations in case of emergency. The thing is, most people refused to use the technology. "We can't make people take them out," Eric Doig of Nunavut Emergency Services told the CBC. "We can tell people they are available. We can tell people how they work. We can say, 'Look, it's simple, just throw it in your back pack and if something happens, just activate it and we'll come and get you.'" The beacons were rarely used. Doig said the reason is simple: People believe they have the skills to survive on the land and do not need the technology.

Are the Inuit blindly antagonistic to new technology? Their high adoption rates of the Internet and telemedicine suggest otherwise. A more plausible explanation is that the Inuit as a society can remember a time when having finely rendered internal maps was a matter of survival. Living on what can be called Atomic Earth, the Inuit learned of their world through their senses and nerve endings — unmediated transactions with nature, atom to atom. In this world, the finest, most reliable mapping technology was the lump of pink muscle suspended inside the skull. Anything that compromised that "technology" compromised the chance to return home safely. Living on Digital Earth, we now see the world through the haze of zeroes and ones airborne on capsules of light. Orientation is automated and spatial information is delivered in music-video-type bites. Which leads to a series of questions: If we are spoon-fed coordinates and learn about our place in the real world by touring virtual worlds, will we be as aware of our natural surroundings? Will our mental maps be as rich? And, in the context of this exploration on the social significance of maps, will we be in a better — or worse — position to understand Northrop Frye's Canadian riddle: Where is here? (The answer: Here is wherever the GPS receiver says we are.)

In his book *The Ends of Our Exploring*, Hooley McLaughlin of the Ontario Science Centre in Toronto took a sober look at the pivotal role of maps — the ones we make and the ones made for us. "We couldn't possibly live without maps," he told me. "All our dealings with the world stem from how we create maps." McLaughlin, trained as a developmental biologist, makes the distinction between teleological maps — those with an end in mind, such as road maps and remote sensing images, and dialectical maps — those that are made as the journey progresses and that reflect the emotional and physical experience of the map-maker. Westerners tend to believe teleological maps are the most useful of the two, since they purport to mirror reality. "Many people would say that a 'photograph' of the earth's surface taken from space is the best map you could hope for," McLaughlin wrote. "It is rendered perfectly — there are no distortions." In reality, such images are idealized; they are often composites of satellite images taken over time, perhaps with colours added and clouds removed. They say nothing about the give and take of natural forces on the ground. Our journeys on earth are experienced directly, he pointed out, and our maps should reflect that.

I am not suggesting we all travel to Digital Earth's horizon and jump off. Virtual globes and map-making by the masses will undoubtedly allow for new and enriching ways of looking at the world. Perhaps most promising are those digital tools that will encourage the making of community-based maps. *National Geographic*'s MapXchange, for example, is an on-line cartographic community where qualified individuals swap user-specific map information. Dog lovers in Halifax, for example, can use MapXchange to collaborate on making a map of where to take their dogs for a walk without a leash, then post the result on the Internet.

I am suggesting that future mapping and wayfaring technology be designed with sufficient headroom that allows for the use of Atomic Earth technology — the human brain and associated senses. In my own travels through the outer limits of cartography, the one technological development that I've kept returning to is the "talking" map being developed for the blind. It is an ambitious effort to give someone who is visually impaired and trying to walk to a post office or a restaurant access to navigational information — names of street corners, positions of buildings — from GPS satellites. The instinct of the developers is to build a heavily engineered mapping system that feeds as much information as possible to the blind walker. Heeding feedback from potential users, however, the developers in Montreal are now working on a much simpler and less detailed system based on landmarks rather than the usual geographical coordinates of conventional maps. They have come to realize that, for some orienting cues, the blind are better served by their own senses.

I suppose we are all ricocheting off landmarks in our own lives. That is how the Inuit and Dene travelled overland, creating zigzag patterns in their wakes. And that is how Canada was built: by the connecting of nodes one to another by railroads, telecommunication cables and highways, until the parts could barely be seen in the piece. Between these points of contact you will find our Atomic Earth maps and memories, encrusted, like a Landon Mackenzie painting, with the stories of our country.

Appendix: Timeline

Significant Dates in Canadian Surveying, Mapping and Charting

c. 1400 Estimated date of the *Vinland* map. If it is authentic, it is the oldest known map to show a part of Canada.

1497 John Cabot makes his landfall somewhere in Atlantic Canada. His map has not survived.

1510–20 Juan de la Costa draws a map of the world embodying the cartographic record of Cabot. If the *Vinland* map is not accepted, this is the oldest known map to show a part of Canada.

1541 Nicolas Desliens's map shows Newfoundland as a cluster of islands.

c. 1547 *Harleian Map* is the first to use the name Canada.

1560–90 European cartographers evolve a generally accurate representation of Newfoundland as a single island, notably Desliens's *Mappemonde* of 1560 and Bartolomeu Lasso's manuscript charts of 1575–90.

1578–79 Sir Francis Drake coasts north to approximately forty-eight degrees North latitude in the Pacific Ocean. He may have sighted Vancouver Island.

1579 Martin de Hoyarsabal publishes *Voyages Adventureux*, the first rutter (an early form of nautical chart) for Canada's east coast waters.

1604　Samuel de Champlain maps the east coast of North America from Canso to Nantucket.

1610　Henry Hudson discovers Hudson and James bays. His maps have not survived.

1612　Hessel Gerritsz's chart of Hudson Bay includes Hudson's discoveries.

1613　Champlain makes the first successful attempt to lay down latitudes and longitudes for a map of part of Canada in his 1613 map of the Atlantic coast.

1631–32　Camping on Charlton Island in James Bay, Captain Thomas James and his expedition observe a lunar eclipse that is observed simultaneously by Professor Henry Gellibrand at Gresham College in London. From the observations, Gellibrand calculates the longitude of Charlton Island to be 79° 30', which is essentially correct. It is the first successful astronomic observation for longitude in Canada.

1635–60　Jean Bourdon conducts surveys of seigneuries and other large-scale mapping in support of public works in New France. He is also active in small-scale mapping (e.g., the *Chemin des Iroquois* map and the so-called Bourdon map) and is the probable author of the famous map *Novvelle France* of 1641.

1670–71　The first map showing the entire Lake Superior is included in Father Claude Dablon's *Relations* of 1670–71.

1671　Jean-Louis Baptiste Franquelin begins production of maps and charts of New France.

1675　John Seller's *Atlas Maritimus* appears. It contains Captain Henry Southwood's two charts of Newfoundland's English Shore: *The Coast of Newfoundland from Salmon Cove to Cape Bonavista* and *Cape Race to Cape St Francis*. These are the first large-scale charts of Newfoundland, naming more than one hundred and fifty ports and features.

1686　Jean Deshayes measures the first baseline for a triangulation survey in Canada, running from Lower Town Quebec across the ice to Pointe Lévis. This is the start of the survey of the St Lawrence from Quebec to what is now Sept-Îles. The survey necessitates the reading of about three hundred triangles.

1690–92　Henry Kelsey explores inland to the prairies, seeking trade with the Indians.

1702   *Carte de la Rivière de St. Laurens,* surveyed by Deshayes in 1686, is published by Deshayes. This is the first printed chart of the St Lawrence.

1709   Gédéon de Catalogne surveys the seigneuries along the St Lawrence, and Jean-Baptiste Decouragne prepares cadastral maps that lay out property lines and ownership designations. These maps remain popular in Quebec for the tracing of family roots.

1731   The Cree chief Ochagach draws the first depiction of the land between Lake Superior and the prairies for Pierre de La Vérendrye.

1738   La Vérendrye is the first European to reach the junction of the Red and Assiniboine rivers.

1749   Chossegros de Léry, a military engineer and surveyor, lays out lots along a 2.5-mile frontage of the Detroit River, across from the settlement at Detroit, thereby conducting the first land survey in what is now Ontario. In his report, the first mention is made of measuring rods for land survey in Canada.

      At Grindstone Island, Captain Charles Morris, the first Surveyor General of Nova Scotia, takes the first accurate determination of latitude and longitude in what is now New Brunswick.

1755   Dr John Mitchell produces the first and second editions of his famous *A Map of the British Colonies in North America.* The second edition would be used by the military during the Seven Years War and later would help define the southern boundary of Quebec. Inaccuracies in this edition caused problems in defining the boundary between the United States and the British Colonies. It was on a print of this map that the contentious American Red Line was drawn to illustrate the U.S. position regarding the boundary line. In the mid-1800s, further difficulties were caused by inaccuracies in this map when disputes arose during the attempt to define the western boundary of Ontario.

1758   Samuel Holland and James Cook work together to chart portions of the St Lawrence River and Gulf.

1760–63   Samuel Holland and others map the St Lawrence Valley, under orders from General James Murray, the first British governor of New France.

1764　John Collins begins the survey of the boundary between Quebec and New York State.

1769　The first scientific observations for latitude and longitude in Western Canada are made at Fort Prince of Wales (now Churchill) in preparation for observing the transit of Venus.

1772　Samuel Hearne compiles his *Map of Part of the Inland Country to the Northwest of Prince of Wales Fort.*

1774　Captain Juan Perez reaches Canada's west coast. He is the first European to make a confirmed sighting of this part of the country.

1777　The first edition of DesBarres' *Atlantic Neptune* is published.

1778　Philip Turner begins to map parts of north central Canada for the Hudson's Bay Company. He uses sextant measurements for both latitude and longitude.

　　　　Captain Cook arrives at Nootka on the west coast. His chart, *North West Coast of America*, delineates the true shape of the coast and ends "imaginary cartography" of the region.

1781　A four-mile strip of land along the Niagara River is purchased from the Mississauga and Chippewa, the first purchase of Native land for white settlement in what is now Ontario.

1783　Governor Haldimand issues instructions to Samuel Holland to make exploratory surveys for settlement of the Loyalists, setting in motion the process of survey and settlement that would form Southern Ontario.

　　　　Land surveying in what is now Ontario commences with John Collins's survey of Kingston Township. It is first surveyed with an outline six miles square, but on instructions from London received in October, it is altered to a six-by-ten outline with lots of two hundred acres.

1784–85　Based on his own explorations, Peter Pond produces a map that discloses the canoe route from the prairies into the Athabasca and Mackenzie rivers. His map is the first to depict part of the Mackenzie basin.

1788　Captain Gother Mann carries out the first British hydrographic surveys of importance on the Great Lakes, charting stretches of the Georgian Bay shoreline.

1789　Alexander Mackenzie reaches the Arctic Ocean at the mouth of the river that now bears his name.

1792 George Vancouver begins his hydrographic survey of the west coast.

1793 Mackenzie reaches the Pacific Ocean travelling overland.

The Province of Upper Canada issues its first land patent.

1794 The survey of Yonge Street is started. When completed, this would provide a military road to Lake Simcoe, and from there, a water and portage route to Lake Huron.

The first United States–Canada boundary commission is created by the Jay's Treaty.

Likely the first map of New Brunswick is published in *Kitchen's Atlas*.

1795 Samuel Gale and John B. Duberger publish the first map of Quebec's Eastern Townships.

1797 Thomas Wright (representing Great Britain) and Samuel Webber (representing the United States) set up an observatory near St Andrews. Their purpose is to determine the latitude and longitude of the point to help decide which of two rivers is the St Croix mentioned in the Treaty of 1783.

1798 Upper Canada's first survey act, *An Act to Ascertain and Establish the Boundary Lines of the Different Townships of the Province*, is enacted. The Act requires the planting of monuments of stone or other durable material at township corners and governing points, and provides the death penalty for wilful defacement, alteration or removal of the monuments.

1813 David Thompson completes the manuscript of his famous *Map of America between Latitude 40 and 70 North and Longitude 80 and 150 West*.

1814 Peter Fidler is employed by Lord Selkirk to lay out thirty-six river lots along the Red River, the first property surveys on the prairies.

1815 Joseph Bouchette publishes his text *The British Dominations in North America*. It includes a general map of British North America and a map of Lower Canada at 2.5 miles to an inch.

Henry Bayfield, aged twenty, starts his hydrographic career with Captain W. F. W. Owen on the Great Lakes. Bayfield would continue his surveys in Canadian waters until 1856.

1819　Edward Parry explores Lancaster Sound north of Baffin Island and sails west through Viscount Melville Sound to Melville Island. The long traverse, together with the mapping of Canada's mainland Arctic coast (1819–46), provides "base-lines" for the subsequent mapping of Arctic islands.

1819–22　John Franklin leads an expedition that explores and maps the Coppermine River and the coastline from the Coppermine to Bathurst Inlet. It is the first step in the mapping of Canada's Arctic seaboard.

1824　David Thompson conducts surveys to locate the "most north-west point of the Lake of the Woods." Under Article Seven of the Treaty of Ghent, the international boundary runs through the Great Lakes to this point, then due south to the forty-ninth parallel. Thompson decides this ill-defined point should be either at the present position of Kenora or at the northern point of an inlet now known as Northwest Angle Inlet.

1825　Dr Tiarks, a British astronomer, decides that the point chosen by Thompson at Northwest Angle Inlet is the point referred to in the Treaty of Ghent. The decision is accepted by the Americans.

1825–27　Franklin and Dr John Richardson map the mainland coast from the mouth of the Mackenzie River west to Prudhoe Bay (Franklin) and east to the Coppermine River (Richardson).

1832　Joseph Bouchette publishes his second and improved map of Lower Canada.

1834　W. MacKay compiles a map of Nova Scotia more accurate and complete than any before.

1837　Samuel Morse invents the electric telegraph. By 1850, it would be used for the transmission of time signals. Bayfield uses it to determine the longitude of Canadian cities.

1837–39　Peter Dease and Thomas Simpson explore and map the Arctic mainland coast from the Coppermine River to Chantry Inlet.

1838　Beginning of the geological survey of Newfoundland under J. B. Jukes. Jukes's fieldwork, 1839–40, is confined to what he can observe from the coast.

1842　The Geological Survey is established in Montreal. Topograph-ical surveys to provide geological maps are begun.

Adolphus Lee Lewes is the first person to be formally employed as a surveyor in British Columbia. The Hudson's Bay Company hires him to map the Company's new establishment at Fort Victoria. He produces a map titled *Ground Plan of portion of Vancouver Island selected for New Establishment taken by James Douglas, Esq.*, the earliest known example of map-making by a land surveyor on Vancouver Island.

1843–44 Canada's first precise traverse is run by Captain W. F. W. Owen on the frozen Saint John River.

1843–45 The survey of the boundary between Quebec and the United States is completed.

1846 The Oregon Treaty is signed, giving the British undisputed sovereignty to land north of the forth-ninth parallel as well as Vancouver Island.

1846–47 Dr John Rae surveys Canada's coastline from Foxe Basin to Boothia Peninsula, virtually completing the mapping of Canada's Arctic mainland seaboard.

1846–48 Royal Engineers survey routes for the Intercolonial Railway. The final surveyed right-of-way is 1,863 kilometres long, and borders the St Lawrence River and Gulf for the most part of its run from Halifax to Quebec City.

1848 The search for John Franklin begins. This effort, which would continue until 1859, discloses much about the geography of the Canadian Arctic islands.

1850 John M'Clure enters the Arctic Ocean from the Pacific and coasts eastward to Cape Parry. He then turns north and sails through Prince of Wales Strait to the northeast angle of Banks Island, thus reaching Viscount Melville Sound from the west. This virtually completes the exploration of one of the Northwest Passages.

1856 "Electric observations" (i.e., telegraphic time signals) are used to find the accurate longitude of Collingwood, Kingston, Montreal, Ottawa, Quebec City, Toronto and Windsor.

1856–77 Maps of thirty-four Ontario counties are published, most of them produced by George C. Tremaine and Henry F. Walling.

1856 Survey of the first baseline in Northern Ontario is started. Known as the Salter Line, it is extended from Lake Nipissing to Sault Ste Marie, laying the foundation for the later surveying of Northern Ontario.

1857   Captain Richards RN, of HMS *Plumper*, makes observations in Semiahmoo Bay for the determination of the Treaty of Oregon of 1846. This provides a starting point for the westward survey of the parallel.

1858   The first Canadian fire insurance plan is published. This is titled the *Boulton Atlas of Toronto*.

1859   Thomas Devine, head of the Surveys Branch of Upper Canada, publishes the first official map of Canada titled *Government Map of Canada from the Red River to the Gulf of St Lawrence*. He apparently uses Sir William Logan's base map to position western detail.

1867   Simon Dawson surveys the "Dawson Route" from Port Arthur to the Red River. This road is based on his 1858 explorations and is used until the opening of the CPR.

1869   Lieutenant-Colonel J. S. Dennis, accompanied by Major Wallace, Captain Boulton, Milner Hart PLS, William Durie, William Dow and J. D. Wilkins, arrives in the Red River Settlement and begins surveying for land settlement. Major A. C. Webb joins them later. Webb's survey is stopped on October 11 by a party of seventeen Metis under Louis Riel. Further surveying would be discontinued because of the resistance and the approach of winter.

The Dominion Land Survey of the prairies begins. Plans of survey of townships are published at one mile to two inches.

Sandford Fleming explores the Lake of the Woods–Red River Country for the proposed CPR line.

1871–77   The survey for the CPR from Mattawa to Vancouver, a distance of about 4,636 kilometres, is carried out. The routes explored amount to nearly 42,000 kilometres, of which 18,507 are chained and levelled.

1872–74   The International Boundary from the northwest corner of the Lake of the Woods to the Rocky Mountains is surveyed.

1875   The first of the thirty-two county atlases of Ontario is published. The last atlas is produced in 1881, though other editions appear in 1903 and 1906.

1877   The first survey of an Indian reserve in Western Canada (Berens River) is carried out.

1880   British rights to the Arctic islands are passed to Canada.

1881   Manitoba is enlarged from the "Postage Stamp Province" up to the twelfth baseline.

1883–1907   Missionary Rev. Adrian Morice maps a two-hundred-mile square area, centred on Fort St James, between 1883 and 1904. He publishes *Map of the Northern Interior of British Columbia* in 1907.

1886   The Department of Marine and Fisheries publishes the first Canadian hydrographic chart.

Photo-topographical surveys start in the Rocky Mountains, following successful experimental work in 1885.

Staff Commander Boulton establishes a benchmark at Little Current, Manitoulin Island, thus commencing observations for Great Lakes water levels.

A map of the Cariboo District is drafted by Amos Bowman, assisted by James McEvoy. This is said to be the first accurate large-scale map of a part of British Columbia.

Map Showing Mounted Police Stations and Patrols, a map of the prairies is published by the Department of the Interior. The map, drawn at sixteen miles to one inch, shows the settlement of the prairies, including the railways and telegraph lines.

1887–88   George Mercer Dawson, William Ogilvie and Richard McConnell start the mapping of the southwest Yukon at six miles to the inch. Numerous points are fixed in latitude and chronometer longitudes.

1892   Photo-topographical surverys are started in British Columbia by Thomas Kains, following the successful use of the method in the Rocky Mountains by federal surveyors since 1886.

1896   The subdivision of Southern Ontario into townships is completed.

1897   The Geographic Board of Canada is formed primarily to regulate the application of geographical names.

1900   The Ontario government initiates a systematic exploration of Northern Ontario. Ten exploration parties, led by land surveyors (with one exception) and accompanied by a geologist and timber assessor, are instructed to report on timber resources and geology, including the economic potentials of found minerals. The parties are also required to report on flora, fauna, and rivers and lakes suitable for communication routes and power-generating sites. The results of the survey accelerate the survey of new townships in what is beginning to be called New Ontario.

1902　The first precise gravity measurements are made in Canada by Dr O. J. Klotz in Ottawa, Montreal and Toronto using a modified Mendenhall Pendulum Apparatus.

1903　The Department of Militia and Defence establishes Canada's military mapping unit, initially called the Mapping Branch of the Intelligence Department. Survey operations begin the following year.

1906　The first edition of *The Atlas of Canada* appears.

1911　The first Canadian coastal chart engraved in Canada is published.

1912　A Geographic Section is established in the Surveyor General's Branch of British Columbia, to produce lithographed "pre-emptor" sheets to accommodate requests for maps from land-seeking settlers. (A pre-emptor sheet was a map used by the homesteader to select his or her parcel of land.)

1916　The first transcontinental line of geodetic precise levels, run along railways from Halifax to Vancouver, is completed. ("Geodetic" is the horizontal and vertical positioning of a survey location.)

1920　The first commercial flight is made into Northern Canada. No air charts were available in Canada at this time.

1921　Ontario utilizes aircraft to make sketch maps of forested areas.

1922　The first aerial photographs of Manitoba are taken to assess their value for mapping.

1923　The Ontario Department of Public Highways publishes the first Ontario road map.

1925　The Royal Canadian Air Force (RCAF) purchases Vickers Vidette flying boats. Oblique photographs taken from these aircraft are used for four-mile mapping.

Aerial photographs are taken of the proposed route of the railway from The Pas to Churchill.

1926   Canada's first aeronautical chart is published by the Department of the Interior.

1929   The first extensive aerial photographic survey in British Columbia is carried out. The photography is performed by the RCAF, and by the end of the 1930 flying season, approximately 41,437 square kilometres would be covered.

1930   The Hydrographic Service makes first use of aerial photography for the mapping of shorelines.

1938   The Manitoba Department of Highways publishes the first road map of the province.

1947   Canada's first long-range mapping program is approved by the Cabinet Defence Committee. Among other items, it calls for the completion of the *Four-Mile Series* (on the scale of 1:253,440) within twenty years.

       After 164 years of surveying its townships, Ontario starts to annul townships and parts of townships. Annulments are carried out where the survey fabric has become so obliterated that it is no longer economical or advisable to continue surveying in relation to old township boundaries or subdivision lines.

1948   The British Columbia Department of Lands and Forests charters a helicopter for survey work. In the same summer, a geodetic survey party under F. P. Steers uses a helicopter for work along the Alaska Highway. They are the first Canadian survey agencies to use this new form of transportation.

1957   The Tellurometer, an electronic measuring device in which distances are computed by timing the transmission of radio waves, is first used in Canada.

1963   The National Research Council completes construction of the world's first analytical plotter.

       Canadian Geographic Information System is initiated by the Agriculture Rehabilitation and Development Agency. It is the world's first GIS.

1970   The Gestalt Photomapper is developed by Hobrough Limited of Vancouver.

1977   Energy, Mines and Resources Canada establishes the Task Force on National Surveying and Mapping under the leadership of Dr P. A. Lapp. The Task Force calls for topographical data in digital form; the National Topographic Data Base (a digital database) is established to fill this need.

The Commission de toponymie du Québec is established within the framework of the Charter of the French Language.

1979   After some one hundred and eighty years of use, the last entry is made in Ontario's Domesday Books. Instituted in the early 1800s, the Domesday Books contain a record of all lands alienated by the province since the first patent was issued in 1793. The books were first replaced in a computer-based land index listing. In 1991, this would be replaced by a more modern land index system.

1980   A Global Positioning System (GPS) is used for the first time in Canada. This system obtains the precise position of a receiver by measuring the distance of the receiver from four or more passing satellites whose orbits are known precisely.

1982   Digital mapping is now standard practice in the Quebec Department of Energy and Resources.

1987–93   *The Historical Atlas of Canada* is published in three volumes by the University of Toronto Press.

1992   The height of Mount Logan, Canada's highest mountain, is obtained by GPS methods. The height is 5,959 metres plus or minus 3 metres. The uncertainty is due to lack of knowledge of the geoid in the Mount Logan area.

Adapted from *Significant Dates in Canadian Surveying, Mapping, and Charting,* A. C. Hamilton and L. M. Sebert, Canadian Institute of Geomatics, 1996.

INDEX

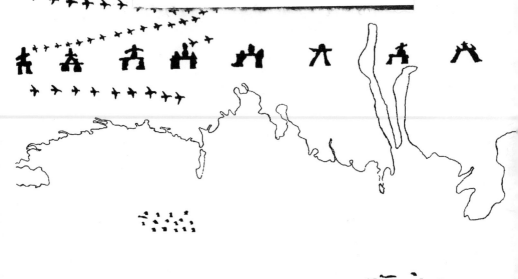